AF775306

Advances in Information Recording

DIMACS

Series in Discrete Mathematics
and Theoretical Computer Science

Volume 73

Advances in Information Recording

Paul H. Siegel
Emina Soljanin
Adriaan J. van Wijngaarden
Bane Vasić
Editors

Center for Discrete Mathematics
and Theoretical Computer Science
A consortium of Rutgers University, Princeton University,
AT&T Labs–Research, Bell Laboratories,
NEC Laboratories America, and Telcordia Technologies
(with partners at Avaya Labs, HP Labs, IBM Research,
Microsoft Research, and Stevens Institute of Technology)

American Mathematical Society

This DIMACS volume presents the proceedings from the DIMACS Working Group on Theoretical Advances in Information Recording held at Rutgers University, March 22–24, 2004, and the DIMACS Workshop on Theoretical Advances in Information Recording held at Rutgers University, March 25–26, 2004.

2000 *Mathematics Subject Classification.* Primary 68P20, 68P30, 92D20; Secondary 37B10, 93E10, 94A14, 94A15, 94A17, 94A40, 94B12.

Library of Congress Cataloging-in-Publication Data

Advances in information recording / Paul H. Siegel... [et al.], editors.
p. cm. — (DIMACS series in discrete mathematics and theoretical computer science ; vol. 73)
Includes bibliographical references.
ISBN 978-0-8218-3752-8 (alk. paper)
1. Computer storage devices. 2. Information theory. 3. Coding theory. I. Siegel, Paul H., 1953– II. Soljanin, Emina, 1962– III. Van Wijngaarden, Adriaan J., 1968– IV. Vasić, Bane, 1964– V. Series.

TK7895.M4.A3195 2008
621.39—dc22 2007060569

Copying and reprinting. Material in this book may be reproduced by any means for educational and scientific purposes without fee or permission with the exception of reproduction by services that collect fees for delivery of documents and provided that the customary acknowledgment of the source is given. This consent does not extend to other kinds of copying for general distribution, for advertising or promotional purposes, or for resale. Requests for permission for commercial use of material should be addressed to the Acquisitions Department, American Mathematical Society, 201 Charles Street, Providence, Rhode Island 02904-2294, USA. Requests can also be made by e-mail to reprint-permission@ams.org.

Excluded from these provisions is material in articles for which the author holds copyright. In such cases, requests for permission to use or reprint should be addressed directly to the author(s). (Copyright ownership is indicated in the notice in the lower right-hand corner of the first page of each article.)

© 2008 by the American Mathematical Society. All rights reserved.
The American Mathematical Society retains all rights
except those granted to the United States Government.
Copyright of individual articles may revert to the public domain 28 years
after publication. Contact the AMS for copyright status of individual articles.
Printed in the United States of America.

∞ The paper used in this book is acid-free and falls within the guidelines
established to ensure permanence and durability.
Visit the AMS home page at http://www.ams.org/

10 9 8 7 6 5 4 3 2 1 13 12 11 10 09 08

Contents

Foreword

This DIMACS volume on Information Recording is a collection of refereed contributions written by leading researchers in the area of information theory. The articles focus on problems concerning efficient and reliable storage of information. The articles were developed from a DIMACS Working Group and a DIMACS Workshop on Theoretical Advances in Information Recording held at Rutgers University, Piscataway, NJ, on March 22-24, 2004 and March 25-26, 2004, respectively. These two events were part of the 2001–2005 Special Focus on Computational Information Theory and Coding, which aimed to explore interconnections among coding theory, theoretical computer science, information theory, and related areas of computer science and mathematics. It addressed some of the challenges for the next 50 years – in particular wireless communication, magnetic/optical storage, the role of signal processing in networks, network information theory, and the creation of quantum information theory.

We would like to express our appreciation to Paul Siegel, Emina Soljanin, Adriaan J. van Wijngaarden and Bane Vasić for organizing this successful working group and workshop and for editing this volume. We extend our thanks to Robert Calderbank, Chris Rose, Amin Shokrollahi, Emina Soljanin and Sergio Verdú for their efforts as Special Focus organizers.

The Special Focus was made possible by funding from the National Science Foundation, the New Jersey Commission on Science and Technology, the DIMACS partners at Rutgers University, Princeton University, AT&T Research Labs, Bell Laboratories, NEC Research Institute and Telcordia Technologies, and its affiliate partners at Avaya Labs, HP Labs, IBM Research and Microsoft Research.

Fred S. Roberts
Director

Robert Tarjan
Co-Director for Princeton

Preface

It is widely known that, over the past 40 years, the pace of progress in information storage technology has rivaled that seen in semiconductor-based computing technology. In commercially-available hard disk drives using magnetic recording, the highest areal density – the number of bits of information stored per unit of area – has sky-rocketed from 100 kilobits per square inch in 1965 to 180 gigabits per square inch in 2007. This represents a 1.8 million-fold increase. With the latest "perpendicular" magnetic recording technology, a single 3.5-inch drive can provide a terabyte of information storage for a desktop computer, with maximum data transfer rates that approach 900 megabits per second.

This impressive technological progress, coupled with an equally remarkable reduction in the cost of storage, has had a significant impact in consumer electronics, as well. Personal audio and video players the size of a deck of cards now boast 1.8-inch disk drives capable of storing up to 100 gigabytes of multimedia information. Similarly, in the realm of optical recording, removable storage devices such as Compact Disc (CD), Digital Versatile Disc (DVD), and Blue-ray Disc (BD) drives for audio and video applications reflect enormous technological strides. Today, a dual-layer BD disk can store 50 gigabytes of information and transfer data at 54 megabits per second. Recently, non-volatile solid-state memory technology has experienced significant improvements, as well. The latest 1.8-inch flash memory devices can store as much as 32 gigabytes of data, and these "flash drives" are finding widespread use in a number of portable storage applications.

In an apparently endless synergistic cycle, remarkable multidisciplinary advances in data storage technology, such as those mentioned above, are enabling more complex and sophisticated information-based applications, while imaginative new developments in computing, business, entertainment, science, and transportation are continuing to demand practical storage devices with increased capacity, performance, and space efficiency.

The question is how future demands for information storage will be met. Near-term improvements in recording media, read-write transducers, mechanical interfaces, and signal processing techniques are expected to double or triple areal densities. To reach higher densities, researchers are exploring more complex recording approaches, such as heat-assisted magnetic recording and magnetic bit-patterned media recording, which offer the prospect of an order of magnitude increase in areal density over conventional techniques. Beyond that, however, novel information recording methods that differ more radically from those of the present day will likely be required.

Therefore, researchers are investigating more exotic techniques, such as holographic optical recording, thermo-mechanical recording with arrays of nanoscale probes, and molecular-scale electronic memory cells built from layered nanowires. Efforts are even being made to devise storage devices that are inspired by biomolecular mechanisms observed in living cells. As noted by Matt Ridley in his book *Genome*, the principles underlying natural data storage are as old as the time "when life divided the labour between two separate activities: chemical work and information storage, metabolism and replication." Uncovering and exploiting these principles is another compelling research direction that is very relevant to the field of information recording.

With this as background, we come to the theme underlying this volume, namely, that information theory, including the related disciplines of communication theory and coding theory, has played an important role in the evolution of information storage technology, and it will continue to do so, independent of the physical recording mechanism. Information-theoretic considerations can guide the development of useful mathematical models for the underlying data storage and retrieval process. Analysis of these models can then provide insights into fundamental limits on achievable storage densities and data transfer rates. These insights, in turn, can serve as the impetus for the invention of new communication and coding techniques that make it possible for practical systems to approach or achieve the fundamental limits.

The collection of peer-reviewed articles in this volume evolved from the DIMACS Working Group and DIMACS Workshop on Theoretical Advances in Information Recording held at Rutgers University, Piscataway, NJ, on March 22–24, 2004 and March 25–26, 2004, respectively. These meetings were part of a series of workshops organized under the auspices of the "DIMACS 2001–2005 Special Focus on Computational Information Theory and Coding," a program funded by the National Science Foundation. The DIMACS working group and workshop successfully brought together experts in information storage from a range of different fields. The working group comprised 11 keynote presentations and was attended by 27 participants. The two-day DIMACS workshop consisted of 10 invited presentations with 24 participants. The lists of presentations given at these two events are included at the end of this volume.

The first three contributions in this collection explore extensions to present-day storage technologies. The paper by W. M. J. Coene and A. H. J. Immink describes modulation coding for a novel optical recording approach, known as "Two-Dimensional Optical Storage" or, simply, TwoDOS. In TwoDOS, bits are stored on a broad spiral consisting of multiple rows of bits arranged in a hexagonal lattice pattern. The bit rows in the spiral are recovered jointly using a multi-spot laser and a two-dimensional (2D) detection algorithm. The authors identify bit patterns which are most error-prone for this optical recording channel, and they then design modulation codes which avoid these bit patterns, so as to minimize the read-out errors.

The work by R. Radhakrishnan, B. Vasić, F. Erden and C. He introduces an enhanced magnetic recording technology called "Heat Assisted Magnetic Recording" or HAMR. The HAMR approach uses a laser to heat the recording medium during the write process, permitting the use of magnetic media that allow for significantly higher recording densities. The paper provides the concepts and mathematical model required for analysis of the HAMR system from a communication theory perspective.

The third contribution by A. Nayak, J. R. Barry, and S. W. McLaughlin explores bounds on the performance of timing recovery for channels with intersymbol interference (ISI). The authors derive the Cramér-Rao bound on timing estimation error variance for such channels in the presence of a frequency offset and a random walk timing component. The analysis also provides insight into new placement strategies for training symbols within a recorded sector of data.

The next three articles explore the connections between data storage, information theory, and genetics. The work on macro-molecular data storage by M. Mansuripur and P. Khulbe presents preliminary results that demonstrate the potential for reliable, high-speed information recording and retrieval using macro-molecular DNA sequences as the storage medium. G. Battail, in his contribution, draws on concepts from information theory to support the hypothesis that error correcting codes with "soft constraints" are used to encode genetic information, hence ensuring reliable transmission to next generation. The paper on data storage in cells, by O. Milenkovic, introduces a novel line of investigation for studying storage and processing of information in cells using a range of concepts and techniques drawn from information theory, coding theory, and computer science.

The final contribution, by N. Kashyap and P. H. Siegel, describes a framework for using constrained coding techniques, whose development over the past few decades has been motivated largely by problems arising in information recording, to combat a certain nonlinear signal distortion that arises in high bit-rate, long haul optical fiber data transmission. The paper demonstrates the applicability of results and methods motivated by the study of information storage systems to other communication-theoretic settings.

The working group and workshop comprised several other presentations, some of which have been documented as papers elsewhere. Four presentations explored extensions to present-day storage technologies and achievable information rates for such systems. G. Cherubini of IBM Research, Zürich, presented a nanotechnology-based approach for highly-parallel, ultra-dense data storage.[1] E. Kurtas and R. Venkataramani of Seagate Research, Pittsburgh, Pennsylvania, reported on the capacity of magnetic recording channels, in particular, longitudinal and perpendicular systems. P. H. Siegel of the University of California, San Diego, California, presented information rates for two-dimensional recording technologies, such as holographic memories.[2]

Several presentations focused on coding for constrained systems, timing recovery and error control coding. B. H. Marcus of the University of British Columbia, Vancouver, gave an introductory presentation on optimal block-decodable encoders for constrained systems, and P. Chaichanavong of the University of California, San Diego, California, and T. L. Poo of Stanford University, Stanford, California, presented material on constrained systems with unconstrained positions.[3] B. E. Moision of the Jet Propulsion Laboratory, Pasadena, California, presented material on coded modulation. K. R. Narayanan of Texas A&M University, College Station,

[1] E. Eleftheriou, T. Antonakopoulos, G. K. Binnig, G. Cherubini et al., "Millipede – a MEMS-based scanning-probe data-storage system," *IEEE Trans. Mag.,* vol. 39, no. 2, pp. 938–945, Mar. 2003.

[2] J. Chen and P. H. Siegel, "On the symmetric information rate of two-dimensional finite-state ISI channels," *IEEE Trans. Inf. Theory,* vol. 52, no. 1, pp. 227–236, Jan. 2006.

[3] T. L. Poo, P. Chaichanavong and B. H. Marcus, "Tradeoff functions for constrained systems with unconstrained positions," *IEEE Trans. Inf. Theory,* vol. 52, no. 4, pp. 1425–1449, Apr. 2006.

Texas, presented a soft-input soft-output decoding algorithm for Reed-Solomon codes.[4] N. Varnica of Harvard University, Cambridge, Massachusetts, presented an improved belief-propagation decoder for low-density parity-check codes based on channel information correction which can be utilized for any memoryless or intersymbol interference channel.[5] W. Ryan of the University of Arizona, Tucson, Arizona presented an information-theoretic approach to obtaining optimal code rates for error control codes for a magnetic storage channel approximated by a Lorentzian model.[6] J. R. Barry of Georgia Institute of Technology, Atlanta, Georgia, and A. Kavčić of Harvard University, Cambridge, Massachusetts, presented iterative methods that jointly perform the tasks of timing recovery and error control decoding.[7]

The working group also included a presentation by P. Winkler of Bell Laboratories and Institute for Advanced Study, Princeton, New Jersey on a combinatorial analysis of statistical facts about the human genome and a presentation by C. Rose of Rutgers University, Piscataway, New Jersey on the efficiency of communicating over interstellar distances using electromagnetic radiation versus transporting physical artifacts with inscribed information.

It is a great pleasure to acknowledge Fred Roberts, Director of DIMACS, and Mel Janowitz, Associate Director of DIMACS, for creating and maintaining the excellent infrastructure for the working group and workshop, and Robert Calderbank, Chris Rose, Amin Shokrollahi, Emina Soljanin and Sergio Verdú for organizing the Special Focus on Computational Information Theory and Coding. We are grateful to Linda Casals, Sarah Donnelly, Christine Houck, Jessica Herold and Maria Mercado of DIMACS for their assistance during the workshop organization, and to Sergei Gelfand and Christine Thivierge of the American Mathematical Society for their assistance in the preparation of this volume. We are indebted to the National Science Foundation for the financial support of the workshop and to the American Mathematical Society for publishing this volume. Finally, we wish to thank the authors for their outstanding contributions and their cooperation in the reviewing process.

Paul H. Siegel
Emina Soljanin
Adriaan J. van Wijngaarden
Bane Vasić

---

[4] J. Jiang and K. R. Narayanan, "Iterative soft-input soft-output decoding of Reed-Solomon codes by adapting the parity-check matrix," *IEEE Trans. Inf. Theory*, vol. 52, no. 8, pp. 3746–3756, Aug. 2006.

[5] N. Varnica, M. P. Fossorier and A. Kavčić, "Augmented belief propagation decoding of low-density parity check codes," *IEEE Trans. Commun.*, vol. 55, no. 7, pp. 1308–1317, July 2007.

[6] S. Yang, A. Kavčić, and W. Ryan, "Optimizing the bit aspect ratio of a recording system using an information-theoretic criterion," *IEEE Trans. Magn.*, vol. 39, no. 5, pp. 2228–2230, Sept. 2003.

[7] W. Zeng, A. Kavčić, and R. Motwani, "Extraction of timing error parameters from readback waveforms," *IEEE Trans. Magn.*, vol. 42, no. 2, pp. 194–199, Feb. 2006.

DIMACS Series in Discrete Mathematics
and Theoretical Computer Science
Volume **73**, 2008

Modulation Coding for a Two-Dimensional Optical Storage Channel

Wim M. J. Coene and Andre H. J. Immink

Abstract. In optical storage, data can be arranged on the disc in a meta-spiral consisting of a large number of bit-rows (or tracks) with a small track-pitch. Successive revolutions of the meta-spiral are separated by a narrow guard band. The channel bits can be arranged on a 2D hexagonal lattice. The read-out channel has low-pass characteristics, which makes some very specific 2D patterns more error-prone than others. This paper presents a scheme for 2D modulation coding that eliminates these worst-case patterns. The scheme is based on a radial concatenation of strips consisting of a small number of bit-rows, alternated by single bit-rows. Strips and single bit-rows are each encoded with their specific modulation code such that the radially concatenated bitstream satisfies the 2D constraint. Finally, a Bliss-like error correction scheme is presented for the meta-spiral format.

1. Introduction

A new concept for two-dimensional optical storage is currently being developed, in which the information on the disc fundamentally has a two-dimensional character [**1, 2**]. The format of the current generations of optical recording (CD, DVD, and more recently, Blu-ray Disc, BD) has been based on a single-track spiral. The 3rd generation, BD, uses a blue laser diode with a wavelength λ= 405 nm and a lens with a Numerical Aperture given by NA = 0.85 [**3, 4**] and has a storage capacity of 25 GB. The aim of our new concept is to realize an increase in storage density over BD with a factor of 2, in combination with a factor of 10 in data rate (for the same physical parameters of the optical read-out system). For this purpose, the bits are organized in a so-called *meta*-spiral as shown in Fig. 1. Such a spiral consists of a number of bit-rows stacked upon each other with a fixed phase relation in the radial direction (which is orthogonal to the direction of the meta-spiral), so that the bits are arranged on a 2D lattice. A 2D closed-packed hexagonal ordering of the bits is chosen because it has a 15% higher packing fraction than the square lattice as used in [**5, 6**]. Successive revolutions of the meta-spiral are separated by a guard

---

2000 *Mathematics Subject Classification.* 68P20, 68P30, 94A40, 94B12, 94B60.

Key words and phrases. Optical recording, 2D modulation coding, 2D inter-symbol interference, 2D worst-case patterns, enumerative coding, 2D hexagonal bit-lattice.

This research has been carried out within the framework of a European IST-funded Project, called "TwoDOS" (Project No. IST-2001-34168).

©2008 American Mathematical Society

band consisting of one empty bit row (Fig. 1). A multi-spot light-path for parallel readout is realized, where each spot has BD characteristics. The signal processing with equalization, timing recovery and bit-detection is carried out in a 2D fashion, that is, *jointly* over all the bit-rows within the meta-spiral [**2**]. For the subject of bit-detection for the considered 2D format that is based on a meta-spiral with a small track pitch, the interested reader is referred to [**7**].

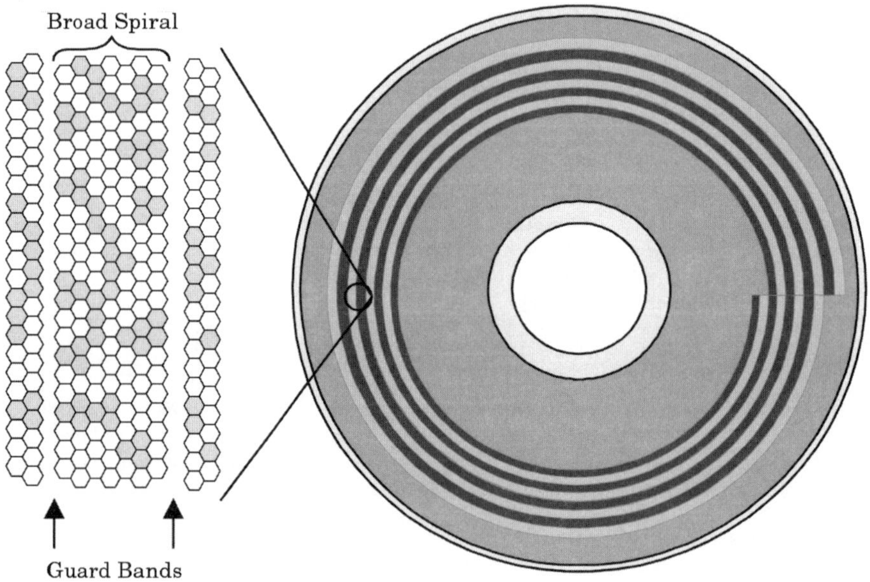

FIGURE 1. Schematic format for two-dimensional optical storage (for simplicity a 7-row meta-spiral is shown).

In the public literature, 2D storage is studied mainly in the area of optical storage. Also magnetic storage can be adapted towards a 2D format, and some papers start to appear in the literature (see e.g., [**8**]). For 2D optical storage, we refer to the competing work in [**6**], [**9**], [**10**], albeit on *square* instead of hexagonal 2D bit-lattices. Another difference with our approach is that [**6**] uses a 2D modulation code with $d = 1$ run-length-limited (RLL) constraint in both the tangential and the radial direction (respectively parallel and orthogonal to the direction of the meta-spiral): in this paper, we will propose a format with a high-rate modulation code that prohibits a very specific type of worst-case patterns that is characteristic for the 2D optical storage channel based on the 2D hexagonal bit-lattice. Our 2D-constraint can be seen as the 2D extension of the well known *maximum transition run* constraint (MTR), that has been developed in 1D runlength limited coding [**11**] in order to reduce the signal energy at the Nyquist frequency.

1.1. Structure of the Article. The article is structured as follows. In Section 2, we describe the characteristics of the 2D optical storage channel. The indexing of bits on the 2D *direct space* hexagonal bit-lattice, and of the 2D Fourier components on the *reciprocal space* lattice is given in Section 3. Section 4 discusses the 2D bit-patterns that are most critical with respect to transfer over the channel: these bit-patterns are also referred to as *worst-case patterns*. In Section 5, the basic concept of a 2D modulation code is presented that prohibits the occurrence of these critical patterns: the code is based on two building blocks, for which separate modulation codes are described in Section 6 and Section 7, respectively. In Section 8, we propose a scheme combining error-correction coding and modulation coding for the 2D meta-spiral. Finally, in Section 9, we formulate our conclusions.

2. Channel Characteristics

In case we approximate the optical channel as a linear system, it can be characterized by a modulation transfer function (MTF) that has a low-pass behavior with a hard cut-off frequency at $\nu_c = \frac{2\,\mathrm{NA}}{\lambda}$. Its MTF can be expressed as (see [**12, 13**]):

$$\mathrm{MTF}(\nu_s,\theta)=\begin{cases}\frac{2}{\pi}\left[\arccos(\frac{\nu_s}{\nu_c})-\frac{\nu_s}{\nu_c}\sqrt{1-\left(\frac{\nu_s}{\nu_c}\right)^2}\right] & \nu_s\leq\nu_c,\\ 0 & \nu_s>\nu_c.\end{cases} \tag{1}$$

In Eq. (1), ν_s is the spatial frequency of the information on the disc, and θ is the azimuth in the 2D spatial frequency plane. This circularly symmetric function is shown in Fig. 2. The analysis in [**12**] that leads to this shape for the MTF is based on diffraction of the laser spot by the bit-patterns on the disc. Note that the 2D bit-patterns we consider require a 2D frequency analysis in order to assess the transfer by the 2D channel. On the 2D bit-lattice, we can distinguish one-dimensional sections at different inclinations, that connect a set of bits in the 2D plane: we will refer to these sections as *bit-lines*. As a rule-of-thumb, we can state that a set of bit-lines with a smaller inter-line distance will give rise to diffraction at larger angles, which corresponds to higher spatial frequencies (and worse transfer by the channel).

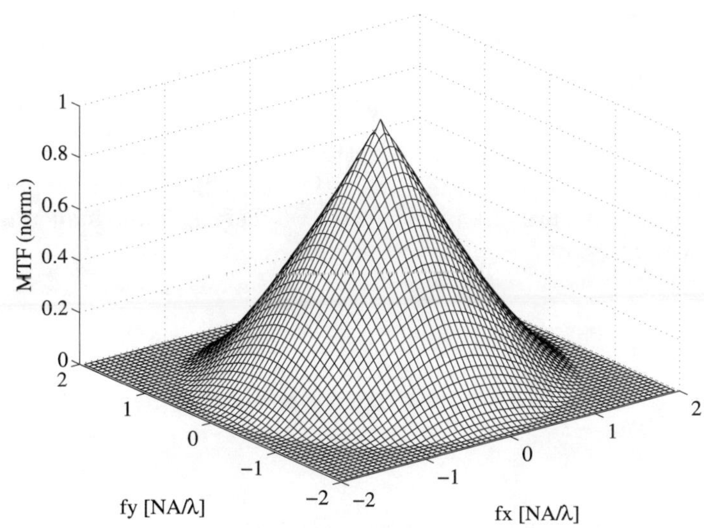

FIGURE 2. 2D Modulation Transfer Function (MTF). Spatial frequencies are denoted in units of $\frac{\mathrm{NA}}{\lambda}$. The channel's cut-off frequency is given by $\nu_c = \frac{2\,\mathrm{NA}}{\lambda}$.

3. Notation

3.1. Indexing in the 2D "Direct Space" Lattice. The 2D hexagonal bit-lattice with its six-fold rotational symmetry has three basic axes. In terms of an xy Cartesian coordinate system that is defined with respect to the tangential (x) and radial (y) direction of the meta-spiral, these i- and j- axes of the hexagonal lattice correspond to the unit vectors :

$$(2) \qquad i: \; u_0 = \begin{pmatrix} 1 \\ 0 \end{pmatrix} \; j: \; u_1 = 1/2 \begin{pmatrix} -1 \\ \sqrt{3} \end{pmatrix}.$$

In Eq. (2), it is assumed that the so-called "lattice constant" which is defined as the closest distance between two neighboring bits, is normalized to unity. The above lattice is usually known as the "direct space" lattice. A convenient way to denote such a lattice is by means of its "generating matrix" [**14**], given by:

$$(3) \qquad L_u = \begin{bmatrix} u_{0x} & u_{1x} \\ u_{0y} & u_{1y} \end{bmatrix} = \begin{bmatrix} 1 & -1/2 \\ 0 & \sqrt{3}/2 \end{bmatrix}.$$

The direct space lattice is drawn in Fig. 3, together with two types of bit-lines. The first type of bit-lines, shown in Fig. 3 (a), are diagonal bit-lines that are parallel to the u_1-axis; the second type of bit-lines, shown in Fig. 3 (b), have a shorter inter-line distance. The 2D bit-lines are indicated by their so-called Miller-indices (pq): this is common practise in three-dimensional crystallography where 2D lattice planes in the 3D lattice are the equivalent of our 1D bit-lines. Further, the direct space lattice and reciprocal space lattice (see next subsection) are some of the basic concepts in the field of crystallography and diffraction analysis. Diffraction at a set of bit-lines occurs in the direction *orthogonal* to these lines. The vector pointing in the latter direction, and with a length equal to the inverse of the repeat period (or distance) of the lines, is commonly referred to as the *diffraction vector* of these bit-lines. The set of all these diffraction vectors constitute another 2D lattice, which is called the "reciprocal space" lattice (in the 2D spatial frequency plane).

3.2. 2D "Reciprocal Space" Lattice. The basic vectors of the reciprocal space lattice (of the 2D hexagonal bit-lattice with lattice vectors (u_0, u_1)) are denoted (v_0, v_1), and have the property that (where the dot indicates the inner-product of two vectors):

$$(4) \qquad u_k \cdot v_l = \delta_{kl}.$$

This is equivalent to stating that the generating matrix L_v of the reciprocal space lattice is equal to the inverse transposed of the generating matrix of the direct space lattice, that is,

$$(5) \qquad L_v = (L_u^{-1})^T.$$

The direct space hexagonal lattice (with base vectors making an angle of 120°) has as reciprocal space lattice again an hexagonal lattice (with base vectors making an angle of 60°, and u_0 and v_0 making an angle of 30°; the length of v_0 and v_1 equals $2/\sqrt{3}$). It is shown in Fig. 4. The 2D reciprocal space can be filled by a contiguous tiling of a 2D fundamental domain, which has an hexagonal shape, and which can be

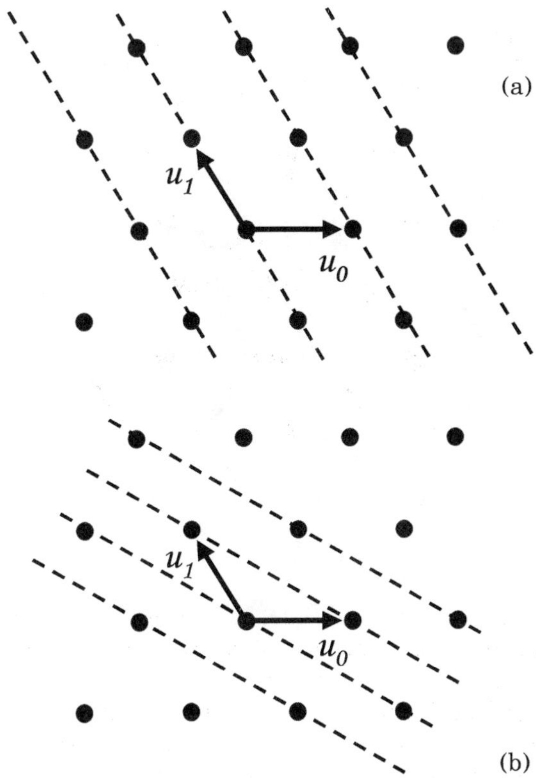

FIGURE 3. "Direct space" bit-lattice with two types of bit-lines drawn, with Miller indices equal to: (a) (10), and (b) (11).

constructed as a "Wigner-Seitz cell" or "first Brilloin zone" [**15**] based on the basic lattice vectors in reciprocal space. This 2D fundamental domain is in fact simply the 2D version of the Nyquist interval in the one-dimensional case (defined by its boundaries $[-\frac{1}{2T}, +\frac{1}{2T}[$, where T is the distance between two sampling points in the 1D-case). Fig. 4 further shows the diffraction vector of the (11) bit-lines (which is orthogonal to these lines), indicated by $\mathbf{B}_{(11)}$.

4. Critical Patterns

4.1. 1D-Case with the MTR-Constraint. In traditional 1D storage, it is well known that the Nyquist sequence of alternating bits $\cdots + - + - + - \ldots$ is badly transmitted by the channel (because of its *low-pass* characteristics). Based on this knowledge, a class of so-called *maximum transition run* (MTR) runlength-limited (RLL) codes has been derived in [**11**]. The MTR-constraint specifies the maximum number of consecutive "1"-bits in the (d, k) bitstream (where a "1" indicates the start of a new run). Note that the channel bits that are written to the medium (which we refer to as RLL bits) are obtained from the (d, k) bitstream after feeding it to a so-called 1T-precoder, which is essentially a modulo-2 integrator. Thus, in the RLL bitstream, the MTR constraint limits the number of consecutive 1T

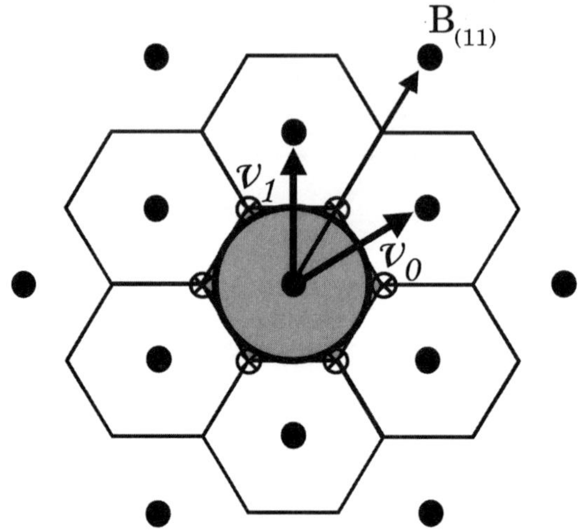

FIGURE 4. "Reciprocal space" lattice with the fundamental hexagonal domain, for a disc capacity where the "cut-off" circle of the channel MTF forms an inscribed circle (for a high storage density equal to 2× that of BD; for an 11-row meta-spiral, this corresponds with a lattice parameter, which is the shortest distance between bits, equal to 138 nm). The symbol ⊗ indicates the frequency components of the worst-case patterns of Section 4.

runs. Originally, in [**11**], the maximum number of consecutive "1"-bits in the (d, k) bitstream was limited to 2, which implies that only isolated 1T runs are present in the RLL bitstream. A pure Nyquist sequence of alternating bits obviously corresponds with the highest spatial frequency of the system. Similar concepts apply to the two-dimensional case.

4.2. 2D-Case on Hexagonal Bit-Lattice. Recall that the boundary points of the 1D Nyquist interval in frequency space represent the most critical frequencies in the 1D signal processing. Similarly, the corner points of the 2D hexagonal fundamental domain represent the most critical two-dimensional periodic structures (also called *super-structures* here, in analogy to the usual terminology in crystallography) on the 2D hexagonal bit-lattice that are subject to the worst transfer by the MTF of the channel (this is due to the low-pass characteristics of the MTF of Fig. 2, so that higher spatial frequencies correspond with a lower value of the MTF, and thus a worse transfer). These super-structures consist of a repeated stacking of the (11) type of bit-lines as shown in Fig. 5: there are three consecutive bit-lines in the repeat period, each bit-line containing only one type of bits, such that the repeat period reads as $\cdots + - - + - - + - - \ldots$ (for one polarity of the bitstream). Since the repeat period equals $3 \times d_{(11)}$ where $d_{(11)}$ is defined as the lattice spacing of the $d_{(11)}$ bit-lines, the corresponding 2D frequency vector lies at 1/3 of $\mathbf{B}_{(11)}$ as is shown in Fig. 4. The latter observation can also be derived as follows. The super-structure can be described in terms of its generating matrix in direct space given by (e.g., for the diamond-shaped pattern at the top of Fig. 5):

$$L_u^{ss} = \frac{1}{2}\begin{bmatrix} 3 & 3 \\ -\sqrt{3} & \sqrt{3} \end{bmatrix} \tag{6}$$

The corresponding generating matrix (for the super-structure) in reciprocal space then becomes:

$$L_v^{ss} = \frac{1}{\sqrt{3}}\begin{bmatrix} \frac{\sqrt{3}}{3} & \frac{\sqrt{3}}{3} \\ -1 & 1 \end{bmatrix} \tag{7}$$

which can be seen in Fig. 4 to constitute the corner points of the fundamental domain in reciprocal space. It can be easily analyzed in Fig. 5 that this super-structure consists of a concatenation of two types of clusters: one cluster having a "+"-bit at its center, and surrounded by six "−"-bits as its nearest neighbors, the other cluster having a "−"-bit at its center with a Nyquist ring consisting of the six alternating bits "+ − + − +−" as its nearest neighbors. It is further obvious from Fig. 5, that the periodic super-structure can also be described in terms of a repetition of the same type of bit-lines along the two equivalent directions (the direction perpendicular to these two sets of bit-lines makes an angle of 60° and 120° degrees respectively, with the direction perpendicular to the first set of bit-lines). Since the directions normal to a set of bit-lines correspond with their diffraction vector in reciprocal space, the three sets of bit-lines of the periodic super-structure correspond to three consecutive corner points of the 2D fundamental domain in reciprocal space.

We will briefly discuss the other type of bit-lines, mentioned above with respect to Fig. 3, that is, the (10) bit-lines. The diffraction vector $\mathbf{B}_{(10)}$ coincides with the basic lattice vector v_0 of the reciprocal lattice. In case these bit-lines are alternatingly filled with all "+"-bits or all "−"-bits, a superstructure is formed with a repeat period equal to $2 \times d_{(10)}$ with $d_{(10)}$ the lattice spacing of the $d_{(10)}$ bit-lines. The corresponding 2D frequency vector lies at 1/2 of $\mathbf{B}_{(10)}$ so that it coincides with the point of intersection between the boundary of the 2D fundamental domain and the inscribed circle at the cut-off of the MTF (see Fig. 4).

Thus, in conclusion, although at first sight the alternating "+" and "−" (10)-bit-lines seem to be the 2D-equivalent of the 1D Nyquist sequence, it is the 2D superstructure based on the (11)-bit-lines with "+ − −" repeat period that is the most critical pattern on the 2D hexagonal bit-lattice.

5. 2D Modulation Coding for Meta-Spiral: Two Building Blocks

Similar to the case of the MTR-constraint [**11**] in modulation coding for 1D storage, we propose a 2D modulation code that forbids the occurrence of the super-structure patterns on the 2D hexagonal bit-lattice that give rise to frequency components at the set of Nyquist frequencies as defined above. In order to realize this 2D constraint, we consider two types of building blocks to construct a multi-track meta-spiral. A first type of building block consists of strips as used in *strip-based* 2D coding proposed in [**5, 16**]: the 2D area is divided into consecutive strips. A strip is aligned "horizontally", that is, along the tangential direction of the meta-spiral, and consists of a small number of bit-rows, for example 3. Coding is carried out

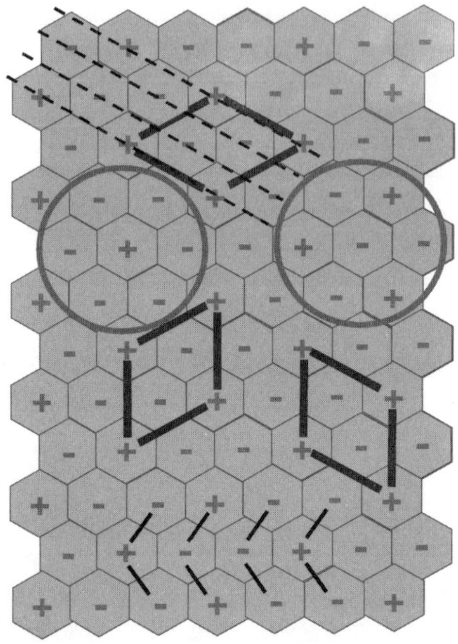

FIGURE 5. Worst-case pattern of channel bits on the 2D hexagonal bit-lattice. Three equivalent orientation variants are shown. The two types of bit-clusters that generate the 2D pattern are encircled: one has a "+"-bit at its center, the other a "−"-bit. At the bottom, the repetitive pattern of fish-bone-shaped bit-triplets is indicated.

along this horizontal direction, and becomes essentially one-dimensional. Strips are concatenated one upon the other in the radial direction. In the formalism of [**5, 16**], codewords do not cross the boundaries of a strip. In addition, we consider a second type of building block for the 2D modulation code: these are single bit-rows that are 1D encoded such that these rows serve as *merging bit-rows* gluing consecutive strips together. The code constraints for both types of building blocks are described by a state-transition diagram (STD) where each branch between a given departure state and the corresponding arrival state has one of the possible channel symbols as its label. The STD defines the direction of evolution of the code. Note that in the meta-spiral, there is one single direction of evolution for both types of modulation codes (of 2D *strips* and 1D *merging bit rows*).

6. Modulation Coding for Building Block Type I: 2D-Encoded 3-Row Strips

We consider as a practical case strips consisting of 3 bit-rows. Note however that the basic idea is also generic for any number of rows larger than three.

6.1. 3-row NRZ and NRZI Channel Symbols. For the case of 3-row strips, we have 8-ary channel symbols that comprise three NRZI bits (as they are written on the disc), one bit per bit-row in the strip. We propose a staggered stacking of the 3 NRZI bits in one symbol, so that these symbols may be reminiscent to fish-bones (see Fig. 5 at the bottom). We have designed our 2D code such that it generates NRZ symbols. Just as in 1D modulation encoding, a basic ingredient of the 2D modulation encoding is a 1T-precoder, carried out in a row-wise manner along the tangential direction of the meta-spiral: this 1T-precoder transforms the NRZ bits (or (d,k)-bits of the runlength-limited (RLL) code in the traditional 1D RLL terminology) into NRZI bits. Therefore, and since our 2D constraint does not depend on the overall polarity, we define 4 STD-states for a 3-row strip as defined in Table 1. Please note that $b \in \{-1, 1\}$ and $\bar{b} \equiv -b$).

TABLE 1. STD-states for a 3-row strip.

STD-State σ_1	STD-State σ_2	STD-State σ_3	STD-State σ_4
b / b \ b	b / $\bar{b}$ \ $\bar{b}$	b / $\bar{b}$ \ b	b / b \ $\bar{b}$

Each of the transitions in the STD from one STD-state to another is labeled by an 8-ary NRZ symbol. Each of the NRZ bits of the bit-triplet corresponds to a given bit-row in the 3-row strip. For the sake of completeness, we recall that an NRZ-bit equal to "1" indicates a transition in the NRZI bitstream along the considered bit-row, a "0"-bit indicates the absence of such a transition. For a 3-row strip, this is illustrated in Table 2 (the superscript index denotes the bit-row in the strip, the subscript index denotes the symbol number along the strip).

TABLE 2. 8-ary NRZ and NRZI symbols for a 3-row strip.

k-th NRZI Symbol	k-th NRZ Symbol	$(k+1)$ th NRZI Symbol
b_k^0	$\rightarrow i \rightarrow$	$b_{k+1}^0 = b_k^0(-1)^i$
b_k^1	$\rightarrow j \rightarrow$	$b_{k+1}^1 = b_k^1(-1)^j$
b_k^2	$\rightarrow l \rightarrow$	$b_{k+1}^2 = b_k^2(-1)^l$

6.2. Generation of Worst-Case Super-Structure Patterns. The periodic super-structure patterns (in a 3-row strip) that we want to forbid, can be described as a succession of a number of bit-triplets (or fish-bones), given by:

$$\begin{array}{ccccccc}
\cdots & b & \bar{b} & b & b & \bar{b} & \cdots \\
 & / & / & / & / & / & \\
\cdots & \bar{b} & b & b & \bar{b} & b & \cdots \\
 & \backslash & \backslash & \backslash & \backslash & \backslash & \\
\cdots & b & \bar{b} & b & b & \bar{b} & \cdots
\end{array}$$

The repeat period of this pattern comprises exactly three fish-bones. Note that the first state in the above pattern equals σ_3. The corresponding NRZ-symbols are derived as (with the NRZ symbols denoted S, with $S = i + 2j + 4l$ where i, j and l represent the NRZ-bits along each of the three bit-rows):

$$\longrightarrow \sigma_3 \quad \underset{(S=\mathbf{7})}{\overset{\begin{pmatrix} i \\ j \\ l \end{pmatrix} = \begin{pmatrix} 1 \\ 1 \\ 1 \end{pmatrix}}{\longrightarrow}} \quad \sigma_3 \quad \underset{(S=\mathbf{5})}{\overset{\begin{pmatrix} i \\ j \\ l \end{pmatrix} = \begin{pmatrix} 1 \\ 0 \\ 1 \end{pmatrix}}{\longrightarrow}} \quad \sigma_1 \quad \underset{(S=\mathbf{2})}{\overset{\begin{pmatrix} i \\ j \\ l \end{pmatrix} = \begin{pmatrix} 0 \\ 1 \\ 0 \end{pmatrix}}{\longrightarrow}} \quad \sigma_3$$

The last state is again equal to the first state (σ_3), and the sequence can be repeated to form a longer worst-case pattern.

6.3. Forbidden Sequences. The worst-case patterns can be eliminated by forbidding particular sequences of NRZ-symbols that would leave from certain STD-states. As an example, we propose to truncate the sequence as soon as two consecutive NRZI bit-triplets result that form part of the worst-case pattern. This implies that, for instance, for STD-state σ_3, after emission of NRZ-symbol $S = \mathbf{7}$, it is forbidden to emit as subsequent symbol $S = \mathbf{5}$. There are two additional cases that have to be prevented: for STD-state σ_3, after emission of NRZ-symbol $S = \mathbf{5}$, one may not emit as subsequent symbol $S = \mathbf{2}$, and for STD-state σ_1, after emission of NRZ-symbol $S = \mathbf{2}$, it must be forbidden to emit as subsequent symbol $S = \mathbf{7}$.

6.4. Connection Matrix and Capacity. The adaptation of the state transition diagram (STD) in order to consider the forbidden sequences is done as follows. Three additional states are generated. The first one, denoted σ_5, can only be reached when emitting symbol $S = \mathbf{7}$ from state σ_3; further, the fan-out of σ_5 is identical to that of σ_3 (the state that is reached in the original STD when emitting $S = \mathbf{7}$ from state σ_3), with the single exception that emission of symbol $S = \mathbf{5}$ is not allowed:

$$\rightarrow \sigma_3 \underset{\mathbf{7}}{\rightarrow} \sigma_5 \underset{\not{\mathbf{5}}}{\rightarrow}$$

The second additional STD-state, denoted σ_6, can only be reached when emitting symbol $S = \mathbf{5}$ from state σ_3; further, the fan-out of σ_6 is identical to that of σ_1 (the state that is reached in the original STD when emitting $S = \mathbf{5}$ from state σ_3). Now, the single exception is that emission of symbol $S = \mathbf{2}$ is not allowed from σ_6:

$$\rightarrow \sigma_3 \underset{\mathbf{5}}{\rightarrow} \sigma_6 \underset{\not{\mathbf{2}}}{\rightarrow}$$

Finally, the third additional STD-state, denoted σ_7, can only be reached when emitting symbol $S = \mathbf{2}$ from state σ_1; further, the fan-out of σ_7 is identical to that of σ_3 (the state that is reached in the original STD when emitting $S = \mathbf{2}$ from state σ_1). Again, the single exception is that emission of symbol $S = \mathbf{7}$ is not allowed from σ_7:

$$\begin{array}{ccccc} \rightarrow & \sigma_1 & \rightarrow & \sigma_7 & \rightarrow \\ & & \mathbf{2} & & \mathbf{7} \end{array}$$

The state-transition diagram (STD) for the 2D-constraint in the 3-row strip is given in Table 3 (with the additional states underlined, and with the forbidden symbols indicated by "X"). This 7-state STD has the following connection matrix (which indicates how many branches exist that connect one state to another):

$$D = \begin{bmatrix} 2 & 2 & 1 & 2 & 0 & 0 & 1 \\ 2 & 2 & 2 & 2 & 0 & 0 & 0 \\ 1 & 2 & 1 & 2 & 1 & 1 & 0 \\ 2 & 2 & 2 & 2 & 0 & 0 & 0 \\ 1 & 2 & 1 & 2 & 1 & 0 & 0 \\ 2 & 2 & 1 & 2 & 0 & 0 & 0 \\ 1 & 2 & 1 & 2 & 0 & 1 & 0 \end{bmatrix} \tag{8}$$

The largest eigenvalue of D, denoted $\lambda_{\max}$, is equal to 7.91697. The capacity corresponding with the 2D constraint for a 3-row strip is given by:

$$C = \frac{1}{3} \log_2(\lambda_{\max}) = 0.994983. \tag{9}$$

The factor 1/3 originates from the fact that each symbol comprises three channel bits.

TABLE 3. State-Transition Diagram (STD) for a 3-row strip.

	NRZ Symbol							
STD-state	(0)	(1)	(2)	(3)	(4)	(5)	(6)	(7)
σ_1	σ_1	σ_2	$\underline{\sigma_7}$	σ_4	σ_4	σ_3	σ_2	σ_1
σ_2	σ_2	σ_1	σ_4	σ_3	σ_3	σ_4	σ_1	σ_2
σ_3	σ_3	σ_4	σ_1	σ_2	σ_2	$\underline{\sigma_6}$	σ_4	$\underline{\sigma_5}$
σ_4	σ_4	σ_3	σ_2	σ_1	σ_1	σ_2	σ_3	σ_4
$\underline{\sigma_5}$	σ_3	σ_4	σ_1	σ_2	σ_2	X	σ_4	$\underline{\sigma_5}$
$\underline{\sigma_6}$	σ_1	σ_2	X	σ_4	σ_4	σ_3	σ_2	σ_1
$\underline{\sigma_7}$	σ_3	σ_4	σ_1	σ_2	σ_2	$\underline{\sigma_6}$	σ_4	X

6.5. 2D k-Constraint. In traditional 1D storage, very long runs lead to inaccuracies in the *timing recovery*, which is dealt with by a device called a phase-locked loop (PLL). The PLL regenerates the internal "clock" that is matched to the length of the bits on the medium: the bit clock is adjusted at each variation in the detected signal waveform. Areas on the medium with too few transitions may cause "clock-drift". Similarly, in a 2D-encoded strip, it is necessary that the 2D channel bitstream shows some variation which can be used as timing information. Therefore, we want to limit the number of successive $S = \mathbf{0}$ symbols to a small number, denoted k, similarly to the k-constraint in 1D RLL channel coding. Such a *joint* k-constraint over a number of contiguous bit-rows has already been proposed in [**17, 18**].

When our 2D-constraint is to be combined with such a joint k-constraint, we proceed as follows. First, we identify all branches in the STD of Table 3 that correspond with the $S = \mathbf{0}$ symbol; with these branches, we construct a 7×7 sub-matrix Y. Further, we define the sub-matrix X as the original connection matrix of Eq. (8) *minus* Y. X is thus that part of the original connection matrix that corresponds to the emission of symbols other than the $\mathbf{0}$-symbol. With these two sub-matrices, the number of times a $\mathbf{0}$-symbol is emitted is easily controlled via a new connection matrix (*including* the k-constraint) that is denoted $D[k]$. It is obtained as a $7(k+1) \times 7(k+1)$ matrix, which can be written as a $(k+1) \times (k+1)$ block matrix:

$$D[k] = \begin{pmatrix} X & Y & 0 & \cdots & 0 & 0 \\ X & 0 & Y & \cdots & 0 & 0 \\ \cdots & \cdots & \cdots & \cdots & \cdots & \cdots \\ X & 0 & 0 & \cdots & 0 & Y \\ X & 0 & 0 & \cdots & 0 & 0 \end{pmatrix} \tag{10}$$

where "0" denotes a 7×7 all-zero matrix, and where the sub-matrices X and Y are given by:

$$X = \begin{pmatrix} 1 & 2 & 1 & 2 & 0 & 0 & 1 \\ 2 & 1 & 2 & 2 & 0 & 0 & 0 \\ 1 & 2 & 0 & 2 & 1 & 1 & 0 \\ 2 & 2 & 2 & 1 & 0 & 0 & 0 \\ 1 & 2 & 0 & 2 & 1 & 0 & 0 \\ 1 & 2 & 1 & 2 & 0 & 0 & 0 \\ 1 & 2 & 0 & 2 & 0 & 1 & 0 \end{pmatrix} \tag{11}$$

and

$$Y = \begin{pmatrix} 1 & 0 & 0 & 0 & 0 & 0 & 0 \\ 0 & 1 & 0 & 0 & 0 & 0 & 0 \\ 0 & 0 & 1 & 0 & 0 & 0 & 0 \\ 0 & 0 & 0 & 1 & 0 & 0 & 0 \\ 0 & 0 & 1 & 0 & 0 & 0 & 0 \\ 1 & 0 & 0 & 0 & 0 & 0 & 0 \\ 0 & 0 & 1 & 0 & 0 & 0 & 0 \end{pmatrix} \tag{12}$$

It is interesting to note that the matrix in Eq. (10) has a structure that is reminiscent of the connection matrix for a 1D RLL constrained sequence with $d = 0$ and a finite k-constraint (just replace X and Y in Eq. (10) by unity).

For $k = 2$, the capacity amounts to $C[k] = 0.994123$: hence, a rate $R = 152/153 = 0.99346$ code is possible for the 2D-encoded strip (with 3 bit-rows). This code-mapping is obtained as follows. The number 152 is the largest number

n of user bits that satisfies three conditions: (*i*) it is a multiple of 8 (since we use byte-oriented error-correction coding), (*ii*) $n+1$ is a multiple of 3 (the number of bits in a fish-bone symbol), and (*iii*) $R = n/(n+1) \leq C[k=2]$.

6.6. Enumerative Coding Scheme. A convenient way to implement the high-rate 152-to-153 2D modulation code is by means of enumerative coding (see [**19, 20**], where it is applied to 1D runlength limited (RLL) coding). Since the channel symbols in the 3-row wide 2D-encoded strips comprise three bits ($M=8$), we have to make use of the M-ary version for the lexicographic ordering as given by Cover [**19**], which yields for the rank i_S of a channel word $\mathbf{x}$:

$$i_S(\mathbf{x}) = \sum_{j=1}^{n} \sum_{m=0}^{x_j-1} n_S(x_1, x_2, \ldots, x_{j-1}, m) \tag{13}$$

In this equation, a 2D channel word $\mathbf{x}$ comprises n channel symbols (bit-triplets or fish-bones) denoted $x_1, x_2, \ldots, x_{n-1}, x_n$. Further, $n_S(x_1, x_2, \ldots, x_{j-1}, x_j)$ represents the number of channel words of length n for which the first j channel symbols are equal to $x_1, x_2, \ldots, x_{j-1}, x_j$. Note that in the binary case with 1D d-constraint RLL coding, the set of numbers $n_S(x_1, x_2, \ldots, x_{j-1}, x_j)$ is simplified to $x_j N_d(n-j)$ (with x_j the binary bit value of the (d,k) bitstream, with n the channel-word length, and with $N_d(p)$ the number of d-constrained sequences of length p). A similar reduction cannot be made for our current case. Instead, we use the following procedure.

Let us indicate the current state *after* emission of symbol with index j with Σ_j, where Σ_j is one of the basic STD-states, that is, $\Sigma_j \in \{\sigma_1, \sigma_2, \ldots, \sigma_7\}$. We start the encoding of a channel word always from the same STD-state in order to avoid channel errors to propagate from one word into the next one. Let us denote this initial state Σ_0, which can be chosen as $\Sigma_0 \equiv \sigma_2$ (the reason for this particular choice will become clear at a later stage). For the index sets n_S that are to be used in Eq. (13), we actually need to know what the resulting state will be when symbol m is emitted to reach symbol position j, hereby considering the history of the previously emitted channel symbols $x_1, x_2, ..., x_{j-1}$ (which represent the coding path through the state-transition diagram). This is shown schematically below, with the resulting state denoted Σ_j^m, where the superscript m is used to indicate that for symbol number j, we have $0 \leq m < x_j$:

$$\Sigma_0 \xrightarrow{x_1} \Sigma_1 \xrightarrow{x_2} \Sigma_2 \xrightarrow{x_3} \Sigma_3 \ldots \xrightarrow{x_{j-1}} \Sigma_{j-1} \xrightarrow{m} \Sigma_j^m.$$

So we have that

$$n_S(x_1, x_2, ..., x_{j-1}, m) = n_S^{'}(\Sigma_j^m), \tag{14}$$

where $n_S^{'}(\Sigma_j^m)$ indicates the total fan-out from state Σ_j^m up to any possible arrival state q after completion of the channel word (with emission of the $n-j$ extra symbols so that a total of n channel symbols in the channel word is realized). Therefore, we have that

$$n_S^{'}(\Sigma_j^m) = \Sigma_q D_{\Sigma_j^m, q}^{n-j} \tag{15}$$

where D is the connection matrix of the state-transition diagram, the required power is $n - j$ (the remaining number of symbols to be emitted), the required matrix element is (Σ_j^m, q) and the sum is over all possible arrival states q.

In our practical case, we have that $n = 51$. Concatenation of consecutive channel words is realized by means of an extra merging symbol, that redirects the coding path to the initial coding state that was agreed upon (e.g., $\Sigma_0 \equiv \sigma_2$, see above). At this stage, a sufficient condition for a proper choice of the initial state Σ_0 is that it can be reached from any other state of the STD by emission of a single symbol: therefore, the three states that were added to realize the 2D constraint, σ_5, σ_6 and σ_7, are no potential candidates for Σ_0. In case we additionally want to realize DC-control along one of the bit-rows of the 2D 3-row strip, as we will discuss in the next subsection, then an extra condition will further restrict the candidates for Σ_0.

6.7. DC-Control. In a 2D optical drive, servo systems are used for tracking of the position of the laser spot array along the radial direction of the meta-spiral, and for focusing of the laser spot on the information layer. These servo systems typically require a DC-free data signal. The signals used for the servo control are derived from one of the laser spots that are scanning the 2D meta-spiral, and thus result from a single bit-row within the meta-spiral. If the spectral power density of a considered bit-row reveals a "notch" (or zero) at DC, then the signal is considered to be "DC-free".

The sequence of the considered bit-row $b_1, b_2, \ldots$ is called *DC-free* if its *running digital sum* (RDS)

$$\mathrm{RDS}_i = \sum_{j=-\infty}^{i} b_j$$

takes on only finitely many different values. In that case, the power spectral density function vanishes at DC.

A well known procedure to restrict the value of the RDS is by insertion of an extra NRZ channel symbol that offers the freedom to flip the polarity of the subsequent channel bitstream (and thus the *sign* of its contribution to the RDS, not its magnitude). Note that a "1" instead of a "0" in the NRZ bitstream of a single bit-row changes the polarity of the subsequent RLL (or NRZI) bitstream due to the use of the 1T-precoder.

For our case with the 2D-encoded 3-row wide strips, we want to realize DC-control for only one out of the three bit-rows (in view of servo-control in the 2D optical drive using an 11-row meta-spiral, see Section 8.3). For this purpose, we intend to use the same NRZ-symbol that was required for the merging of two consecutive channel words so that the coding path could be redirected towards the same initial state Σ_0 in the STD.

Let us represent by S_0 and S_1 two complementary NRZ symbols, that is, $S_0 + S_1 = \mathbf{7}$. By selection of either S_0 or S_1 as merging NRZ symbol, we can flip the polarity of all three bit-rows at once. Note that we want to control the RDS of only a single bit-row; therefore, we can select any of the three bit-rows to be made DC-free. Note that, upon emission of either S_0 or S_1, it is required to arrive in the same initial state Σ_0: this extra condition eliminates the STD-states σ_1 and σ_3 from the list of potential candidates for Σ_0. Let us choose $\Sigma_0 \equiv \sigma_2$. We can then distinguish the following 4 cases: (i) if the last state of the preceding

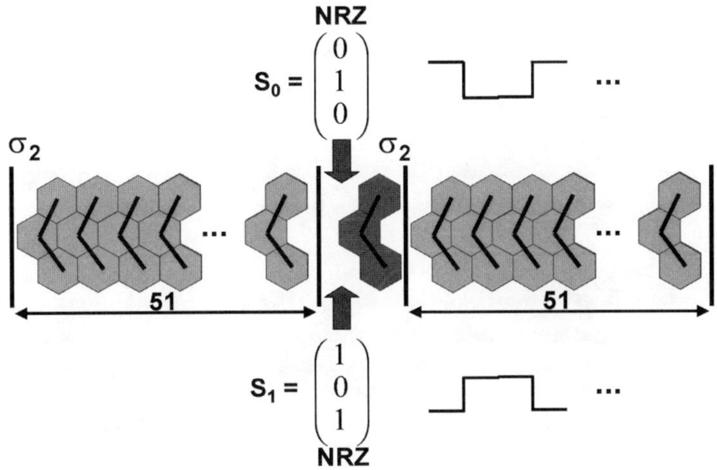

FIGURE 6. DC-control for one bit-row of the 2D-encoded 3-row strip via the extra symbol that is also used to redirect the coding path of the enumerative coding to STD-state σ_2 as the initial state Σ_0. The situation is shown where a choice has to be made between NRZ-symbols $S_0 = \mathbf{2}$ and $S_1 = \mathbf{5}$.

n-symbol channel word equals σ_1 or σ_6, then the two symbols S_0 and S_1 equal **1** and **6**; (*ii*) if said last state equals σ_2, then the two symbols S_0 and S_1 equal **0** and **7**; (*iii*) if said last state equals σ_3, σ_5 or σ_7, then the two symbols S_0 and S_1 equal **3** and **4**; and (*iv*) if said last state equals σ_4, then the two symbols S_0 and S_1 equal **2** and **5**: the latter situation is depicted in Fig. 6. A similar reasoning would apply if we had chosen for the alternative initial state, that is, $\Sigma_0 \equiv \sigma_4$.

7. Modulation Coding for Building Block Type II: 1D-Encoded Single Bit-Rows

In strip-based coding as proposed in [**5, 16**], strips are constructed so that concatenation of strips in the radial direction does not lead to violations of the constraints across the strip boundaries: for this purpose, the clusters at the boundary of a strip have to satisfy a special boundary constraint. In our case, the 2D encoded strips cannot be freely concatenated in the radial direction. Therefore, when strips are stacked upon each other, we can identify at the boundary area of the two strips two other 3-row wide areas that overlap with the two considered strips. It is obvious that, although the 2D constraint applies to all strips, it may be violated for each of these two 3-row wide areas at the boundary between strips.

The purpose of the building blocks of the second type, which are the 1D encoded bit-rows positioned in between two consecutive strips as shown in Fig. 7, is to glue these consecutive strips together such that the 2D constraint also applies in the boundary area of the strips.

7.1. Forbidden Sequences in 1D-Encoded Single Bit-Rows. In order to satisfy the 2D constraint also in the boundary area of consecutive strips, it is sufficient to forbid the following two repetitive sequences in the NRZI bitstream of the

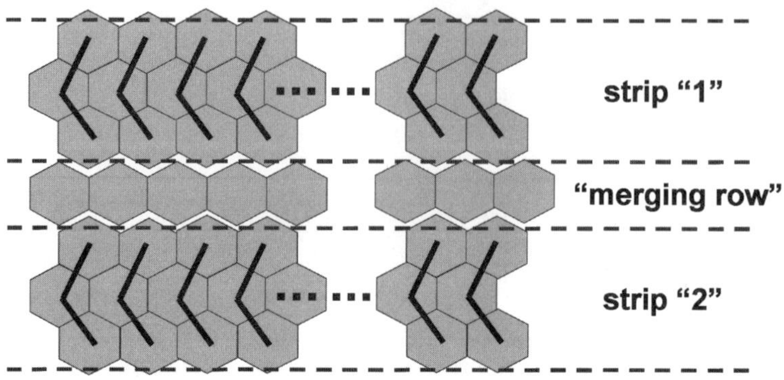

FIGURE 7. Stacking of two 3-row strips with a merging bit-row in between.

1D encoded single bit-rows: $\cdots 00100100100100 \cdots$, and $\cdots 11011011011011 \cdots$. These two NRZI sequences correspond with the single NRZ sequence given by: $\cdots 0110110110110 \cdots$. By means of this constraint on the single bit-rows, the actual phase of the modulation codes of the two building blocks has become irrelevant.

Therefore, we design the 1D modulation code such that the NRZ pattern 11011 is prohibited. The corresponding state-transition diagram (for a $k = 5$ constraint) is shown in Fig. 8.

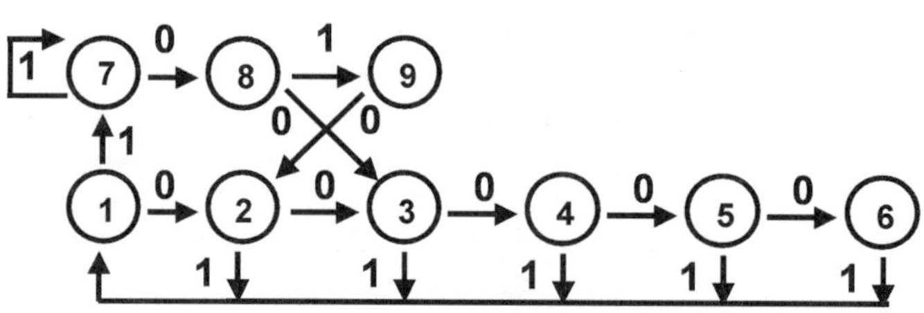

FIGURE 8. State-transition diagram for the 1D modulation code of the merging bit-rows.

7.2. Modulation Code. We construct a *sliding block* code for the above 1D constraint using the well known state-splitting algorithm or ACH-algorithm [**21**]. The code maps user words of 12 user bits onto channel words of 13 channel bits (code rate $R = 12/13$). Its k-constraint is chosen to be $k = 5$. The approximate eigenvector equals $\mathbf{v} = \{2, 2, 2, 2, 1, 1, 2, 1, 1\}$. The code is not designed to be DC-free (DC-control is reserved for one of the bit-rows of the 3-row strips).

8. Bliss-like Scheme for Modulation Coding and ECC Coding

Our scheme uses two modulation codes. The first modulation code that is to be applied for the 3-row strips has a high coding rate, and is implemented via a coding scheme that uses very long codewords (with a mapping of 152 user bits onto

153 channel bits). It is used for the largest fraction of the source data. For such a high-rate code, the traditional *"Figure 1"* is not very well suited. Its very long codewords that comprise (at the user side) a number of consecutive ECC symbols (or bytes) are subject to excessive error-propagation: a single channel error during read-out will affect one complete channel codeword, but will lead to a large number of erroneous bytes prior to ECC decoding.

For traditional high-rate 1D RLL codes to be used in conjunction with error-correction coding, Bliss [**22**] has proposed a variant on *"Figure 1"* that does not suffer from the above drawbacks. We first briefly explain the Bliss-scheme for traditional 1D modulation encoding. In the *encoder* (shown in Fig. 9), there are two modulation codes instead of a single one. The first modulation code (step (1)) is positioned *before* the ECC encoder, unlike the traditional *"Figure 1"*. The first modulation code has a (very) high code rate, which necessitates to make use of long codewords, but leads to severe error propagation. Subsequently, the ECC encoder (step (2)) operates on the constrained sequence that is produced by the first modulation encoder. Because of the high rate of the latter, the ECC is only slightly less effective than in the case the ECC would be applied on the original source data (since the first modulation encoder with its high rate adds only limited correlation). The parities generated by the ECC encoder are then encoded by the second modulation encoder (step (3)),which has not that very high rate (of the first modulation encoder), and which does not suffer from severe error-propagation. The constrained sequence for the parity part, produced by the second modulation encoder, is then cascaded in step (4) with the constrained sequence for the data part, produced by the first modulation encoder: the cascading process might require some *merging* procedure.

In the *decoder* of the Bliss-scheme, the part of the channel bitstream corresponding to the parities is decoded first by the second modulation decoder (which yields only little error-propagation). Then, the ECC decoder operates with as input the (decoded) parities and the part of the channel bitstream corresponding to the data: the ECC decoder produces at its output the error-free channel bitstream. In this way, channel errors that occur in the channel bitstream corresponding to the data part do not lead to error propagation. Finally, the decoder of the first channel code produces the corresponding source data for the user.

In our 2D modulation scheme, the second modulation code that is to be applied for the single merging bit-rows has a lower coding efficiency (with a 12-to-13 mapping), but (unlike the first code) does not suffer from excessive error-propagation. Recall that an additional purpose of this second modulation code is to glue 3-row wide strips together while maintaining the 2D constraint also at the boundary area. The second modulation code is used for the ECC parities, and for a certain fraction of the source data. We describe now the encoder and decoder for our 2D modulation scheme in conjunction with a Bliss-like scheme for the error-correction coding.

8.1. Encoder. The different steps at the side of the *encoder* are shown in Fig. 10. In a first step (step-1), the source data is partitioned into two parts, denoted *Part-1* and *Part-2*. This subdivision is convenient since, for an 11-row meta-spiral, the two single bit-rows (second type of building block, Section 7) represent a data capacity that exceeds the overhead that is typically needed for the ECC parity symbols. Then, the source data *Part-1* is encoded with (the first) modulation encoder-1 (in step-2), producing the channel bitstream in the distinct building

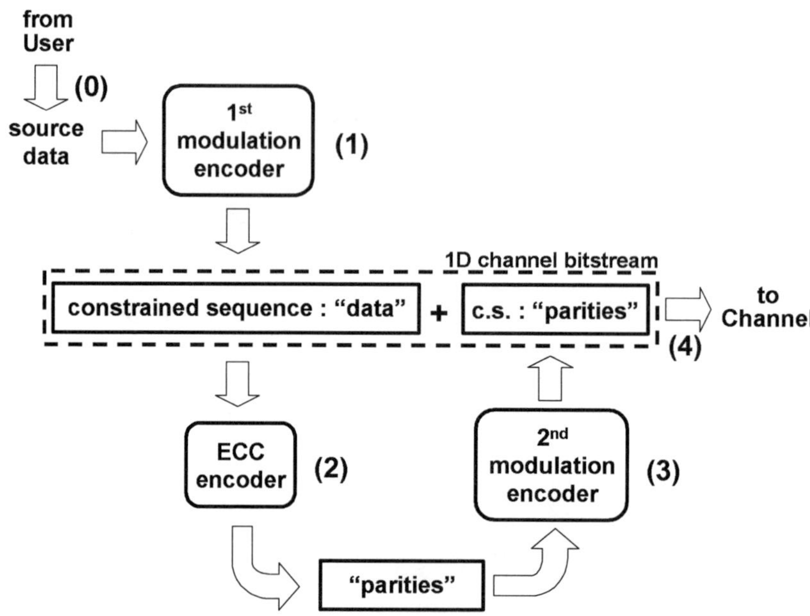

FIGURE 9. Encoder for Bliss-variant [**22**] of *"Figure 1"* for 1D RLL Coding.

blocks of the first type. The latter channel bitstream together with the source data *Part-2* are then the inputs (denoted as (3.a)) for the ECC encoder (step-3), which produces ECC parities (3.b) at its output. Subsequently, the source data *Part-2* together with the ECC parities are the input of (the second) modulation encoder-2 (in step-4), producing the channel bitstream in the distinct building blocks of the second type (in this case, the single merging bit-rows). In step-5, the different building blocks are assembled (or *multiplexed*) to generate the overall channel bitstream of the full strip. The latter overall bitstream is then ready to be transferred over the channel (step-6).

8.2. Decoder. The different steps at the side of the *decoder* in our 2D coding scheme are shown in Fig. 11. In a first step (step-1), the as-detected overall channel bitstream is de-multiplexed into the respective parts corresponding to the 3-row strips and merging bit-rows. In step-2, modulation decoder-2 decodes the as-detected channel bitstream of the building blocks of the second type into ECC parities and source data *Part-2*. Modulation decoder-2 has only little error-propagation (it is based on 12-bit input words, which are 1.5 bytes long). ECC decoding is performed in step-3: at its input (3.a), the ECC decoder uses the as-detected channel bitstream of the building blocks of the first type, the ECC parities and the source data *Part-2*: all these may contain channel errors produced by the bit-detection module that uses the read-out signals. At its output (3.b), the ECC decoder (of step-3) produces the error-free (corrected) channel bitstream of the building blocks of the first type, and the corrected source data *Part-2*. Next, the error-free channel bitstream of the building blocks of the first type are decoded by modulation

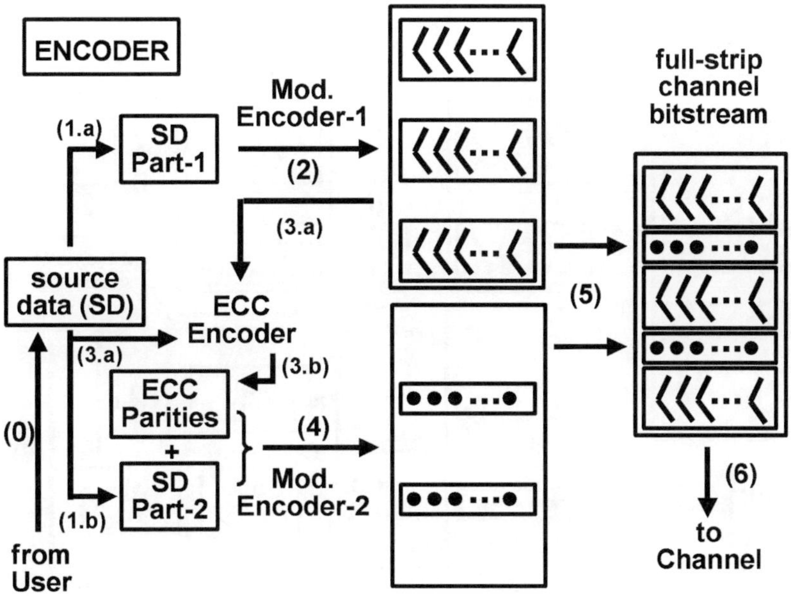

FIGURE 10. Encoder for 2D coding with joint ECC encoding and modulation encoding in a 2D meta-spiral consisting of 3 strips (each of 3 bit-rows) and 2 separate bit-rows.

decoder-1 (step-4), hereby generating the source data *Part-1*. In step-5, the two parts of source data are reassembled to generate the overall source data, that are to be sent to the user in step-6.

8.3. Data-Allocation in the Meta-Spiral. We consider the data allocation for the practical case of an 11-row meta-spiral consisting of three 3-row stripes and two merging bit-rows. DC-control is applied in the outer two bit-rows of the meta-spiral for the purpose of the radial tracking servo, and in the center bit-row for the focusing servo: these bit-rows are the top and bottom outer bit-rows of the corresponding two outer 3-row strips, and the center bit-row for the central 3-row strip. No DC-control is applied on the merging bit-rows. Consequently, for each block of 52 channel symbols (including one merging symbol) along the tangential direction of the meta-spiral, we have 19 (152/8) byte-symbols for each 3-row strip, and 6 ($1/8 \times 12/13 \times 52$) byte-symbols for each merging bit-row. Thus, for each 52 symbols along an 11-row meta-spiral, we have a total of 69 bytes that can be encoded.

9. Conclusions

We have derived a scheme for a two-dimensional modulation code that prohibits specific worst-case patterns for the 2D optical storage channel with the channel bits located on a 2D hexagonal bit-lattice. These worst-case patterns are the 2D extension of the 1D *maximum transition run* constraint. A meta-spiral format consisting

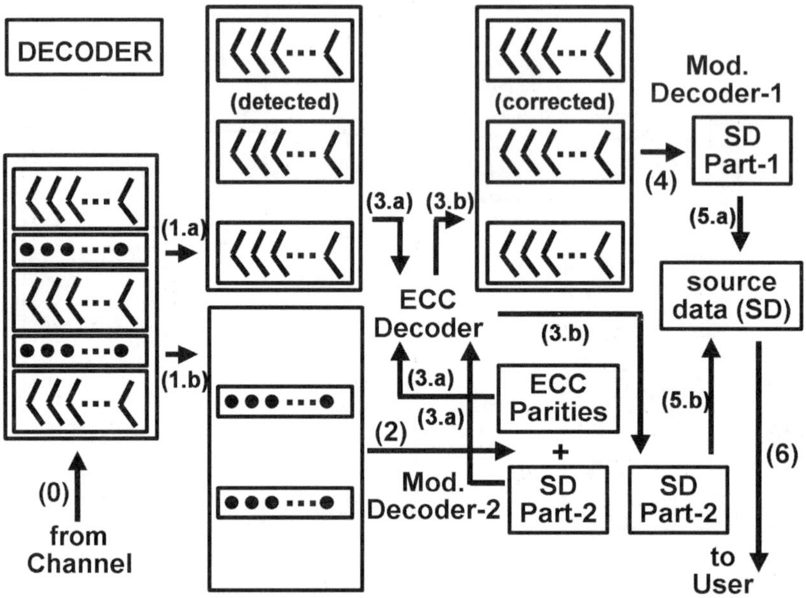

FIGURE 11. Decoder for 2D coding with joint ECC decoding and modulation decoding in a 2D meta-spiral consisting of 3 strips (each of 3 bit-rows) and 2 merging bit-rows.

of alternatingly 3-row strips and single merging bit-rows has been presented, where both types of building blocks have their own modulation code, realizing together the aimed 2D constraint over the complete area of the meta-spiral. Finally, a scheme combining this 2D modulation code with error correction coding has been derived.

10. Acknowledgments

This research is part of a European IST-Project, called "TwoDOS" (Project No. IST-2001-34168). All project-members (Philips Research, University of Limerick, Eindhoven University of Technology, University of Lancaster, Philips ODTC and HW Communications) are acknowledged for their contributions to this work.

References

[1] W. M. J. Coene, "Two-dimensional optical storage", in Technical Digest of Optical Data Storage (ODS) Conference, pp. 90–92. 2003.

[2] A.H.J. Immink, W.M.J. Coene, A.M. van der Lee, C. Busch, A.P. Hekstra, J.W.M. Bergmans, J. Riani, S.J.L. van Beneden, and T. Conway, "Signal processing and coding for two-dimensional optical storage", in *Proc. IEEE Global Telecommunications Conference 2003,* vol. 7, pp. 3904–3908, Dec. 2003.

[3] T. Narahara, S. Kobayashi, M. Hattori, Y. Shimpuku, G. van den Enden, J. Kahlman, M. van Dijk, and R. van Woudenberg, "Optical disc system for digital video recording", *Japanese Journal of Applied Physics*, vol. 39, Pt1, no. 2B, pp. 912–919, 2000.

[4] B. Stek, R. Otte, T. Jansen, and D. Modrie, "Advanced signal processing for the Blu-ray Disc system", in Technical Digest Joint International Symposium on Optical Memory (ISOM) and Optical Data Storage (ODS), pp. 263–265, 2002.

[5] W. Weeks and R.E. Blahut, "The capacity and coding gain of certain checkerboard codes," *IEEE Trans. Inform. Theory*, vol. 44, no. 3, pp. 1193–1203, May 1998.

[6] T. Kato, S. Taira, T. Maeda, Y. Katayama, and T. Nishiya, "Two-dimensional run-length-limited code and partial response maximum likelihood system with multi-track recording," ISOM/ODS 2002, Joint International Symposium on Optical Memory and Optical Data Storage 2002, Post-Deadline Paper WP.23, pp. 51–53, July 2002.

[7] A.P. Hekstra, W.M.J. Coene, and A.H.J. Immink, "Refinements of multi-track Viterbi bit-detection", *IEEE Trans. Magn.*, vol. 43, no. 7, pp. 3333–3339, July 2007.

[8] Y. Wu, N. Singla, J.A. O'Sullivan, and R.S. Indeck, "Iterative detection schemes for two-dimensional ISI channels," in *Proc. Intermag Conf.*, Amsterdam, paper no. 627, 2002.

[9] S. Taira, T. Hoshizawa, T. Kato, Y. Katayama, T. Nishiya, and T. Maeda, "Study of recording methods for advanced optical disks," *Technical Report of IEICE*, vol. 2002-03, pp. 57–64, 2002.

[10] T. Kato, S. Taira, Y. Katayama, T. Nishiya, and T. Maeda, "Two-dimensional partial-response equalization and detection method with multi-track recording for optical disks," *Technical Report of IEICE*, vol. 2002-03, pp. 65–70, 2002.

[11] J. Moon and B. Brickner, "Maximum transition run codes for data storage systems", *IEEE Trans. Magn.*, vol. 32, no. 5, pp. 3992–3994, Sept. 1996.

[12] J. Braat, "Read-out of optical discs", in *Principles of Optical Disc Systems*, Adam Hilger Ltd, Bristol, Chapter 2, pp. 7–87, 1985.

[13] H.H. Hopkins, "Diffraction theory of laser read-out systems for optical video discs," *J. Opt. Soc. Am.*, vol. 69, pp. 4–24, 1979.

[14] T. Kalker, "On multidimensional sampling," in *Digital Signal Processing Handbook*, Chapter 4, CRC Press, 1998.

[15] C. Kittel, "Introduction to solid state physics", Chapter 2, John Wiley & Sons, 1976.

[16] J.J. Ashley, B.H. Marcus, "Two-dimensional low-pass filtering codes", *IEEE Trans. Comm.*, vol. 46, no. 6, pp. 724–727, June 1998.

[17] M.W. Marcellin and H.J. Weber, "Two-dimensional modulation codes", *IEEE Journal Sel. Areas Comm.*, vol. 10, no. 1, pp. 254–266, Jan. 1992.

[18] R.E. Swanson and J.K. Wolf, "A new class of two-dimensional RLL recording codes", *IEEE Trans. Magn.*, vol. 28, no. 6, pp. 3407–3416, Nov. 1992.

[19] T.M. Cover, "Enumerative source coding", *IEEE Trans. Inform. Theory*, vol. IT-19, no. 1, pp. 73–79, Jan. 1973.

[20] K.A.S. Immink, *Codes for mass data storage systems*, Shannon Foundation Publishers, The Netherlands, 1999.

[21] R.L. Adler, D. Coppersmith, and M. Hassner, "Algorithms for sliding block codes. an application of symbolic dynamics to information theory", *IEEE Trans. Inform. Theory*, vol. IT-29, no. 1, pp. 5–22, Jan. 1983.

[22] W.G. Bliss, "Circuitry for performing error correction calculations on baseband encoded data to eliminate error propagation", *IBM Techn. Discl. Bul.*, vol. 23, pp. 4633–4634, 1981.

Philips Research Laboratories, Prof. Holstlaan 4, 5656 AA Eindhoven, The Netherlands

E-mail address: `wim.coene@philips.com`

Philips Research Laboratories, Prof. Holstlaan 4, 5656 AA Eindhoven, The Netherlands

E-mail address: `andre.immink@philips.com`

DIMACS Series in Discrete Mathematics
and Theoretical Computer Science
Volume **73**, 2008

Characterization of Heat-Assisted Magnetic Recording Channels

Rathnakumar Radhakrishnan, Bane Vasić, Fatih Erden, and Ching He

ABSTRACT. The storage capacity of hard disk drives has increased tremendously over the last decade. However, the rate of increase has reached a bottle-neck as the technology approaches a theoretical limit known as the super-paramagnetic limit. Heat-Assisted Magnetic Recording (HAMR) has emerged as one of the important technologies to overcome this limit. The process of heating while writing brings about certain unique characteristics when compared to conventional schemes. In this paper, we introduce heat-assisted recording, explain the techniques used to numerically model the two-dimensional magnetization process in longitudinal HAMR and extend it to perpendicular recording. Utilizing these models, we investigate the transition characteristics that depend, among other factors, on various thermal parameters. In particular, we determine the effects of change in peak temperature and laser spot position on transition length and center.

1. Introduction

Over the last 40 years, hard drives have clearly emerged as the primary means of data storage. A basic hard drive consists of a disk made of magnetic material and a recording head. The disk is divided into many equally spaced tracks where the data is stored as a binary sequence utilizing the two directions of magnetization possible. The process of storing and retrieving information using magnetic recording is illustrated in Fig. 1. The write current to the recording head is modulated according to the information to be stored and consequently it induces a series of magnetic transitions in the medium. During the read process, magnetic transition in the medium induces a readback signal in a magneto-resistive sensor flying over it.

There have been tremendous increases in the storage capacity of hard disk drives over the last few years. Such increases were almost always achieved by scaling down the area of a bit by reducing its length and width. The medium consists of

2000 *Mathematics Subject Classification.* 68P20, 68P30, 94A40.

Key words and phrases. Heat-assisted magnetic recording, hybrid recording, transition location, transition parameter.

This work was performed as part of the INSIC HAMR ATP program with the support of the U.S. Department of Commerce, National Institute of Standards and Technology, Advanced Technology Program, Cooperative agreement number 70NANB1H3051.

©2008 American Mathematical Society

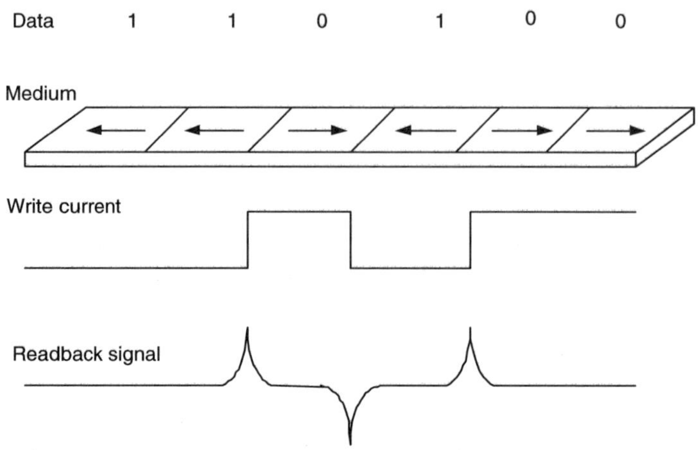

FIGURE 1. Illustration of write and read process in a magnetic recording drive

tiny magnetic particles whose volume needs to be correspondingly scaled down to maintain sufficient signal-to-noise ratio. The anisotropy energy of a grain is defined as $E_a = K_u V$, where K_u is the anisotropy of the grain and V its volume. Since anisotropy energy determines the particle stability; scaling down the volume of magnetic particles reduces their stability. The magnetic industry has reached a critical point where the particle size can no longer be reduced. This is known as the super-paramagnetic limit. The use of a high anisotropic medium to counter this problem makes it difficult to magnetize. Therefore, in order to further increase the areal density, radically new technologies need to be adopted. In this regard, Heat-Assisted Magnetic Recording (HAMR) was proposed as a very attractive option [**1**] where, a high anisotropy medium is heated by a laser at the location of transition during the write process. It is believed that it is possible to achieve an areal density of 1 terabits per square inch (Tb/in^2) with this technology.

In order to exploit the enormous potential of HAMR, there are many challenges that need to be resolved. It is important to study and analyze the system, so as to identify and understand its characteristics. In this paper we introduce HAMR, explain the numerical models used to analyze the system and illustrate some of its important characteristics. The paper is organized as follows. Section 2 describes the principle of heat-assisted magnetic recording. Section 3 introduces the thermal Williams-Comstock model, which is shown to represent a HAMR system appropriately by incorporating all thermal and magnetic properties. Using this model, we show how to determine the magnetic transition characteristics for a given system. Further, in order to accurately capture the effects of finite-width magnetic tracks, we utilize microtrack model described in Section 4. These models enable us to characterize HAMR, especially their dependence on the thermal profile, which is illustrated in Section 5. Finally, we conclude the paper in Section 6.

2. Principle of Heat-Assisted Magnetic Recording

In heat-assisted magnetic recording, during the write process the magnetic media is heated by a laser attached to the write-head assembly. After magnetizing, the

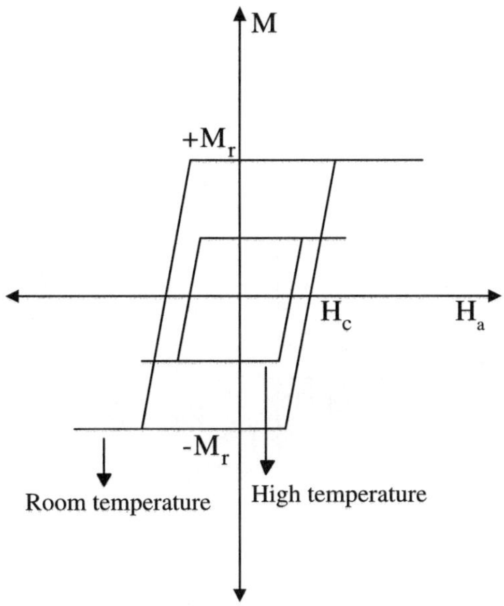

FIGURE 2. Example of an MH loop, illustrating its dependence on temperature

medium is rapidly cooled down to room temperature. The resultant magnetization of the medium is determined by its hysteresis loop (MH loop), which shows the relationship between the applied field (H_a) and the resultant magnetization (M). An example of an MH-loop is shown in Fig. 2. For stable magnetic transitions, a certain field is applied so that even after removing the field, the medium retains a certain level of magnetization. This is called remnant magnetization (M_r). The ease of making a transition in a medium is measured by its coercivity (H_c), which is the field required to reverse the direction of magnetization. The coercivity and remnant magnetization are known to vary approximately linearly with temperature. Therefore, if a transition is written at a temperature higher than room temperature, a smaller field is required to make a transition. But, almost instantaneous cooling ensures that the medium saturates at M_r corresponding to the room temperature.

The process of heating while writing enables sharper magnetic transitions to be made on high coercive materials, thereby achieving higher stability and areal density. The read process in HAMR is identical to that of conventional magnetic recording systems. Though the fundamental idea behind HAMR is simple, the process of rapid heating and cooling brings about a number of practical challenges. More information on these can be obtained from [**4, 5, 6**].

3. The Thermal Williams-Comstock Model

The William-Comstock model is a well-known approximate analytical model that describes the transition characteristics in a conventional magnetic recording system. In [**2**], this model was extended by incorporating thermal gradients in order to determine the transition characteristics of a longitudinal HAMR system. Specifically, this model, known as the *thermal Williams-Comstock model*, captures the effects of heating through the thermal gradients of coercivity and remnant

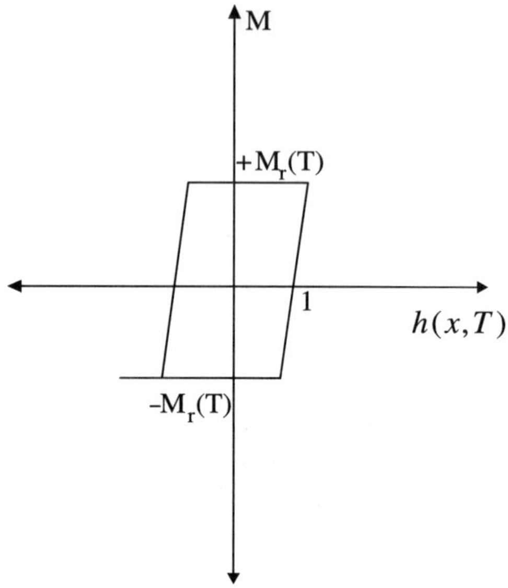

FIGURE 3. MH loop with effective field

magnetization. Application of this model to perpendicular HAMR system is also discussed in this section.

As mentioned earlier, the MH loop of a magnetic material is dependent on the temperature. In order to account for this behavior a new quantity called effective field (h) is introduced. It is defined as the ratio of applied field and coercivity,

$$h(x,T) = \frac{H_a(x)}{|H_c(T(x))|} \tag{1}$$

where $T(x)$ is the temperature profile along the direction of the movement of head (x). Note that the dependence of coercivity on temperature is shown explicitly. The new MH loop defined using h is shown in Fig. 3, where irrespective of the temperature, h is 1 at the point of reversal of magnetization. The magnetization gradient with respect to position is defined as,

$$\frac{dM}{dx} = \frac{dM}{dh}\frac{dh}{dx}. \tag{2}$$

Following a similar approach as in the Williams-Comstock model, the resultant equation, known as the *slope equation* is derived as,

$$\frac{dM(x)}{dx} = \frac{dM(x)}{dH_a}\left[\frac{dH_h(x)}{dx} + \frac{dH_d(x)}{dx} - \frac{dH_c(T)}{dT}\frac{dT}{dx}\right] \tag{3}$$

where, $M(x)$ is magnetization, H_h, H_d are the head and demagnetizing field respectively. Demagnetizing field is defined as the field from the magnetized medium, which opposes the field from the head. Note that the magnetization gradient depends on the coercivity thermal gradient.

Two quantities that completely characterize a magnetic transition are its transition center (or location) and length. Transition center is defined as the point where the magnetization of the medium reverses its direction. It occurs when the net applied field equals the coercivity of the medium. The net applied field is defined as $H_a = H_h + H_d$. Therefore, the transition center is the solution to the equation

$$H_c(x) = H_h(x) + H_d(x) \tag{4}$$

.

Traditionally, magnetic transitions are described using an arctangent profile. Sometimes, hyperbolic tangent is argued to be better suited [**13**]. An arctangent transition is described as

$$M(x) = \frac{2M_r(T(x))}{\pi} \tan^{-1}\left(\frac{x - x_0}{a}\right) \tag{5}$$

where, x_0 is the transition center, a is known as the transition parameter and the expression πa is known as the transition length. The goal of the thermal Williams-Comstock model is to determine a and x_0 of a transition for a given HAMR system set-up. As mentioned before, transition center can be evaluated using Eqn. 4. The transition parameter is evaluated using the slope equation. See [**2**] for the derivation of each quantity of the slope equation.

Demagnetizing field is known to depend on both transition center and parameter. Therefore from Eqn. 3 and Eqn. 4, it can be seen that the two unknowns, transition center and parameter are dependent on each other and cannot be solved analytically. But, if the thermal spot size of the laser used for heating is assumed to be large, then the equations can be simplified and solved analytically. For large spot size, since the thermal gradients are small, demagnetizing field can be ignored in the calculation of transition center, thus making x_0 independent of a. Also, the demagnetizing field gradient equation simplifies, which in turn simplifies the slope equation.

If the spot size is not large, then the demagnetizing field cannot be ignored. Therefore, the system of equations (Eqn. 3 and Eqn. 4) can only be solved iteratively [**3**]. In the first iteration, for a random value of a, x_0 is calculated using Eqn. 4. Then using this value of x_0, Eqn. 3 is evaluated for a. In the second iteration, this new value of a is used to determine the new x_0 and so on. The iteration continues until both x_0 and a converges to some required accuracy.

Thermal Williams Comstock Model can be applied for both longitudinal and perpendicular HAMR. Irrespective of the direction of magnetization, the transition can be considered to follow an arctangent profile. In order to solve the slope equation, the head and demagnetizing field needs to be evaluated. The field expressions for both longitudinal and perpendicular recording is explained in the following sections.

3.1. Longitudinal HAMR. In longitudinal recording, the medium is magnetized in the longitudinal direction (along the media). The set-up of a longitudinal system is shown in Fig. 4, which shows the poles of the head and the medium beneath it. The longitudinal field between the two poles magnetizes the media in the longitudinal direction. Assuming an infinitely long and wide head with a finite gap width, Karlqvist derived an analytical expression for the field intensity in the medium [**8**]. The expression for the longitudinal component of the field is given as

$$H_x(x,y) = \frac{H_0}{\pi}\left[\tan^{-1}\left(\frac{x+g/2}{y}\right) - \tan^{-1}\left(\frac{x-g/2}{y}\right)\right] \tag{6}$$

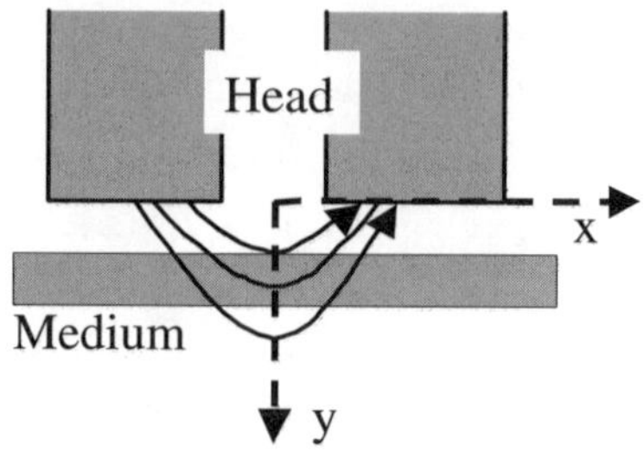

FIGURE 4. Longitudinal head and field

where g is the gap width and H_0 is the deep gap field. For the purpose of thermal Williams-Comstock model, the field is evaluated at the center of the medium. If t is the thickness of the medium and d the distance from the bottom of the head to the medium surface, then H_x is evaluated at $y = d + t/2$. The effect of the H_y component of the field is ignored in longitudinal recording. The demagnetizing field from a transition can be expressed as [**7**]

$$H_d(x) = -\frac{dM}{dx} * H_x^{\text{step}}(x) \tag{7}$$

where the field from a sharp transition at the center of the medium is given as

$$H_x^{\text{step}}(x) = \frac{1}{\pi}\tan^{-1}\left(\frac{t}{2x}\right). \tag{8}$$

Therefore, assuming an arctangent transition, the demagnetizing field can be calculated as below. If the laser spot size is large, then the demagnetizing field equation can be simplified, details of which are given in [**2**].

$$\begin{aligned} H_d(x) = \frac{-2}{\pi^2}\int_{-\infty}^{+\infty}\Bigg[&\frac{M_r(x')a}{a^2+(x_0-x')^2} + \tan^{-1}\left(\frac{x'-x_0}{a}\right) \\ &\frac{dM_r(T(x'))}{dx'}\Bigg]\tan^{-1}\left(\frac{t}{2(x-x')}\right)dx' \end{aligned} \tag{9}$$

3.2. Perpendicular HAMR. In perpendicular recording, the perpendicular field of the head magnetizes the medium in the vertical direction. The actual set-up of a perpendicular system is shown in the top of Fig 5. A highly permeable layer (or keeper) is deposited beneath the medium through which the field is conducted from one pole to the other. Note that the field is in the vertical direction in the medium. The field intensity, derived by Westmijze [**9**], is given as a complex function that needs to be solved numerically. But, by considering the equivalent system set-up (bottom of Fig. 5), an analytical head field expression can be derived [**10, 11**]. An image of the pole head can be considered to be symmetrically placed beneath the medium. When this set-up is turned sideways, the similarity with the longitudinal set-up can be readily seen. Therefore, to a good approximation the field in a perpendicular head can be evaluated using the Karlqvist expression, taking into account the change in coordinate system for the perpendicular recording. Therefore, the perpendicular component of the head field is given as

$$H_y(x,y) = \frac{H_0}{\pi}\left[\tan^{-1}\left(\frac{y+g/2}{x}\right) - \tan^{-1}\left(\frac{y-g/2}{x}\right)\right] \tag{10}$$

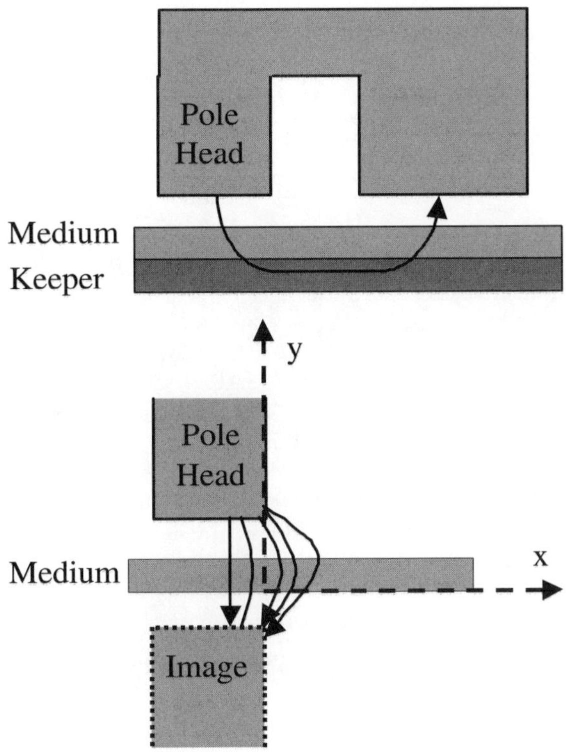

FIGURE 5. Perpendicular head and field: actual head configuration and equivalent set-up

where g is the gap width between the pole head and its image. If d is the head-medium distance and t is the medium thickness, then $g = 2d + 2t$. For the thermal Williams-Comstock model, the field is evaluated at the center of the medium ($y = t/2$). The effect of the H_x component of the field is ignored in perpendicular recording. As mentioned before, the Karlqvist expression is not a reasonable approximation for fields close to the head gap. Therefore, Eqn. 10 is valid only for $x > 0$. Since, in general, the transition occurs away from the pole edge this expression can be faithfully used in the thermal Williams-Comstock model for evaluation of transition characteristics. The demagnetizing field can be calculated using Eqn. 7, but with the perpendicular field component of a sharp transition as shown below.

$$H_d(x) = -\frac{dM}{dx} * H_y^{\text{step}}(x) \tag{11}$$

where the field from a sharp transition at the center of the medium is given as [**12**]

$$H_y^{\text{step}}(x) = \frac{1}{\pi} \tan^{-1}\left(\frac{2x}{t}\right) \tag{12}$$

Therefore, considering an arctangent transition the demagnetizing field can be calculated as,

$$H_d(x) = \frac{-2}{\pi^2}\int_{-\infty}^{+\infty}\left[\frac{M_r(x')a}{a^2+(x_0-x')^2} + \tan^{-1}\left(\frac{x'-x_0}{a}\right)\frac{dM_r(T(x'))}{dx'}\right]\tan^{-1}\left(\frac{2(x-x')}{t}\right)dx' \tag{13}$$

For a large laser spot size, the second term becomes insignificant. Consequently, the demagnetization field can be reduced to,

$$\begin{aligned} H_d(x) &\approx -\frac{2}{\pi^2}\int_{-\infty}^{\infty}\frac{M_r(x')a}{a^2+(x'-x_0)^2}\tan^{-1}\left(\frac{2(x-x')}{t}\right)dx' \\ &= \frac{2M_r(T(x))}{\pi}\tan^{-1}\left(\frac{x-x_0}{t/2+a}\right) \end{aligned} \tag{14}$$

and the gradient of the demagnetizing field can be simplified if we ignore the thermal gradient of the remnant magnetization, i.e.,

$$\frac{dH_d(x)}{dx} \approx -\frac{2M_r(T(x))}{\pi(a+t/2)} \tag{15}$$

Furthermore, similar to the derivation for longitudinal recording in [**2**], we can show that the analytical expression for the transition parameter in perpendicular recording is,

$$a = -\frac{\gamma}{2} + \frac{1}{2}\sqrt{\gamma^2 + \frac{4H_c(1-S)t}{\Delta\pi}}\Bigg|_{x_0}, \tag{16}$$

where,

$$\begin{aligned} \Delta &= \frac{dH_h}{dx} - \frac{dH_c}{dT}\frac{dT}{dx}\bigg|_{x_0} = \frac{H_g g}{\pi(x_0^2+(g/2)^2)} - \frac{dH_c}{dT}\frac{dT}{dx}\bigg|_{x_0}, \\ \gamma &= \frac{2M_r}{\Delta\pi} - \frac{t}{2} + \frac{2H_c(1-S)}{\Delta\pi}. \end{aligned} \tag{17}$$

4. Microtrack Model

The process of heating and magnetization of a medium is two-dimensional. But, the Williams-Comstock model provides only a one-dimensional solution to the problem of determining the transition characteristics. Therefore, they do not accurately model the magnetic transition of a track with finite width. In this section, we explain the microtrack model that closely captures the effects of this two-dimensional process. In this model, a magnetic track is divided into several sub-tracks of equal width as shown in Fig. 6. The temperature profile resulting from the heating is denoted by $T(x, y)$ where, x and y represent the directions along and across the track respectively. If N is the number of sub-tracks and Δz their width, then for each sub-track, the temperature profile is approximated by the one-dimensional function $T(x, y = i \cdot \Delta z)$, $-N/2 \le i \le N/2$. The more sub-tracks, the better the approximation. For a given system set-up, thermal Williams-Comstock model is applied independently to each of these sub-tracks to determine the corresponding transition parameter and center. If the readback response for

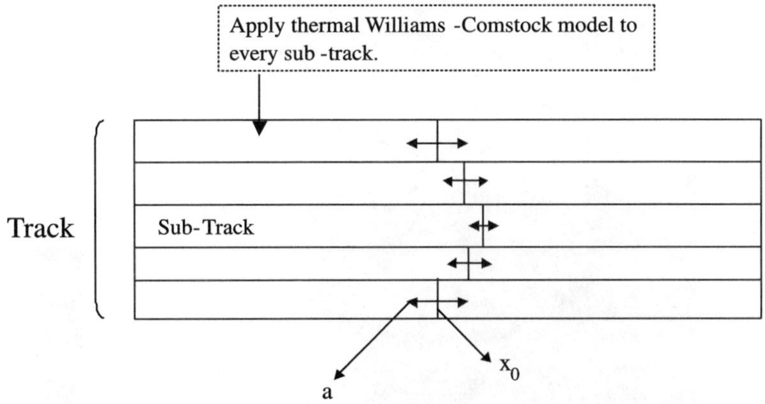

FIGURE 6. Microtrack modeling of HAMR channel

each of these sub-tracks is $h(t, a)$, then the total response of the transition is given as,

$$p(t) = \frac{1}{N} \sum_{i=1}^{N} h(t - \tau_i, a_i) \tag{18}$$

where, τ_i and a_i are the transition center and parameter of the ith sub-track. The isolated transition responses for longitudinal and perpendicular recording are expressed using Lorentzian and error functions respectively [**14**].

5. Transition Characteristics

Designing a HAMR system for optimal performance is a multi-dimensional problem. The system performance is dependent not only on magnetic properties like coercivity and remnant magnetization, but also on their variation with temperature, heating profile (peak temperature, width at half of peak temperature) [**3**], and also on the position of peak temperature [**2**]. The position of the laser spot needs to be properly chosen in order to obtain the optimal performance. Since the laser is attached to the head assembly, it is not known whether it is possible to align the peak temperature with the gap center or whether it is the best possible set-up. In this section, we report on some of the unique characteristics of longitudinal HAMR induced by thermal spot.

For any system parameters, using the thermal Williams-Comstock model and the microtrack model, the transition length, location and magnetization can be determined across a track of finite width. Fig. 7 shows an example of a typical magnetization pattern of a transition in the medium for a longitudinal recording system. This figure illustrates several features of a transition that are induced by heating and are unique to HAMR. Firstly, we note that the transition occurs at different location across the track and secondly, the transition is sharp at the center and decreases progressively toward the edges of the track. Since, the thermal profile is Gaussian in both dimensions, maximum temperature occurs at the center of the track and minimum at the edges of the track. As coercivity varies linearly with

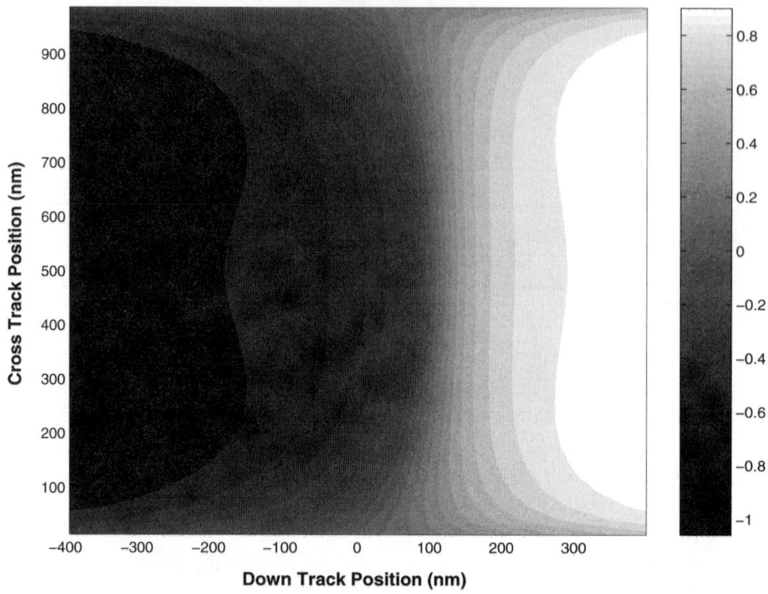

FIGURE 7. Magnetization of the medium after a transition is made

temperature, solution to Eqn. 4 varies for different sub-tracks, inducing the transition curvature across the track. The solution to transition location is a function of y, since temperature T is a function of both x and y. Thermal Williams-Comstock model suggests that high coercivity gradient induces sharper transitions. Since, coercivity gradient along the track is small at the edges, we notice a significant increase in transition length near the edges. From Eqn. 4, we note that the transition location also depends on the head field. Fig. 8 shows the shift in transition location with respect to the gap center at various deep gap fields for a system with $H_c(x,y) = -500 \cdot T(x,y) + 5 \cdot 10^5$ A/m and $M_r(x,y) = -300 \cdot T(x,y) + 3 \cdot 10^5$ A/m. It also clearly shows the transition curvature across the track.

One of the most important quantity that determines the storage capacity of HAMR is the width of the readback signal of its transitions. The width when measured at half their peak value is denoted by PW_{50} and is commonly used for purpose of comparison. Smaller the PW_{50}, greater the storage capacity of the disk. Therefore, it is necessary to investigate the effects of thermal profile on readback signal width. In the following analysis we assume a high coercive material, where $H_c(x,y) = -2000 \cdot T(x,y) + 1.6 \cdot 10^6$ A/m and $M_r(x,y) = -1200 \cdot T(x,y) + 1.2 \cdot 10^6$ A/m. Other system parameters are shown in Table 1. Fig. 9 shows the PW_{50} of the readback signal at various peak temperatures for different deep gap fields. In general, higher temperatures lead to smaller PW_{50}, but show signs of saturating or even increasing at very high temperatures. Though not shown here, this phenomenon is more pronounced with low coercive materials. For a given head field, there is an optimal temperature that achieves minimum PW_{50}. Since, higher temperatures result in lower coercivity, it is natural to expect PW_{50} to be better at high temperatures, but the reason for their saturation or increase at very high temperatures is not obvious.

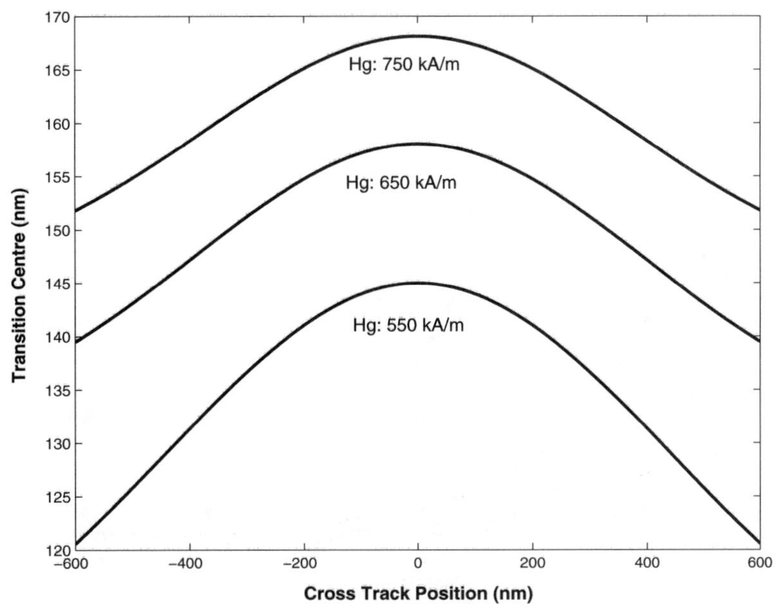

FIGURE 8. Transition center curvature across the track for various deep gap fields. For this system, $H_c(x,y) = -500 \cdot T(x,y) + 5 \cdot 10^5$ A/m and $M_r(x,y) = -300 \cdot T(x,y) + 3 \cdot 10^5$ A/m

The readback width not only depends on the peak temperature, but also on the position of the laser (or consequently the position of the peak temperature) with respect to the head gap. Along the track, the laser can be positioned either in the direction of the head movement (up-track or +X) or opposite to it (down-track or -X). For all cases, the laser is assumed to be at the center of the track in the cross-track direction. Positioning anywhere else is undesirable and is not discussed in this paper. Fig. 10 shows the PW_{50} for the same system as before with peak temperature 350 °C, at different laser spot positions around the head gap center (0 nm). Minimum PW_{50} occurs when the laser is positioned just to the right of the gap center. Moving the laser away from the gap in either direction, greatly increases the readback signal width, though it seems to decrease after reaching a peak for down-track laser spot positions. To explain such a behavior needs careful investigation. Without a proper understanding of the source of these changes, it will be difficult to generalize the behavior of any HAMR system, which has many degrees of freedom for optimization. In the following analysis, we identify the reasons for such changes and argue that it is indeed a general behavior of HAMR with high coercive materials.

The two parameters that determine the PW_{50} of the readback signal of a transition are the transition curvature of the track and parameter of each sub-track. Changing the position of the laser not only changes the temperature profile but also the coercivity of the medium. Consequently, it alters both the transition center and parameter. Fig. 11 shows an example of how the head field and the coercivity look at different laser spot positions along the down-track direction. Observe that the point of intersection of coercivity and head field is different at different laser spot

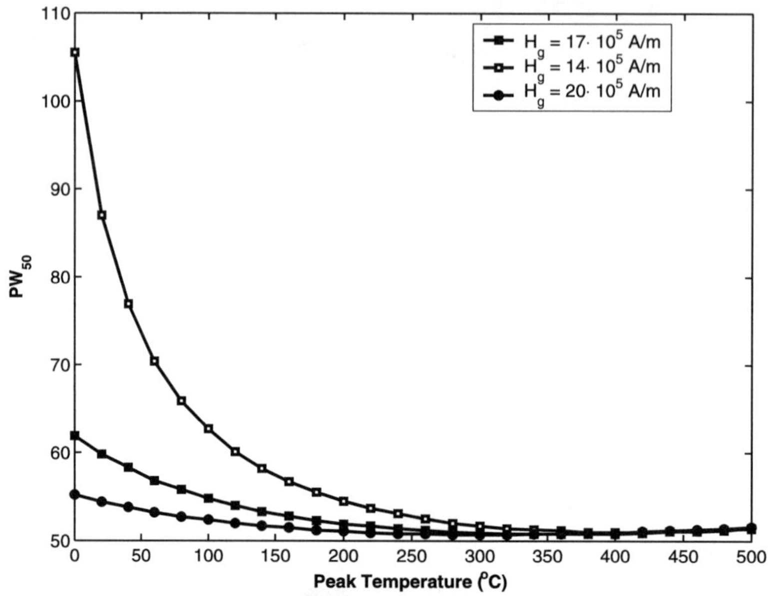

FIGURE 9. Readback signal width at various peak temperatures for different gap fields

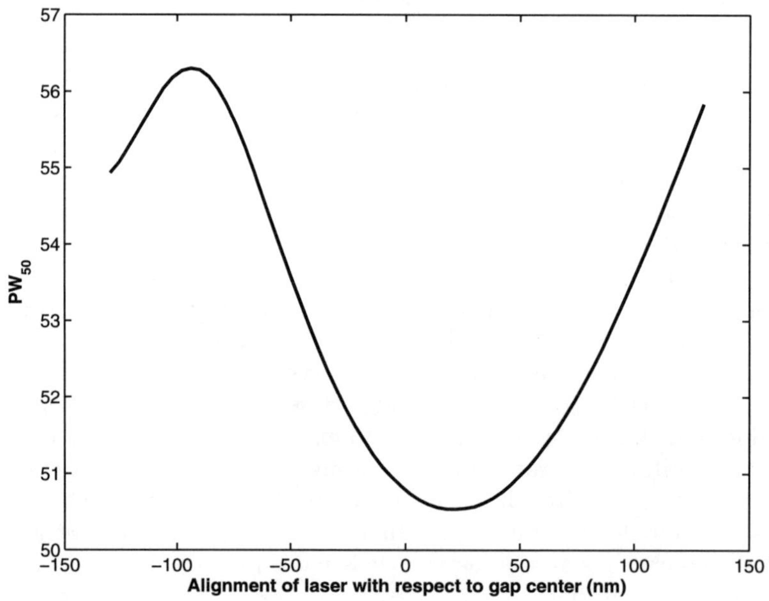

FIGURE 10. PW_{50} at various laser spot positions in Longitudinal HAMR

TABLE 1. System Parameters

Full-width half-max of laser spot	70 nm
Write head gap	100 nm
Distance from pole to medium	20 nm
Read head gap	5 nm
Width of the track	160 nm
Number of microtracks	23

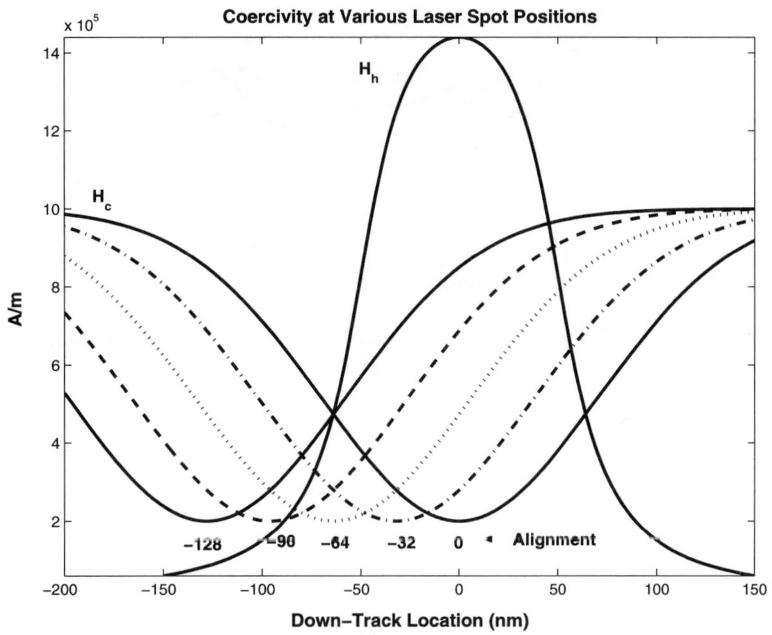

FIGURE 11. Coercivity for various laser spot positions

positions. This figure is a one-dimensional illustration of how the coercivity changes with laser spot, i.e. it is an illustration for one of the sub-tracks.

Fig. 12 shows the transition centers across the track at different laser spot positions in the down-track direction. It reveals two general trends. As the laser is moved down-track from the gap center, transition location initially move away from the gap center until they occur at the positive coercivity gradient region. Thereafter, moving the laser further down-track, moves the location back closer to the gap center. As the transition location moves away from the gap center, the curvature deteriorates, since the center now occurs closer to the peak temperature, where the variation in thermal gradient *across* the track is the highest. Consequently, in this example, the transition curvature is at its worst when the laser is aligned at around -96 nm (location closest to peak temperature) and improves on either side of this position. Fig. 13 shows the cross-track transition parameter profile for the same down-track laser spot positions. As before, two trends are identified. The parameter generally increases when laser is moved down-track toward the lower

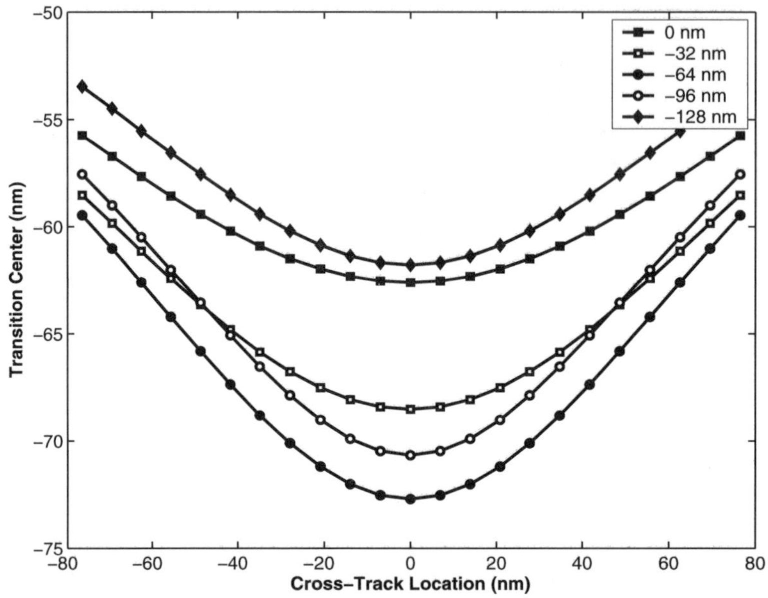

FIGURE 12. Transition centers *across* the track at various laser spot positions in the down-track direction

gradient region. In the figure, at an alignment of -96 nm there is a huge increase largely contributed by almost-zero coercivity gradient and low head field. If the transition location occurs when both coercivity gradient and head field gradient are positive, then higher coercivity gradient would result in a higher transition parameter. Since, coercivity gradient decreases toward track edges, we observe that the parameter at the center of the track increases much faster than the parameter at the edges of the track, when laser is moved down-track. At an alignment of -128 nm, though the parameter at the center remains higher than at the edges, its values have improved on account of better head field gradient at the transition location.

When laser is moved up-track, the coercivity gradient is always negative at the transition location. Also, farther the laser is from the gap center, farther the transition location is from the peak temperature. Therefore, as shown in Fig. 14, there is almost no curvature for positions far to the right of the gap center. For the same reason, as shown in Fig. 15, the change in transition parameter is almost identical throughout every sub-track. However, since the transition location is pushed to the lower temperature regions, where the coercivity gradients are smaller, transition parameter increases. PW_{50} is directly proportional to the transition parameter and is inversely proportional to the extent of curvature. If the transition location of the sub-tracks of a track are misaligned, then their combined readback response will be much wider than the response of a track whose sub-track locations are aligned with each other. As the laser is positioned along the down-track direction, PW_{50} will increase on account of deteriorating curvature though the transition parameter will be less. It will peak when the transition location occurs, where the temperature of the medium is maximum. As the laser is positioned along the up-track direction, PW_{50} will increase on account of increasing

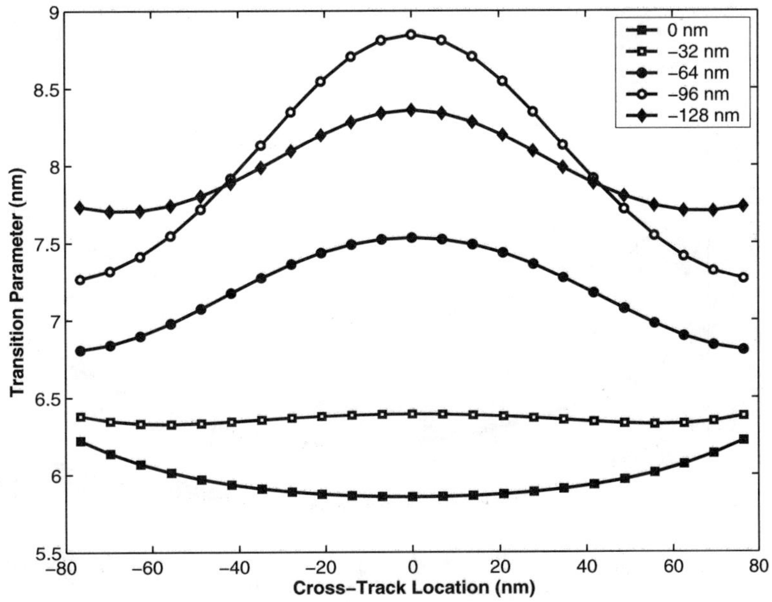

FIGURE 13. Transition parameter *across* the track at various laser spot positions in the down-track direction

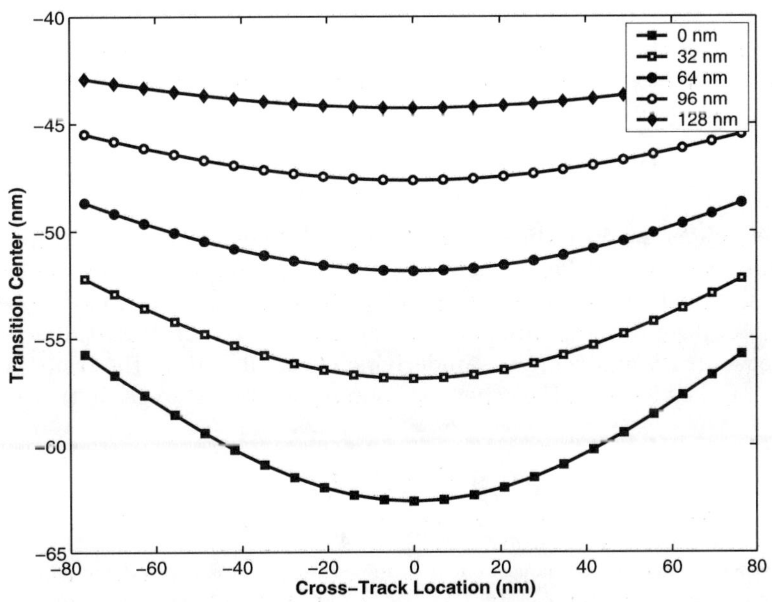

FIGURE 14. Transition centers *across* the track at various laser spot positions in the up-track direction

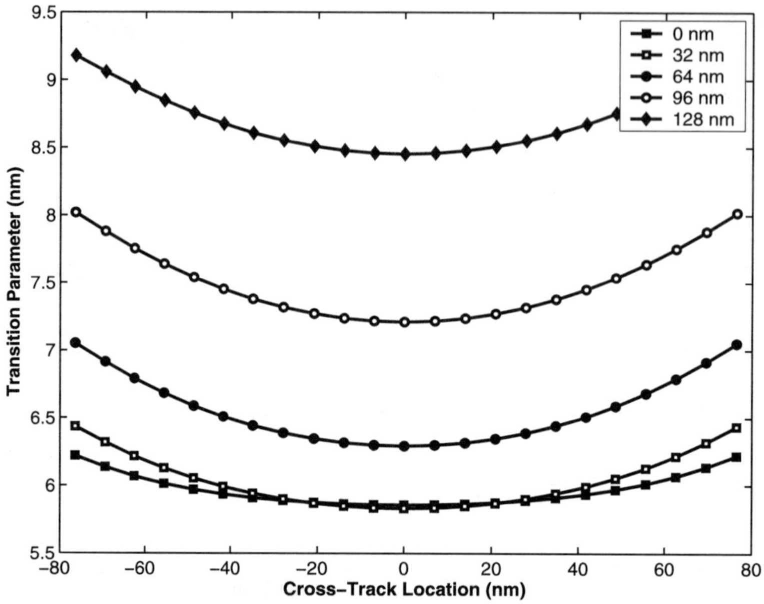

FIGURE 15. Transition parameters *across* the track at various laser spot positions in the up-track direction

transition parameter, though the curvature will improve. The minimum PW_{50} can be obtained for laser spot alignments close to the gap center. This explains the behavior observed in Fig. 10.

6. Conclusion

In this paper we introduced the thermal Williams-Comstock model for both longitudinal and perpendicular heat-assisted recording. Using this model and the microtrack model, several characteristics of HAMR were illustrated. Specifically, the effects of peak temperature and laser spot alignment on the readback response were discussed. By analyzing the underlying effects it had on the transition length and location, we identified the general system behavior to changes in thermal profile.

References

[1] M. H. Kryder, "Future trends in magnetic storage technology", *Joint NAPMRC*, Digest of Technical Papers, p. 68, Jan. 2003.

[2] T. Rausch, "Thermal Williams-Comstock model for predicting transition length in a heat-assisted magnetic recording system", *IEEE Trans. Mag.*, vol. 40, no. 1, pp. 137–147, Jan. 2004.

[3] M. F. Erden, T. Rausch and W. A. Challener, "Cross-track location and transition parameter effects in heat-assisted magnetic recording", *IEEE Trans. Mag.*, vol. 41, no. 6, pp. 2189–2194, June 2005.

[4] T. W. McDaniel and W. A. Challener, "Issues in design of media for hybrid recording", *Trans. Magn. Soc. Jpn.*, vol. 2, pp. 316–321, 2002.

[5] T. W. McDaniel, W. A. Challener and K. Sendur, "Issues in heat-assisted perpendicular recording", *IEEE Trans. Mag.*, vol. 39, no. 4, pp. 1972–1979, Jul. 2003.

[6] W. A. Challener, T. W. McDaniel, C. Mihalcea, K. Mountfield, K. Pelhos and K. Sendur, "Light delivery techniques for heat-assisted magnetic recording", *Jpn. J. Appl. Phys.*, vol. 42, pp. 981–988, 2003.

[7] S. X. Wang and A. M. Taratorin, *Magnetic Information Storage Technology*, Academic Press, 1999.

[8] O. Karlqvist, "Calculation of magnetic field in the ferromagnetic layer of a magnetic drum", *Trans. Roy. Inst. Tech.*, no. 86, 1954.

[9] W. K. Westmijze, "Studies on magnetic recording", *Phillips Res. Rep.*, part II, vol. 8, no. 3, & Part III, vol. 8, no. 4, 1953.

[10] J. C. Mallinson and H. N. Bertram, "On the characteristics of pole-keeper head fields", *IEEE Trans. Mag.*, vol. 20, no. 5, pp. 721–723, Sept. 1984.

[11] J. C. Mallinson and H. N. Bertram, "A theoretical and experimental comparison of longitudinal and vertical modes of magnetic recording", *IEEE Trans. Mag.*, vol. 20, no. 3, pp. 461–467, May 1984.

[12] H. N. Bertram, *Theory of Magnetic Recording*, Cambridge University Press, 2003.

[13] Y. Zhang and H. N. Bertram, "A theoretical study of nonlinear transition shift", *IEEE Trans. Mag.*, vol. 34, no. 4, pp. 1955–1957, July 1998.

[14] B. Vasic and E. M. Kurtas, *Coding and Signal Processing for Magnetic Recording Systems*, chapter 18, pp. 18.1-18.12, CRC Press, 2004.

Department of Electrical and Computer Engineering, University of Arizona, Tucson, Arizona 85721
E-mail address: `rathna@ece.arizona.edu`

Department of Electrical and Computer Engineering, University of Arizona, Tucson, Arizona 85721
E-mail address: `vasic@ece.arizona.edu`

Seagate Research, Pittsburgh, Pennsylvania 15222
E-mail address: `fatih.erden@seagate.com`

Seagate Research, Pittsburgh, Pennsylvania 15222
E-mail address: `ching.he@seagate.com`

DIMACS Series in Discrete Mathematics
and Theoretical Computer Science
Volume **73**, 2008

Cramér-Rao Bound for Timing Recovery on Channels with Inter-Symbol Interference

Aravind R. Nayak, John R. Barry, and Steven W. McLaughlin

Abstract. This paper deals with the Cramér-Rao bound (CRB) on timing estimation error variance for communication across channels with inter-symbol interference (ISI). The CRB for ISI channels with frequency offset is well-known in the literature. We derive the CRB for a more general model that includes a random walk component in addition to a frequency offset. The CRB is useful as a benchmark to evaluate competing timing recovery algorithms. In addition, in this paper, the CRB is used as a tool to derive the optimal training symbol placement strategy for channels that suffer from ISI and a frequency offset.

1. Introduction

Timing recovery is an essential component of digital communication and data storage systems. Most physical communication and data storage channels are analog in nature. Magnetic storage relies on storing data using transitions in the direction of magnetization. The information to be stored is often in the form of bits, which are modulated to suit the analog channel characteristics. The output of the channel, called the readback waveform, needs to be mapped back to the discrete domain at the data detector. To this end, the readback waveform is sampled at instants chosen by the timing recovery block. The system error rate varies drastically with the performance of timing recovery which, in turn, is a strong function of the operating SNR.

In this paper, the general problem of timing recovery for channels with inter-symbol interference and baud rate sampling (*i.e.*, one sample per data symbol) is considered. Magnetic recording channels occur as special cases of these. The Cramér-Rao bound (CRB) [**1**] is used to derive a lower bound on timing estimation error variance. For tractability, an uncoded system with *i.i.d.* data symbols is assumed. This assumption is approximately true for systems that employ capacity-approaching iteratively-decodable codes [**2**] [**3**] [**4**] [**5**] that are being considered for magnetic data storage systems. The CRB for constant timing offset model [**6**] and frequency offset models [**7**] are well-known in the literature. In this paper, the CRB

2000 *Mathematics Subject Classification.* 68P20, 68P30, 93E10, 94A14, 94A15, 94A40.

Key words and phrases. Cramér-Rao bound, random walk, frequency offset, timing recovery, training symbol placement, phase-locked loop.

This research was supported by the Information Storage Industry Consortium.

©2008 American Mathematical Society

is derived for the random walk timing offset model, and for a general model that is a combination of a random walk and a frequency offset.

Finally, the CRB is used to derive the training symbol placement strategy that minimizes the CRB on the timing estimation error variance for channels with frequency offset and ISI. The conventional strategy of placing all the known symbols at the start of the sector is not necessarily optimal. In this paper, arbitrary locations are allowed for the training symbols. For the general problem of timing recovery for channels with ISI and frequency offset, the CRB is intractable due to the presence of both known (training) and unknown (data) symbols. Using a looser bound called the modified CRB (MCRB) [**8**] leads to similar intractability. We were able to solve this problem in two special cases. The first case assumes that only the training symbols are written, *i.e.*, the unknown data symbols are absent. With this rather unrealistic assumption, the MCRB is derived as a function of the training symbol placement strategy. The second case assumes the presence of both the training and data symbols, but the channel model is simplified. A linear model for the timing observations is used, where the known symbols lead to reduced measurement noise in the timing estimator. With the known and the unknown symbols thus accounted for, the CRB for this linearized model is derived as a function of the placement strategy. Finally, the placement strategy that minimizes the bounds in these cases is derived. The optimal strategy that minimizes the CRB and the mean-squared timing estimation error in both these cases is to place the training symbols half at the beginning and half at the end of the sector. This strategy significantly reduces the training overhead needed for the same error-rate performance.

2. Definition

Parameter estimation problems can be modeled as consisting of the following four components: [**1**]

- *Parameter Space.* The parameter $\boldsymbol{\theta}$ is a $P \times 1$ vector consisting of P scalar parameters. The parameter space is the set of all possible values the parameter may take on.
- *Observation Space.* This is the set of all possible observations $\boldsymbol{r}$. In general, $\boldsymbol{r}$ is a vector of dimension $N_r \times 1$.
- *Probabilistic Mapping from Parameter Space to Observation Space.* This is the conditional probability density $f_{\boldsymbol{r}|\boldsymbol{\theta}}(\boldsymbol{r}|\boldsymbol{\theta})$ that determines the effect of the parameter $\boldsymbol{\theta}$ on the observation $\boldsymbol{r}$.
- *Estimation Rule.* This is the mapping rule $\hat{\boldsymbol{\theta}}(\boldsymbol{r})$ that is used to map the observation $\boldsymbol{r}$ into an estimate $\hat{\boldsymbol{\theta}}$ which is again a $P \times 1$ vector.

In the absence of *a priori* information, the parameter $\boldsymbol{\theta}$ is treated as a deterministic but unknown quantity. When the *a priori* distribution $f_{\boldsymbol{\theta}}(\boldsymbol{\theta})$ is available, $\boldsymbol{\theta}$ is treated as a random variable.

First, consider the case without *a priori* information. The estimation error covariance matrix is given by $E_{\boldsymbol{r}}[(\hat{\boldsymbol{\theta}}(\boldsymbol{r}) - \boldsymbol{\theta})(\hat{\boldsymbol{\theta}}(\boldsymbol{r}) - \boldsymbol{\theta})^T]$. An estimator $\hat{\boldsymbol{\theta}}(\boldsymbol{r})$ is called *unbiased* if, for all $\boldsymbol{\theta}$, the average bias $B(\boldsymbol{\theta})$ is zero, where

$$B(\boldsymbol{\theta}) = E[\hat{\boldsymbol{\theta}}(\boldsymbol{r}) - \boldsymbol{\theta}] \triangleq \int_{-\infty}^{\infty} f_{\boldsymbol{r}|\boldsymbol{\theta}}(\boldsymbol{r}|\boldsymbol{\theta})[\hat{\boldsymbol{\theta}}(\boldsymbol{r}) - \boldsymbol{\theta}]\, \mathrm{d}\boldsymbol{r}. \tag{1}$$

For any *unbiased* estimator, the CRB is given by [**1**]

$$E_{\boldsymbol{r}}[(\hat{\boldsymbol{\theta}}(\boldsymbol{r})-\boldsymbol{\theta})(\hat{\boldsymbol{\theta}}(\boldsymbol{r})-\boldsymbol{\theta})^T] \geq \boldsymbol{J}_\theta^{-1}, \tag{2}$$

where $\boldsymbol{J}_\theta$ is a $P \times P$ square matrix called the Fisher information matrix, defined by

$$\boldsymbol{J}_\theta = E_{\boldsymbol{r}}\left\{\left[\frac{\partial}{\partial\boldsymbol{\theta}} \ln f_{\boldsymbol{r}|\boldsymbol{\theta}}(\boldsymbol{r}|\boldsymbol{\theta})\right]\left[\frac{\partial}{\partial\boldsymbol{\theta}} \ln f_{\boldsymbol{r}|\boldsymbol{\theta}}(\boldsymbol{r}|\boldsymbol{\theta})\right]^T\right\}. \tag{3}$$

The matrix inequality $E_{\boldsymbol{r}}[(\hat{\boldsymbol{\theta}}(\boldsymbol{r})-\boldsymbol{\theta})(\hat{\boldsymbol{\theta}}(\boldsymbol{r})-\boldsymbol{\theta})^T] \geq \boldsymbol{J}_\theta^{-1}$ is equivalent to stating that the matrix difference $\left(E_{\boldsymbol{r}}[(\hat{\boldsymbol{\theta}}(\boldsymbol{r})-\boldsymbol{\theta})(\hat{\boldsymbol{\theta}}(\boldsymbol{r})-\boldsymbol{\theta})^T] - \boldsymbol{J}_\theta^{-1}\right)$ is positive semi-definite. This implies that the estimation error variance for the ith parameter θ_i is bounded by the ith diagonal entry of $\boldsymbol{J}_\theta^{-1}$. In symbols,

$$E_{\boldsymbol{r}}[(\hat{\theta}_i(\boldsymbol{r})-\theta_i)^2] \geq \boldsymbol{J}_\theta^{-1}(i,i),$$

where $\hat{\theta}_i(\boldsymbol{r})$ and θ_i denote the ith element of $\hat{\boldsymbol{\theta}}(\boldsymbol{r})$ and $\boldsymbol{\theta}$ respectively.

In the presence of an *a priori* distribution $f_{\boldsymbol{\theta}}(\boldsymbol{\theta})$, we consider the average error covariance matrix $E_{\boldsymbol{r},\boldsymbol{\theta}}[(\hat{\boldsymbol{\theta}}(\boldsymbol{r})-\boldsymbol{\theta})(\hat{\boldsymbol{\theta}}(\boldsymbol{r})-\boldsymbol{\theta})^T]$. As opposed to *unbiased* estimators, we consider *probabilistically unbiased* estimators where the conditional expectation of the error, $B(\boldsymbol{\theta})$, satisfies the following conditions:

$$\begin{aligned} \lim_{\boldsymbol{\theta}\to\infty} B(\boldsymbol{\theta}) f_{\boldsymbol{\theta}}(\boldsymbol{\theta}) &= \mathbf{0}, \\ \lim_{\boldsymbol{\theta}\to-\infty} B(\boldsymbol{\theta}) f_{\boldsymbol{\theta}}(\boldsymbol{\theta}) &= \mathbf{0}. \end{aligned} \tag{4}$$

The limits in the above equations are in the sense that each individual component tends to ∞ or $-\infty$ respectively as the case may be. An *unbiased* estimator is *probabilistically unbiased* and, therefore, the result below holds for a more general class of estimators. For *probabilistically unbiased* estimators, the lower bound is given by [**1**]

$$E_{\boldsymbol{r},\boldsymbol{\theta}}[(\hat{\boldsymbol{\theta}}(\boldsymbol{r})-\boldsymbol{\theta})(\hat{\boldsymbol{\theta}}(\boldsymbol{r})-\boldsymbol{\theta})^T] \geq \boldsymbol{J}_T^{-1}, \tag{5}$$

where $\boldsymbol{J}_T$ is the total information matrix of dimensions $P \times P$, defined by

$$\boldsymbol{J}_T = E_{\boldsymbol{r},\boldsymbol{\theta}}\left\{\left[\frac{\partial}{\partial\boldsymbol{\theta}} \ln f_{\boldsymbol{r},\boldsymbol{\theta}}(\boldsymbol{r},\boldsymbol{\theta})\right]\left[\frac{\partial}{\partial\boldsymbol{\theta}} \ln f_{\boldsymbol{r},\boldsymbol{\theta}}(\boldsymbol{r},\boldsymbol{\theta})\right]^T\right\}, \tag{6}$$

where $f_{\boldsymbol{r},\boldsymbol{\theta}}(\boldsymbol{r},\boldsymbol{\theta})$ is the joint probability density of $\boldsymbol{r}$ and $\boldsymbol{\theta}$. As before, the matrix inequality is in the sense that the difference is positive semi-definite. Note that $\boldsymbol{J}_T$ can be rewritten as

$$\boldsymbol{J}_T = E_{\boldsymbol{\theta}}[\boldsymbol{J}_\theta] + \boldsymbol{J}_a, \tag{7}$$

where the *a priori* information matrix $\boldsymbol{J}_a$ is

$$\boldsymbol{J}_a = E_{\boldsymbol{r},\boldsymbol{\theta}}\left\{\left[\frac{\partial}{\partial\boldsymbol{\theta}} \ln f_{\boldsymbol{\theta}}(\boldsymbol{\theta})\right]\left[\frac{\partial}{\partial\boldsymbol{\theta}} \ln f_{\boldsymbol{\theta}}(\boldsymbol{\theta})\right]^T\right\}. \tag{8}$$

The Fisher information matrix $\boldsymbol{J}_\theta$ has an elegant form when the density function $f_{\boldsymbol{r}|\boldsymbol{\theta}}(\boldsymbol{r}|\boldsymbol{\theta})$ is multivariate normal [**9**]. Specifically, if the distribution of $\boldsymbol{r}$ is

$\mathcal{N}(\boldsymbol{x}(\boldsymbol{\theta}), \boldsymbol{R})$, *i.e.*,

$$f_{\boldsymbol{r}|\boldsymbol{\theta}}(\boldsymbol{r}|\boldsymbol{\theta}) = \frac{1}{\sqrt{(2\pi)^N |\boldsymbol{R}|}} \exp\left(-\frac{1}{2} \left[\boldsymbol{r} - \boldsymbol{x}(\boldsymbol{\theta})\right]^T \boldsymbol{R}^{-1} \left[\boldsymbol{r} - \boldsymbol{x}(\boldsymbol{\theta})\right] \right), \tag{9}$$

then $\boldsymbol{J}_\theta$ can be simplified to

$$\boldsymbol{J}_\theta = \boldsymbol{G}^T \boldsymbol{R}^{-1} \boldsymbol{G}, \tag{10}$$

where $\boldsymbol{G}$ is the *sensitivity matrix*

$$\boldsymbol{G} = \left[\frac{\partial}{\partial \boldsymbol{\theta}} \boldsymbol{x}^T(\boldsymbol{\theta}) \right] = [\boldsymbol{g}_0 \; \boldsymbol{g}_1 \cdots \boldsymbol{g}_{P-1}], \tag{11}$$

P is the size of the vector $\boldsymbol{\theta}$ and the $N \times 1$ column vector $\boldsymbol{g}_i = \frac{\partial \boldsymbol{x}(\boldsymbol{\theta})}{\partial \theta_i}$ denotes the variation in the mean $\boldsymbol{x}(\boldsymbol{\theta})$ with respect to θ_i, the ith element of $\boldsymbol{\theta}$. When the covariance matrix is of the form $\boldsymbol{R} = \sigma^2 \boldsymbol{I}$, this further simplifies to

$$\boldsymbol{J}_\theta = \frac{1}{\sigma^2} \boldsymbol{G}^T \boldsymbol{G}. \tag{12}$$

3. System Model

Consider the pulse amplitude modulated (PAM) system shown in Figure 1. The channel output waveform $y(t)$ is given by

$$y(t) = \sum_{l=0}^{N-1} a_l h(t - lT - \tau_l) + n(t), \tag{13}$$

where T is the bit period, $a_l \in \{\pm 1\}$ are the N *i.i.d.* data symbols, $h(t)$ is the channel impulse response, $n(t)$ is additive white Gaussian noise, and τ_l is the unknown timing offset for the lth symbol. The channel response $h(t)$ is assumed to be band-limited to the frequency range $[-\frac{1}{2T}, \frac{1}{2T})$ with the result that baud-rate samples taken at a sampling rate of $1/T$ provide sufficient statistics. To eliminate out-of-band noise at the receiver, the received waveform $y(t)$ is filtered by a low-pass filter with impulse response $\frac{1}{T}\frac{\sin(\pi t/T)}{\pi t/T}$. Next, the resulting waveform $r(t)$ is sampled at instants kT to arrive at baud-rate samples $\{r_k\}$ given by

$$r_k = \sum_{l=0}^{N-1} a_l h(kT - lT - \tau_l) + n_k, \tag{14}$$

where n_k are zero-mean *i.i.d.* normal random variables with variance σ^2.

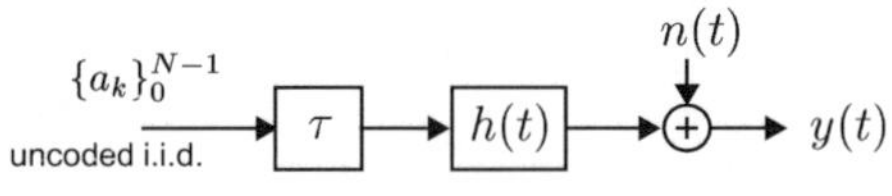

FIGURE 1. System block diagram with timing offsets, channel distortion and additive noise.

The signal-to-noise ratio (SNR) is defined to be SNR $= \frac{E_h}{2\sigma^2}$ where $E_h = \int_{-\infty}^{\infty} |h(t)|^2 \, dt$ is the energy in the channel impulse response $h(t)$. A total of $N + 2M$ samples are collected and stacked in an observation vector $\boldsymbol{r}$, given by $\boldsymbol{r} = [r_{-M} \; r_{-M+1} \cdots r_{N+M-1}]^T$, where eventually $M \to \infty$.

The receiver has to estimate the symbols $\{a_k\}$ and the timing offsets $\{\tau_k\}$ in the general case. In the trained case, where the transmitted symbols $\{a_k\}$ are known at the receiver, the problem is simpler and the receiver only needs to estimate $\{\tau_k\}$. The general timing recovery problem can be phrased as one where $\{a_k\}$ and $\{\tau_k\}$ need to be estimated given $\{r_k\}$ and knowledge of the channel response $h(t)$.

4. Evaluation of the CRB

Before the CRB is evaluated, we make the following simplifying observation. Consider the system model of (14). The parameter $\boldsymbol{\theta}$ consists of two sets of parameters, the *data* parameters $\{a_k\}$ and the *timing* parameters $\{\tau_k\}$.

$$\begin{aligned} \boldsymbol{\theta} &= [a_0\, a_1\, \ldots\, a_{N-1} \mid \tau_0\, \tau_1\, \ldots\, \tau_{N-1}]^T, \\ &= [\boldsymbol{\theta}_d^T \mid \boldsymbol{\theta}_t^T]^T, \end{aligned} \tag{15}$$

where the data parameter vector $\boldsymbol{\theta}_d$ and the timing parameter vector $\boldsymbol{\theta}_t$ are suitably defined. The noise n_k is assumed to be *i.i.d.* normal and, therefore, the Fisher information matrix has the structure described in (12), where the mean $\boldsymbol{x}(\boldsymbol{\theta})$ of (9) is given by

$$[\boldsymbol{x}(\boldsymbol{\theta})]_k = \sum_{l=0}^{N-1} a_l h(kT - lT - \tau_l). \tag{16}$$

The sensitivity matrix $\boldsymbol{G}$ can also be partitioned into data and timing portions, *i.e.*, $\boldsymbol{G} = [\boldsymbol{G}_d\ \boldsymbol{G}_t]$. Therefore, $\boldsymbol{J}_\theta$ has a block structure given by

$$\boldsymbol{J}_\theta = \frac{1}{\sigma^2} \begin{bmatrix} \boldsymbol{G}_d^T \boldsymbol{G}_d & \boldsymbol{G}_d^T \boldsymbol{G}_t \\ \boldsymbol{G}_t^T \boldsymbol{G}_d & \boldsymbol{G}_t^T \boldsymbol{G}_t \end{bmatrix}. \tag{17}$$

In the computation of the total information matrix, we need to take the expectation of $\boldsymbol{J}_\theta$ with respect to $\boldsymbol{\theta}$ (7). For our model, the data symbols are uniformly chosen from $\{\pm 1\}$ and this gives the *a priori* data distribution. If the *a priori* distribution for the timing parameters is not available, it is assumed to be uniformly distributed over the range of these parameters. Now, consider the behavior of the off-diagonal terms $E[\boldsymbol{G}_d^T \boldsymbol{G}_t]$ and $E[\boldsymbol{G}_t^T \boldsymbol{G}_d]$ of (17). Since the data symbols $\{a_k\}$ are zero-mean, taking expectation with respect to $\boldsymbol{\theta}_d$ leads to

$$\begin{aligned} E[\boldsymbol{G}_d^T \boldsymbol{G}_t] &= \mathbf{0} \\ E[\boldsymbol{G}_t^T \boldsymbol{G}_d] &= \mathbf{0}. \end{aligned} \tag{18}$$

Therefore, the off-diagonal entries of the block-diagonal matrix $E[\boldsymbol{J}_\theta]$ are zero. The inverse of this has a block diagonal structure with the diagonal entries being the inverses of the corresponding block diagonal entries of the original matrix, *i.e.*,

$$E[\boldsymbol{J}_\theta] = \begin{bmatrix} \boldsymbol{J}_d & \mathbf{0} \\ \mathbf{0} & \boldsymbol{J}_t \end{bmatrix} \quad \text{and} \tag{19}$$

$$E[\boldsymbol{J}_\theta]^{-1} = \begin{bmatrix} \boldsymbol{J}_d^{-1} & \mathbf{0} \\ \mathbf{0} & \boldsymbol{J}_t^{-1} \end{bmatrix}. \tag{20}$$

If we are concerned only with the CRB on the timing parameters, then we only need to compute the block-diagonal entry of $E[\boldsymbol{J}_\theta]$ corresponding to the timing parameters and invert it. This is what is done in the following subsections for different timing models.

4.1. Constant Offset. We begin by calculating the CRB for constant offset, also done in [**6**]. Denoting the energy in the derivative of the pulse $h(t)$ by $E_{h'}$,

$$E[J_t] = \frac{NE_{h'}}{\sigma^2}, \tag{21}$$

and finally, the CRB is given by [**6**]

$$\sigma_\epsilon^2 \geq \frac{\sigma^2}{NE_{h'}}, \tag{22}$$

where σ_ϵ^2 is the variance of the timing error $\epsilon = \tau - \hat{\tau}$, where $\hat{\tau}$ is an estimate of the timing offset τ. The CRB is inversely proportional to the number of symbols N and directly proportional to the channel noise variance σ^2. The ratio σ^2/N can be viewed as the variance of the averaged noise, and the CRB is the averaged noise variance scaled down by the energy in the derivative of the channel response.

4.2. Frequency Offset. Next, assume an initial timing offset τ_0 and a frequency offset parameter ΔT [**7**]. The timing offsets $\{\tau_k\}$ are given by

$$\tau_k = \tau_{k-1} + \Delta T = \tau_0 + k\Delta T, \tag{23}$$

and the sampled channel model is

$$r_k = \sum_{l=0}^{N-1} a_l h(kT - lT - \tau_0 - k\Delta T) + n_k. \tag{24}$$

The timing parameter to be estimated is $\boldsymbol{\theta}_t = [\Delta T \ \tau_0]$. The average Fisher information evaluates to

$$E[\boldsymbol{J}_t] = \frac{E_{h'}}{\sigma^2}\begin{bmatrix} \frac{(N-1)N(2N-1)}{6} & \frac{N(N-1)}{2} \\ \frac{N(N-1)}{2} & N \end{bmatrix}. \tag{25}$$

Inverting this, the CRB is given by

$$E[\boldsymbol{J}_t]^{-1} = \frac{\sigma^2}{E_{h'}}\begin{bmatrix} \frac{12}{(N-1)N(N+1)} & \frac{-6}{N(N+1)} \\ \frac{-6}{N(N+1)} & \frac{2(2N-1)}{N(N+1)} \end{bmatrix}. \tag{26}$$

The usual parameters of interest are the estimation error variance of the frequency offset parameter ΔT and also that of the initial offset τ_0, and these are the diagonal elements of $\boldsymbol{J}_t^{-1}$. Writing it out, we get

$$\begin{aligned} E[(\Delta T - \hat{\Delta T})^2] &\geq \frac{12\sigma^2}{E_{h'}(N-1)N(N+1)} \\ E[(\tau_0 - \hat{\tau}_0)^2] &\geq \frac{2\sigma^2(2N-1)}{E_{h'}N(N+1)}. \end{aligned} \tag{27}$$

The error variance for ΔT goes asymptotically as N^{-3} whereas the error variance for τ_0 goes as N^{-1}.

4.3. Accumulation Process. Next, consider the accumulation process where the timing offsets are as follows:

$$\tau_{k+1} = \tau_k + w_k = \sum_{j=0}^{k} w_j, \tag{28}$$

where we assume $\tau_0 = 0$ and the sequence $\{\tau_k\}$ is formed by accumulating $\{w_k\}$. If the elements of $\{w_k\}$ are *i.i.d.* zero-mean normal random variables, we get the random walk model which is studied in the next subsection. For the present, no *a priori* information is assumed about the variables $\{w_k\}$. The sample model with uniform sampling is

$$r_k = \sum_{l=0}^{N-1} a_l h(kT - lT - \sum_{j=0}^{l-1} w_j) + n_k$$

$$= x_k + n_k, \tag{29}$$

where x_k is again the noiseless received value. The parameter to be estimated is $\boldsymbol{\tau} = [\tau_1\ \tau_2\ \dots\ \tau_{N-1}]^T$. Instead of directly computing the Fisher information matrix $\boldsymbol{J}_\tau$, we define the parameter $\boldsymbol{w} = [w_0\ w_1\ \dots\ w_{N-2}]^T$, compute $\boldsymbol{J}_w$, and then use the linear transformation relating $\boldsymbol{\tau}$ and $\boldsymbol{w}$ to get $\boldsymbol{J}_\tau$.

First, the computation of $\boldsymbol{J}_w$. The matrix $\boldsymbol{G}$ for the parameter $\boldsymbol{w}$ evaluates to

$$g_{ki} = \frac{\partial x_k}{\partial w_i} = \sum_{l=0}^{N-1} a_l \frac{\partial}{\partial w_i} h(kT - lT - \sum_{j=0}^{l-1} w_j). \tag{30}$$

The derivative of $h(kT - lT - \sum_{j=0}^{l-1} w_j)$ with respect to w_i is zero if w_i does not occur in the summation inside the $h(\cdot)$ term. Therefore,

$$g_{ki} = -\sum_{l=i+1}^{N-1} a_l h'(kT - lT - \sum_{j=0}^{l-1} w_j) = -\sum_{l=i+1}^{N-1} a_l h'(kT - lT - \tau_l). \tag{31}$$

To get the averaged Fisher information, the expectation of $\boldsymbol{G}^T\boldsymbol{G}$ needs to be taken over all data sequences $\boldsymbol{a}$. Since the data symbols are assumed to be uncorrelated, $E[a_{j_1} a_{j_2}] = \delta_{j_1 j_2}$. Using this fact and (31) leads to

$$E[\boldsymbol{G}^T\boldsymbol{G}]_{i_1 i_2} = \sum_{j=\max(i_1,i_2)+1}^{N-1} \left\{ \sum_{k=-M}^{N+M-1} [h'(kT - jT - \tau_j)]^2 \right\}, \tag{32}$$

where the expectation is over $\boldsymbol{a}$. Now, letting $M \to \infty$, the bracketed term is the energy in $h'(t)$, denoted by $E_{h'}$. Therefore,

$$E[\boldsymbol{J}_w]_{i_1 i_2} = \frac{E_{h'}}{\sigma^2} \left((N-1) - \max(i_1, i_2) \right). \tag{33}$$

In long hand,

$$E[\boldsymbol{J}_w] = \frac{E_{h'}}{\sigma^2} \begin{bmatrix} N-1 & N-2 & N-3 & \dots & 1 \\ N-2 & N-2 & N-3 & \dots & 1 \\ N-3 & N-3 & N-3 & \dots & 1 \\ \vdots & \vdots & \vdots & \ddots & \vdots \\ 1 & 1 & 1 & \dots & 1 \end{bmatrix}. \tag{34}$$

To get $\boldsymbol{J}_\tau$ from $\boldsymbol{J}_w$, we use the relationship between $\boldsymbol{\tau}$ and $\boldsymbol{w}$. Recall that $\tau_k = \sum_{j=0}^{k-1} w_j$. In vector notation,

$$\boldsymbol{\tau} = \boldsymbol{T}\boldsymbol{w}, \tag{35}$$

where

$$\boldsymbol{T} = \begin{bmatrix} 1 & 0 & 0 & \dots & 0 \\ 1 & 1 & 0 & \dots & 0 \\ 1 & 1 & 1 & \ddots & \vdots \\ \vdots & \vdots & \vdots & \ddots & 0 \\ 1 & 1 & 1 & \dots & 1 \end{bmatrix} \quad \text{is a lower triangular matrix.} \tag{36}$$

Using this relationship between $\boldsymbol{\tau}$ and $\boldsymbol{w}$, we can write [**10**]

$$\boldsymbol{J}_{\tau} = \boldsymbol{T}^{-T} \boldsymbol{J}_{w} \boldsymbol{T}^{-1}. \tag{37}$$

To compute $\boldsymbol{T}^{-1}$, recognize the fact that we need now the inverse mapping of $\tau_k = \sum_{j=0}^{k-1} w_j$, which is $w_k = \tau_{k+1} - \tau_k$. Therefore,

$$\boldsymbol{T}^{-1} = \begin{bmatrix} 1 & 0 & 0 & \dots & 0 \\ -1 & 1 & 0 & \dots & 0 \\ 0 & -1 & 1 & \ddots & \vdots \\ \vdots & \ddots & \ddots & \ddots & 0 \\ 0 & \dots & 0 & -1 & 1 \end{bmatrix}, \tag{38}$$

which is a lower triangular Toeplitz matrix with only two non-zero diagonals, the main diagonal and an adjacent one. Using (34), (37) and (38) we get

$$E[\boldsymbol{J}_{\tau}] = \frac{E_{h'}}{\sigma^2} \boldsymbol{I}_{N \times N}. \tag{39}$$

Inverting this to get the CRB is simple and we get

$$E[(\tau - \hat{\tau})(\tau - \hat{\tau})^T] \geq \frac{\sigma^2}{E_{h'}} \boldsymbol{I}_{N \times N}. \tag{40}$$

This result implies that for an accumulation process with no *a priori* information, the bound on the estimation error for each component is the same and equal to $\sigma^2 / E_{h'}$, which is the same as the CRB for estimating a constant offset with $N = 1$, *i.e.*, the one-shot transmission case. For the accumulation process, the CRB is independent of N. This result makes intuitive sense since each new observation brings along with it a new parameter to be estimated.

4.4. Random Walk. With a specific *a priori* distribution on the accumulation process, we get the random walk. Consider the random walk given by

$$\tau_{k+1} = \tau_k + w_k = \tau_0 + \sum_{j=0}^{k} w_j, \tag{41}$$

where $w_k \sim \mathcal{N}(0, \sigma_w^2)$ are *i.i.d.* and σ_w^2 determines the severity of the timing jitter. We assume perfect acquisition, *i.e.*, $\tau_0 = 0$.

We now need to compute the total information, which is the sum of the average Fisher information of (39) and the *a priori* information. The *a priori* distribution $\boldsymbol{f}_{\boldsymbol{w}}(\boldsymbol{w})$ is

$$f_{\boldsymbol{w}}(\boldsymbol{w}) = \prod_{j=0}^{N-2} \frac{1}{\sqrt{2\pi\sigma_w^2}} \exp\left(-\frac{w_j^2}{2\sigma_w^2} \right). \tag{42}$$

Therefore, the *a priori* information matrix for $\boldsymbol{w}$ is

$$\boldsymbol{J}_{a\boldsymbol{w}} = \frac{1}{\sigma_w^2} \boldsymbol{I}, \tag{43}$$

and the *a priori* information matrix for $\boldsymbol{\tau}$ is [**10**]

$$\boldsymbol{J}_{a\boldsymbol{\tau}} = \frac{1}{\sigma_w^2}\boldsymbol{T}^{-T}\boldsymbol{T}^{-1}, \tag{44}$$

where $\boldsymbol{T}$ is the linear transformation relating $\boldsymbol{w}$ and $\boldsymbol{\tau}$ defined in (36). Combining (7), (39) and (44) and simplifying leads to

$$\boldsymbol{J}_T = \frac{1}{\sigma_w^2}\begin{bmatrix} \lambda & -1 & 0 & \dots & 0 \\ -1 & \lambda & -1 & \ddots & \vdots \\ 0 & \ddots & \ddots & \ddots & 0 \\ \vdots & \ddots & -1 & \lambda & -1 \\ 0 & \dots & 0 & -1 & \lambda - 1 \end{bmatrix}, \text{ where } \lambda = 2 + E_{h'}\frac{\sigma_w^2}{\sigma^2}. \tag{45}$$

The inverse of $\boldsymbol{J}_T$ is the CRB. This inversion is performed using Cholesky decomposition [**12**]. First, $\sigma_w^2 \boldsymbol{J}_T^{\mathcal{T}}$ is factorized as $\sigma_w^2 \boldsymbol{J}_T^{\mathcal{T}} = \boldsymbol{L}\boldsymbol{L}^T$, where $\boldsymbol{L}$ is a lower triangular matrix. Next, the equation $\boldsymbol{L}\boldsymbol{C} = \boldsymbol{I}$ is solved for $\boldsymbol{C}$. Finally, $\boldsymbol{L}^T\boldsymbol{B} = \boldsymbol{C}$ is solved for $\boldsymbol{B}$, leading to $[\boldsymbol{J}_T^{\mathcal{T}}]^{-1} = \sigma_w^2 \boldsymbol{B}$, and this is given by

$$[\boldsymbol{J}_T^{\mathcal{T}}]_{ij}^{-1} = \sigma_w^2 \frac{a_{\max(i,j)} n_{\min(i,j)}}{n_N - n_{N-1}}, \tag{46}$$

where

$$\begin{aligned} a_j &= \frac{\eta^{N-j} + \eta^{-N+1+j}}{\eta + 1}, \\ n_j &= \frac{(\beta_2\eta - 1)\eta^j + (\eta^2 - \beta_2\eta)\eta^{-j}}{\eta^2 - 1} \quad \text{and} \\ \eta &= \frac{\lambda + \sqrt{\lambda^2 - 4}}{2}. \end{aligned} \tag{47}$$

The CRB on the estimation error for the individual timing estimates τ_k is given by the diagonal elements of $[\boldsymbol{J}_T]^{-1}$, and evaluates to

$$\frac{E[(\hat{\tau}_i(\boldsymbol{r}) - \tau_i)^2]}{T^2} \geq \frac{[\boldsymbol{J}_T]_{ii}^{-1}}{T^2} = h \cdot f(i), \tag{48}$$

where

$$\begin{aligned} h &= \frac{\sigma_w^2}{T^2}\frac{\eta}{\eta^2 - 1} \quad \text{is the steady state value and,} \\ f(i) &= \tanh\left((N + \frac{1}{2})\ln\eta\right)\left[1 - \frac{\sinh\left((N - 2i + \frac{1}{2})\ln\eta\right)}{\sinh\left((N + \frac{1}{2})\ln\eta\right)}\right]. \end{aligned} \tag{49}$$

4.5. General Model: Frequency Offset *and* Random Walk. Next, consider the general timing model given by

$$\tau_{k+1} = \tau_k + \Delta T + w_k = \tau_0 + (k+1)\Delta T + \sum_{j=0}^{K} w_j, \tag{50}$$

where τ_0 is the initial timing offset, ΔT is the frequency offset parameter and $\{w_k\}$ characterize the random walk where $\{w_k\}$ are *i.i.d.* zero-mean normal random variables of variance σ_w^2. The *a priori* distribution of τ_0 is $\mathcal{N}(0, \sigma_{\tau_0}^2)$ and that of

ΔT is $\mathcal{N}(0, \sigma^2_{\Delta T})$. To compute the average Fisher information, we recognize that this is an accumulation process and, therefore, from (39),

$$E[\boldsymbol{J}_\tau] = \frac{E_{h'}}{\sigma^2}\boldsymbol{I}_{N\times N}. \tag{51}$$

To get the *a priori* information matrix, the same procedure is followed as with the random walk model. We define a new parameter $\boldsymbol{\phi}$, which is given by $\boldsymbol{\phi} = [\Delta T\ \tau_0\ w_0\ w_1\ \ldots\ w_{N-2}]^T$, get the *a priori* information matrix $\boldsymbol{J}_{a\boldsymbol{\phi}}$, and finally use the relationship between $\boldsymbol{\phi}$ and $\boldsymbol{\tau}$ to get $\boldsymbol{J}_{a\boldsymbol{\tau}}$.

The *a priori* distribution $\boldsymbol{f}_{\boldsymbol{\phi}}(\boldsymbol{\phi})$ is

$$\begin{aligned} f_{\boldsymbol{\phi}}(\boldsymbol{\phi}) &= \frac{1}{\sqrt{2\pi\sigma^2_{\Delta T}}}\exp\left(-\frac{(\Delta T)^2}{2\sigma^2_{\Delta T}}\right)\times \\ &\quad \frac{1}{\sqrt{2\pi\sigma^2_{\tau_0}}}\exp\left(-\frac{\tau_0^2}{2\sigma^2_{\tau_0}}\right)\times \\ &\quad \prod_{j=0}^{N-2}\frac{1}{\sqrt{2\pi\sigma^2_w}}\exp\left(-\frac{w_j^2}{2\sigma^2_w}\right). \end{aligned} \tag{52}$$

Therefore, the *a priori* information matrix for $\boldsymbol{\phi}$ is

$$\boldsymbol{J}_{a\boldsymbol{\phi}} = \begin{bmatrix} \frac{1}{\sigma^2_{\Delta T}} & & & & \\ & \frac{1}{\sigma^2_{\tau_0}} & & & \\ & & \frac{1}{\sigma^2_w} & & \\ & & & \ddots & \\ & & & & \frac{1}{\sigma^2_w} \end{bmatrix}. \tag{53}$$

The parameter vectors $\boldsymbol{\tau}$ and $\boldsymbol{\phi}$ are related as $\boldsymbol{\tau} = \boldsymbol{M}\boldsymbol{\phi}$, where

$$\boldsymbol{M} = \begin{bmatrix} 0 & 1 & 0 & 0 & \cdots & 0 \\ 1 & 1 & 1 & 0 & \cdots & 0 \\ 2 & 1 & 1 & 1 & \ddots & \vdots \\ \vdots & \vdots & \vdots & \vdots & \ddots & 0 \\ N-1 & 1 & 1 & 1 & \cdots & 1 \end{bmatrix}. \tag{54}$$

The *a priori* information matrices $\boldsymbol{J}_{a\boldsymbol{\tau}}$ and $\boldsymbol{J}_{a\boldsymbol{\phi}}$ are related by $\boldsymbol{J}_{a\boldsymbol{\phi}} = \boldsymbol{M}^T\boldsymbol{J}_{a\boldsymbol{\tau}}\boldsymbol{M}$. [**1**] Since $\boldsymbol{M}$ is not a square matrix, we need a pseudo-inverse of $\boldsymbol{M}$ to get $\boldsymbol{J}_{a\boldsymbol{\tau}}$ from $\boldsymbol{J}_{a\boldsymbol{\phi}}$. Let $\boldsymbol{M}^\dagger = \boldsymbol{M}^T(\boldsymbol{M}\boldsymbol{M}^T)^{-1}$ be the right pseudo-inverse of $\boldsymbol{M}$ such that $\boldsymbol{M}\boldsymbol{M}^\dagger = \boldsymbol{I}$. Then,

$$\boldsymbol{J}_{a\boldsymbol{\tau}} = \boldsymbol{M}^{\dagger T}\boldsymbol{J}_{a\boldsymbol{\phi}}\boldsymbol{M}^\dagger. \tag{55}$$

The pseudo-inverse $\boldsymbol{M}^\dagger$ evaluates to

$$\boldsymbol{M}^\dagger = \begin{bmatrix} -\frac{1}{N} & 0 & & \cdots & & 0 \\ 1 & 0 & & \cdots & & 0 \\ -1+\frac{1}{N} & 1 & \ddots & & & \\ \frac{1}{N} & -1 & \ddots & \ddots & & \vdots \\ \vdots & 0 & \ddots & \ddots & \ddots & \\ \vdots & \vdots & \ddots & \ddots & \ddots & 0 \\ \frac{1}{N} & 0 & \cdots & 0 & -1 & 1 \end{bmatrix}. \tag{56}$$

Using (53), (55) and (56), the *a priori* information matrix $\boldsymbol{J}_{a\boldsymbol{T}}$ is evaluated. Adding this to the average Fisher information matrix leads to

$$\boldsymbol{J}_T = \frac{1}{\sigma_w^2} \begin{bmatrix} \beta & -1 & 0 & \dots & 0 \\ -1 & \lambda & -1 & \ddots & \vdots \\ 0 & \ddots & \ddots & \ddots & 0 \\ \vdots & \ddots & -1 & \lambda & -1 \\ 0 & \dots & 0 & -1 & \lambda-1 \end{bmatrix}, \text{ where} \tag{57}$$

$$\begin{aligned} \lambda &= 2 + E_{h'}\frac{\sigma_w^2}{\sigma^2} \quad \text{and} \\ \beta &= \left(\frac{N^2-N-1}{N^2} + \frac{\sigma_w^2}{\sigma_{\tau_0}^2} + \frac{\sigma_w^2}{N^2\sigma_{\Delta T}^2}\right) + E_{h'}\frac{\sigma_w^2}{\sigma^2}. \end{aligned} \tag{58}$$

Observe that the *a priori* information parameters $\sigma_{\tau_0}^2$ and $\sigma_{\Delta T}^2$ occur in the denominator of the fractions in β. When these are zero, this means we have perfect knowledge of the initial timing offset and the frequency offset and the estimation problem is simply that of estimating the random walk. Therefore, we assume that $\sigma_{\tau_0}^2$ and $\sigma_{\Delta T}^2$ are non-zero with the understanding that the zero case can be handled by eliminating suitable parameters from the estimation problem. Proceeding as with the random walk case, the CRB evaluates to

$$[\boldsymbol{J}_T]_{ij}^{-1} = \sigma_w^2 \frac{a_{\max(i,j)} n_{\min(i,j)}}{n_N - n_{N-1}}, \text{ where} \tag{59}$$

$$\begin{aligned} a_j &= \frac{\eta^{N-j} + \eta^{-N+1+j}}{\eta+1}, \\ n_j &= \frac{(\beta\eta-1)\eta^j + (\eta^2-\beta\eta)\eta^{-j}}{\eta^2-1} \quad \text{and} \\ \eta &= \frac{\lambda+\sqrt{\lambda^2-4}}{2}. \end{aligned} \tag{60}$$

5. Using the Cramér-Rao Bound to Derive the Optimal Training Symbol Locations

In the following sections, the CRB is used as a tool to derive the training symbol placement strategy to minimize the CRB on timing estimation error for channels that suffer from ISI and a frequency offset.

The CRB for the model specified of (14) is intractable when both known and unknown data symbols are present in the set $\{a_k\}$. In this section, a simplified system model is considered, where only the training symbols are present. In other words, the data payload bits are assumed to be all zero. This translates to a PAM system model where the channel output waveform is given by:

$$y(t) = \sum_{l \in \boldsymbol{I}} a_l h(t - lT - \tau_l) + n(t), \tag{61}$$

where $\boldsymbol{I}$, the set of K training locations, is a subset of the universal set given by $\boldsymbol{U} = \{0, 1, \ldots, N-1\}$. The other parameters are as defined for the system of (14). After low-pass filtering, uniform samples of the resulting waveform $r(t)$ are taken, and the kth uniform sample is given by:

$$r_k = \sum_{l \in \boldsymbol{I}} a_l h(kT - lT - \tau_l) + n_k, \tag{62}$$

where $\{n_k\}$ are *i.i.d.* zero-mean Gaussian random variables of variance σ^2. A total of $N+2M$ samples are assumed to be taken, and stacked into an observation vector $\boldsymbol{r} = [r_{-M} \; r_{-M+1} \; \ldots \; r_{N+M-1}]^T$, where eventually, $M \longrightarrow \infty$. The problem now is to evaluate the CRB for the estimation of the timing parameter $\boldsymbol{\theta} = [\Delta T \; \tau_0]^T$ given the set of observations $\boldsymbol{r}$. This is, in general, a function of the set of training symbols $\{a_l\}$.The average CRB, averaged over all training symbol patterns, is got by taking the expectation of $\boldsymbol{J}_\theta^{-1}$ with respect to the training symbols. This is intractable for the system model considered here. Instead, a looser, more tractable lower bound, called the modified CRB (MCRB), is employed. The modified CRB is given by [**8**]:

$$E[(\hat{\theta}_i(\boldsymbol{x}) - \theta_i)^2] \geq E[\boldsymbol{J}_\theta]^{-1}(i,i), \tag{63}$$

where the expectation is now over $\boldsymbol{r}$ and $\{a_l\}$. For ease of notation, the MCRB is referred to as the CRB in the sequel.

The average Fisher information for this case evaluates to [**12**]

$$E[\boldsymbol{J}_\theta] = \frac{E_{h'}}{\sigma^2} \begin{bmatrix} \sum_{k \in \boldsymbol{I}} k^2 & \sum_{k \in \boldsymbol{I}} k \\ \sum_{k \in \boldsymbol{I}} k & K \end{bmatrix}, \tag{64}$$

where $E_{h'}$ is the energy in the derivative of the pulse shape $h(t)$. Inverting this, the CRB on estimating the timing parameters during acquisition is given by

$$\begin{aligned} E[(\hat{\Delta T}(\boldsymbol{r}) - \Delta T)^2] &\geq V_{\Delta T}, \\ E[(\hat{\tau_0}(\boldsymbol{r}) - \tau_0)^2] &\geq V_{\tau_0}, \end{aligned} \tag{65}$$

where

$$\begin{aligned} V_{\Delta T} &= \frac{\sigma^2}{K E_{h'}} \frac{1}{\text{var}(\boldsymbol{I})}, \\ V_{\tau_0} &= \frac{\sigma^2}{K E_{h'}} \left(1 + \frac{\text{mean}(\boldsymbol{I})^2}{\text{var}(\boldsymbol{I})}\right), \end{aligned} \tag{66}$$

where the set $\boldsymbol{I}$ has been redefined in terms of its K ordered elements x_k, $k = 0, 1, \ldots, K-1$, such that $0 \leq x_0 < x_1 < \cdots < x_{K-1} \leq (N-1)$. The mean and variance of any given vector $\boldsymbol{S} = [s_0, s_1, \cdots, s_{K-1}]$ are defined by $\text{mean}(\boldsymbol{S}) = \frac{1}{K}\sum s_k$ and $\text{var}(\boldsymbol{S}) = \frac{1}{K}\sum s_k^2 - \left(\frac{1}{K}\sum s_k\right)^2$. The problem of choosing the best training locations, therefore, is the same as choosing the set $\boldsymbol{I} = \{x_k\}_0^{K-1}$.

The problem statement thus far has been that of estimating ΔT and τ_0, given the set of observations $\boldsymbol{r}$. This can be generalized to the problem of estimating ΔT and τ_m, for any m. For the generalized problem, the CRB on the estimation of ΔT is the same as before, and the CRB for τ_m is given by

$$V_{\tau_m} = \frac{\sigma^2}{KE_{h'}}\left(1 + \frac{(\text{mean}(\boldsymbol{I}) - m)^2}{\text{var}(\boldsymbol{I})}\right). \tag{67}$$

Therefore, the CRB on the estimation of ΔT is independent of the particular choice of m. The CRB on the estimation of τ_m is minimized when $m = \text{mean}(\boldsymbol{I})$.

The relative importance of estimating the two parameters ΔT and τ_m can be quantified by the mean squared error (MSE) defined by

$$\text{MSE} = \frac{1}{N}\sum_{k=0}^{N-1} E[(\tau_k - \hat{\tau}_k)^2]. \tag{68}$$

The mean squared error can be rewritten as

$$\text{MSE} = \frac{1}{N}\sum_{k=0}^{N-1} E[(\tau_m + (k-m)\Delta T - \hat{\tau}_m - (k-m)\hat{\Delta T})^2], \tag{69}$$

where m is chosen as the reference index. For CRB-achieving estimates of ΔT and τ_m, the MSE is given by

$$\text{MSE} = \frac{\sigma^2}{KE_{h'}}\left\{1 + \frac{\text{var}(\boldsymbol{U}) + (\text{mean}(\boldsymbol{U}) - \text{mean}(\boldsymbol{I}))^2}{\text{var}(\boldsymbol{I})}\right\}, \tag{70}$$

where $\boldsymbol{I}$ is the set of acquisition indices, and $\boldsymbol{U}$ is the universal set of indices. The expression for the MSE is independent of the choice of the reference index m. The ultimate goal of the timing estimation problem is to minimize the MSE. In the next section, the training symbol arrangement that minimizes the CRB on ΔT is first derived, and then it is shown that this arrangement minimizes the MSE.

6. Optimal Training Locations

6.1. Minimizing $V_{\Delta T}$. From (66), picking the index set $\boldsymbol{I}$ to minimize the CRB on frequency estimation, $V_{\Delta T}$, is the same as picking the set $\boldsymbol{I}$ with the maximum variance. The following theorem specifies this set.

THEOREM 6.1. *Let K be an even natural number. Let $\boldsymbol{I} = [i_0, i_1, \cdots, i_{K-1}]$ be any vector of integers satisfying $0 \le i_0 < i_1 < \cdots < i_{K-1} \le (N-1)$ and let $\boldsymbol{I}_o$ be given by $\boldsymbol{I}_o = [0, 1, \cdots, \frac{K}{2} - 1, N - \frac{K}{2}, \cdots, N-2, N-1]$. Then $var(\boldsymbol{I}_o) \ge var(\boldsymbol{I})$, with equality iff $\boldsymbol{I} = \boldsymbol{I}_o$.*

PROOF. Let $\boldsymbol{I}_o = [i_{o0}, i_{o1}, \cdots, i_{o(K-1)}]$, *i.e.*

$$\begin{aligned} i_{ok} &= k,\ 0 \le k \le \frac{K}{2} - 1, \\ &= (N-K) + k,\ \frac{K}{2} \le k \le K-1. \end{aligned} \tag{71}$$

The mean of $\boldsymbol{I}_o$ is $\mu_o = \frac{N-1}{2}$. The variance of a vector does not change if a constant is added to or subtracted from all the elements. Therefore, two new vectors $\boldsymbol{I}^1$ and

$\boldsymbol{I}_o^1$ are now formed by subtracting μ_0 from $\boldsymbol{I}$ and $\boldsymbol{I}_o$. In symbols,

$$\begin{aligned} \boldsymbol{I}^1 &= [x_0, x_1, \cdots, x_{K-1}], \\ \boldsymbol{I}_o^1 &= [x_{o0}, x_{o1}, \cdots, x_{o(K-1)}], \\ x_k &= i_k - \mu_o, \\ x_{ok} &= i_{ok} - \mu_o. \end{aligned} \tag{72}$$

The subtraction does not change the variance, and therefore, $\text{var}(\boldsymbol{I}^1) = \text{var}(\boldsymbol{I})$ and $\text{var}(\boldsymbol{I}_o^1) = \text{var}(\boldsymbol{I}_o)$. An alternative notation is

$$\boldsymbol{I}^1 = \boldsymbol{I}_o^1 + \boldsymbol{\epsilon}, \tag{73}$$

where $\boldsymbol{\epsilon} = [\epsilon_0, \epsilon_1, \cdots, \epsilon_{K-1}]$ and $\epsilon_i = x_i - x_{oi}$. The set $\boldsymbol{\epsilon}$ is the set of perturbations needed to go from set $\boldsymbol{I}_o^1$ to the set $\boldsymbol{I}^1$, and satisfies the following constraints.

$$\begin{aligned} 0 \le \epsilon_0 \le \epsilon_1 \le \cdots \le \epsilon_{\frac{K}{2}-1} &\le (N-K) \\ -(N-K) \le \epsilon_{\frac{K}{2}} \le \epsilon_{\frac{K}{2}+1} \le \cdots \le \epsilon_{K-1} &\le 0 \\ \epsilon_{\frac{K}{2}-1} - \epsilon_{\frac{K}{2}} &\le (N-K). \end{aligned} \tag{74}$$

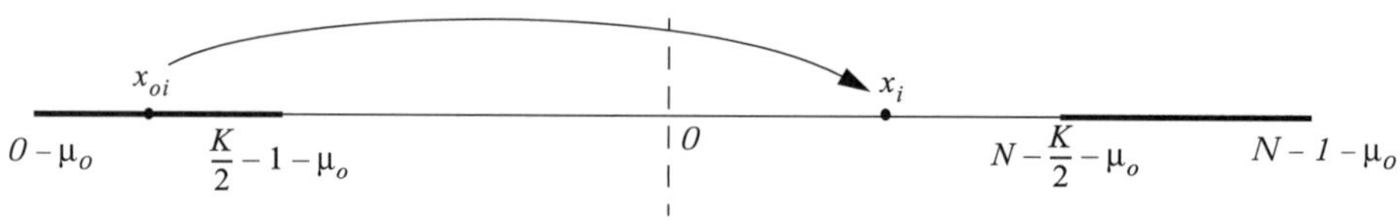

FIGURE 2. The various constraints of $\boldsymbol{\epsilon}$.

Figure 2 explains the constraints on $\boldsymbol{\epsilon}$. The elements of $\boldsymbol{I}_o^1$ are marked along the real line. The left-half elements are all negative and the only perturbations allowed are positive. The perturbations $\{\epsilon_i\}_0^{\frac{K}{2}-1}$ form an increasing sequence with the maximum being $N-K$, which happens when $i_{\frac{K}{2}-1} = N - \frac{K}{2} - 1$. Similarly, the second restriction arises from the right-half. The third restriction arises from the fact that there are N slots and K distinct, ordered elements, and therefore, no two consecutive elements can be separated by more than $N-K$.

The variances $\text{var}(\boldsymbol{I}_o)$ and $\text{var}(\boldsymbol{I})$ can now be rewritten as

$$\begin{aligned} \text{var}(\boldsymbol{I}_o) &= \frac{1}{K}\sum x_{ok}^2, \\ \text{var}(\boldsymbol{I}) &= \frac{1}{K}\sum x_k^2 - \left(\frac{1}{K}\sum \epsilon_k\right)^2. \end{aligned} \tag{75}$$

Next, consider the left half, i.e., $0 \le k \le \frac{K}{2} - 1$. The intuition for the following steps is as follows. For the left half, all the x_{ok}s are negative and positive ϵ_ks will ensure that $|x_k| < |x_{ok}|$ as long as x_k does not exceed $-x_{ok}$ for all possible ϵ_k.

From (71), (72), and (74),

$$0 \le \epsilon_k \le N - K, \tag{76}$$
$$\implies x_{ok} \le x_{ok} + \epsilon_k \le N - K + x_{ok}, \tag{77}$$
$$\implies i_{ok} - \mu_o \le x_k \le i_{ok} - \mu_o + N - K, \tag{78}$$
$$\implies |x_k| \le \max(|i_{ok} - \mu_o|, |i_{ok} - \mu_o + N - K|), \tag{79}$$
$$\implies |x_k| \le \max(\frac{N-1}{2} - k, N - K + \frac{N-1}{2} + k), \tag{80}$$
$$\implies |x_k| \le \frac{N-1}{2} - k, \tag{81}$$
$$\implies |x_k| \le |x_{ok}|. \tag{82}$$

The equality condition is satisfied iff $\epsilon_k = 0$ since $\frac{N-1}{2} - k > N - K + \frac{N-1}{2} + k$ for the left half. By proceeding similarly, it can be shown that the same holds for the right half. Combining the two leads to

$$|x_k| \le |x_{ok}| \quad \text{for} \quad 0 \le k \le (K-1), \tag{83}$$

with equality iff $x_k = x_{ok}$ for all k.

Combining (75), (83) and the fact that $\left(\frac{1}{K}\sum \epsilon_k\right)^2 \ge 0$ with equality iff $\boldsymbol{\epsilon} = \mathbf{0}$ leads to the desired result, *i.e.*,

$$\text{var}(\boldsymbol{I}_o) \ge \text{var}(\boldsymbol{I}), \tag{84}$$

with equality iff $\boldsymbol{I} = \boldsymbol{I}_o$. □

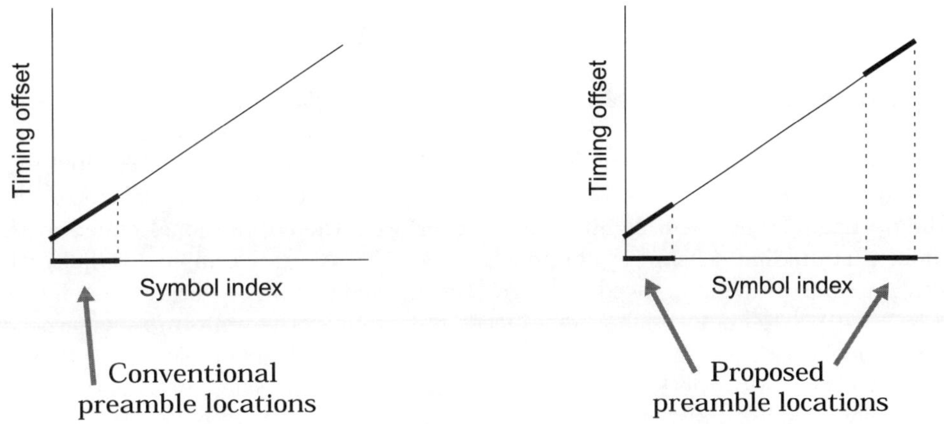

FIGURE 3. Proposed training symbol placement strategy.

Therefore, to minimize $V_{\Delta T}$, the optimum strategy is the split-preamble strategy, where the available training symbols are split into two equal halves and placed at the beginning and at the end of the packet, as shown in Figure 3. The intuition behind the split-preamble strategy is that the observations need to be as far apart as possible while estimating the slope of a straight line.

6.2. Minimizing the MSE. Recall from (70) that the MSE for the CRB-achieving timing estimator is given by

$$\text{MSE} = \frac{\sigma^2}{KE_{h'}}\left\{1 + \frac{\text{var}(\boldsymbol{U}) + (\text{mean}(\boldsymbol{U}) - \text{mean}(\boldsymbol{I}))^2}{\text{var}(\boldsymbol{I})}\right\}. \tag{85}$$

The index set for the split-preamble strategy, $\boldsymbol{I}_o$, has the following properties:

- It has the highest variance among all index sets $\boldsymbol{I}$.
- $\text{mean}(\boldsymbol{I}_o) = \text{mean}(\boldsymbol{U})$.

Combining these properties with the MSE expression leads to the conclusion that the split-preamble arrangement minimizes the MSE.

7. Performance Evaluation of the Split-Preamble Arrangement

In the previous section, the split-preamble strategy was shown to minimize the CRB on frequency estimation, and also the mean squared error. In this section, three schemes are compared for performance with respect to estimating ΔT:

- all known symbols at the start of the packet $(\boldsymbol{I}_1)$ with error variance V_1;
- the split-preamble arrangement $(\boldsymbol{I}_2)$ with error variance V_2;
- sprinkle the known symbols uniformly throughout the packet $(\boldsymbol{I}_3)$ with error variance V_3.

The CRB on the timing estimation error variance for these three schemes can be evaluated using (66), and this leads to

$$\begin{aligned} C_1 &= \frac{V_1 E_{h'}}{\sigma_n^2} = \frac{12}{K(K^2-1)}, \\ C_2 &= \frac{V_2 E_{h'}}{\sigma_n^2} = \frac{1}{\frac{K(K^2-1)}{12} + \frac{KN(N-K)}{4}}, \\ C_3 &= \frac{V_3 E_{h'}}{\sigma_n^2} = \frac{(K-1)^2}{(N-1)^2}\frac{V_1}{\sigma^2}, \end{aligned} \tag{86}$$

where the normalized error variance coefficient C is defined above.

Figure 4 compares the performance of the three training symbol arrangements for $N = 4000$, and K ranging from 1 to 4000. The block length $N = 4000$ was chosen to be similar to the ones currently used for digital magnetic recording. The optimal arrangement significantly outperforms the conventional one, and the uniform sprinkling scheme is not much worse off. As an example, compare the total number of symbols needed to get the normalized error variance coefficient $C = 2 \times 10^{-9}$. The optimal scheme needs 86 symbols, the uniform scheme needs 248 symbols, whereas the conventional scheme needs 1588 symbols of the 4000 to be known! The MSE performance comparison of the three schemes leads to similar conclusions, and is omitted for brevity.

8. Joint Acquisition and Tracking

In Sections 5 and 6, acquisition was considered in isolation, where only the training symbols were transmitted. In this section, a simple version of the problem of joint acquisition and tracking is considered. The payload section is not assumed to be zero. The timing offset model once again consists of an initial timing offset τ_0 and a frequency offset parameter ΔT. The presence of both trained and unknown data makes the CRB, and also the MCRB, intractable. To facilitate analysis, a

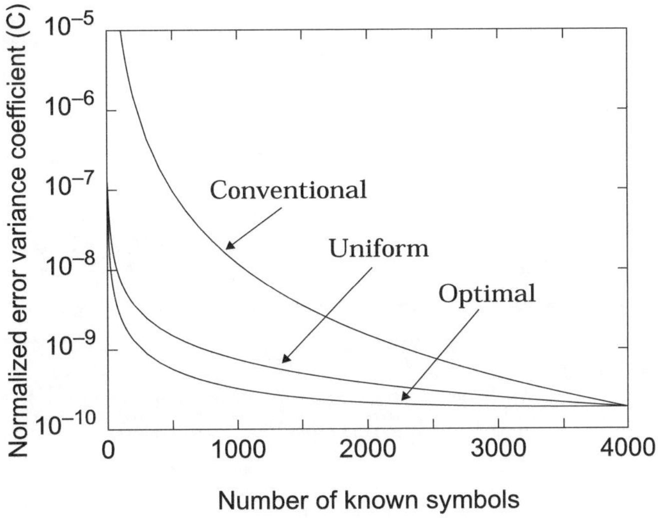

FIGURE 4. Split-preamble outperforms the conventional strategy.

linear observation model based on the characteristics of the timing error detector (TED) is first derived. Based on this model, the CRB on estimating the timing parameters and also the MSE are computed, and finally, it is shown that the split-preamble arrangement minimizes the MSE in this case.

8.1. Linear Model. A phase-locked loop (PLL) consists of a sampling device, a timing error detector (TED), a loop filter and a voltage-controlled oscillator (VCO). The sampling device samples the incoming continuous-time waveform according to sampling instants $\{\hat{\tau}_k\}$ generated by the VCO. The resulting samples are acted upon by the TED to generate estimates $\{\hat{\epsilon}_k\}$ of the timing error $\epsilon_k = \tau_k - \hat{\tau}_k$. These error estimates are filtered by the loop filter which is usually a low-pass filter to reduce the sensitivity of the PLL to channel noise. The loop filter output drives the VCO, completing the phase-locked loop.

An ideal timing error detector would output $\hat{\epsilon}_k = \epsilon_k$. In the presence of noise, a linear TED would output $\hat{\epsilon}_k = \epsilon_k + \nu_k$, where ν_k is independent of ϵ_k. Practical TEDs are linear for an SNR-dependent range around $\epsilon_k = 0$, and in addition, show a correlation between ν_k and ϵ_k. However, in the tracking mode, the operating ϵ_k values are usually small enough for the linearity assumption to hold. In the trained mode, the TED is linear over a much larger range, and therefore, the TED linearity assumption holds even with the large timing offsets faced during acquisition. For a linear TED,

$$\hat{\epsilon}_k = \epsilon_k + \nu_k, \tag{87}$$

$$= \tau_k - \hat{\tau}_k + \nu_k. \tag{88}$$

Constructing $y_k = \hat{\tau}_k + \hat{\epsilon}_k$ leads to the following linear observation model:

$$y_k = \tau_k + \nu_k. \tag{89}$$

Therefore, to arrive at the desired linear model, corresponding outputs from the PLL and the TED need to be added. The PLL outputs an estimate of τ_k assuming that only observations $\{r_l\}_0^{k-1}$ are available. This is, therefore, an *a priori* estimate of τ_k. The TEDs estimate $\hat{\epsilon}_k$, is based on the present observation r_k as well. Hence, y_k, which is the sum of $\hat{\tau}_k$ and $\hat{\epsilon}_k$, is an *a posteriori* estimate of τ_k and the quality of this estimate depends on the quality of the TED output. The linear observation model is valid where the TED characteristics are linear.

In vector notation, the linear measurement model can be written as follows:

$$\boldsymbol{y} = \boldsymbol{\tau} + \boldsymbol{\nu}, \tag{90}$$

where $\boldsymbol{y} = [y_0 \; y_1 \; \dots \; y_{K-1}]^T$, $\boldsymbol{\tau} = [\tau_0 \; \tau_1 \; \dots \; \tau_{K-1}]^T$, and $\boldsymbol{\nu} = [\nu_0 \; \nu_1 \; \dots \; \nu_{K-1}]^T$. The noise variables $\{\nu_k\}$ were assumed to be independent zero-mean normal random variables. The timing recovery block assumed for this section takes advantage of the K known symbols in the training phase, leading to a measurement noise variance σ_a^2 for the observations corresponding to the known symbols (acquisition), and σ_t^2 for the observations corresponding to the data symbols (tracking) such that $\sigma_a^2 < \sigma_t^2$. An example is the PLL-based timing recovery system, where the timing estimation error variance is lesser with training than otherwise. Though the timing estimation error variance as a function of the bit position does not show the step-function type behavior assumed here, but rather varies in a gradual fashion, this observation noise model is used as an approximation.

8.2. CRB for the Linear Model. Let the parameter to be estimated be $\boldsymbol{\theta} = [\Delta T \; \tau_0]^T$, and let $\boldsymbol{x}(\boldsymbol{\theta})$ be the noiseless observation. For the linear model of (90), the kth component of $\boldsymbol{x}(\boldsymbol{\theta})$ is just $x_k = \tau_k = k\Delta T + \tau_0$. The noise variables are not *i.i.d.* The Fisher information matrix evaluates to

$$\boldsymbol{J}_\theta = \frac{1}{\sigma_a^2} \sum_{k \in \boldsymbol{I}_a} \begin{bmatrix} k^2 & k \\ k & 1 \end{bmatrix} + \frac{1}{\sigma_t^2} \sum_{k \in \boldsymbol{I}_t} \begin{bmatrix} k^2 & k \\ k & 1 \end{bmatrix}, \tag{91}$$

where the ordered vectors $\boldsymbol{I}_a$ and $\boldsymbol{I}_t$ contain the indices corresponding to the training and the data symbols respectively. The elements of $\boldsymbol{I}_a$ and $\boldsymbol{I}_t$ together span all the integers from 0 to $N-1$. Let m_a and m_t be the mean of $\boldsymbol{I}_a$ and $\boldsymbol{I}_t$ respectively, and let the respective variances be V_a and V_t. The determinant of $\boldsymbol{J}_\theta$ is

$$|\boldsymbol{J}_\theta| = \left\{ \frac{K}{\sigma_a^2} + \frac{N-K}{\sigma_t^2} \right\} \left\{ \frac{K}{\sigma_a^2} V_a + \frac{N-K}{\sigma_t^2} V_t \right\} + \frac{K}{\sigma_a^2} \frac{N-K}{\sigma_t^2} (m_a - m_t)^2. \tag{92}$$

The CRB then evaluates to

$$\begin{aligned} V_{\Delta T} &= \frac{1}{|\boldsymbol{J}_\theta|} \left[\frac{K}{\sigma_a^2} + \frac{N-K}{\sigma_t^2} \right], \\ V_{\tau_0} &= \frac{1}{|\boldsymbol{J}_\theta|} \left[\frac{K}{\sigma_a^2}(V_a + m_a^2) + \frac{N-K}{\sigma_t^2}(V_t + m_t^2) \right]. \end{aligned} \tag{93}$$

8.3. Minimizing the CRB. With only training symbols alone being transmitted, minimizing $V_{\Delta T}$ was equivalent to maximizing the variance of the set of acquisition indices. To minimize $V_{\Delta T}$ with joint acquisition and tracking, from (93), the acquisition indices need to be picked to maximize the determinant $|\boldsymbol{J}_\theta|$. As before, a constant is subtracted from all the indices so that the new indices are of the form $i - (N-1)/2$ for $i = 0$ to $N-1$, and these are apportioned into the vectors $\boldsymbol{I}'_a$ and $\boldsymbol{I}'_t$ with mean and variance being m'_a, V'_a and m'_t, V'_t respectively. Shifting by a constant does not change the variance, and therefore, $V'_a = V_a$ and $V'_t = V_t$. Also, since all the indices are shifted by the same amount, $m'_a - m'_t = m_a - m_t$. Using these in (92), we see that this subtraction does not affect the determinant.

Next, consider the split-preamble arrangement of Section 6. Let this be the candidate set of acquisition indices for joint acquisition and tracking, $\boldsymbol{I}_a^o$, where

$$\boldsymbol{I}_a^o = [0, 1, \cdots, \frac{K}{2} - 1, N - \frac{K}{2}, \cdots, N-2, N-1]. \tag{94}$$

For this set-up, the means of the shifted vectors, m_a' and m_t', are zero and the determinant can be rewritten as

$$\begin{aligned}
|\boldsymbol{J}_\theta|^o &= \left\{\frac{K}{\sigma_a^2} + \frac{N-K}{\sigma_t^2}\right\}\left\{\frac{1}{\sigma_a^2}\sum_{k\in\boldsymbol{I}'^o_a} k^2 + \frac{1}{\sigma_t^2}\sum_{k\in\boldsymbol{I}'^o_t} k^2\right\}, \\
&= \left\{\frac{K}{\sigma_a^2} + \frac{N-K}{\sigma_t^2}\right\}\left\{\frac{1}{\sigma_t^2}\sum_{k\in\boldsymbol{U}'} k^2 + \left(\frac{1}{\sigma_a^2} - \frac{1}{\sigma_t^2}\right)\sum_{k\in\boldsymbol{I}'^o_a} k^2\right\}, \\
&= C_1\left(C_2 + C_3\sum_{k\in\boldsymbol{I}'^o_a} k^2\right), \qquad (95)
\end{aligned}$$

where $\boldsymbol{U}'$ is the ordered vector containing all shifted indices $i-(N-1)/2$ for $i=0$ to $i=N-1$, which is a constant, independent of the choice of $\boldsymbol{I}_a$. The definition of the constants C_1, C_2 and C_3 follow from equations above. $|\boldsymbol{J}_\theta|^o$ is a function of only the variance of $\boldsymbol{I}'^o_a$.

For an arbitrary choice $\boldsymbol{I}_a$, the determinant evaluates to

$$|\boldsymbol{J}_\theta| = C_1\left(C_2 + C_3\sum_{k\in\boldsymbol{I}'_a} k^2\right) - C_3^2\left(\sum_{k\in\boldsymbol{I}'_a} k\right)^2. \tag{96}$$

It was shown in Section 6 that the choice $\boldsymbol{I}_a = \boldsymbol{I}_a^o$ maximizes the squared term $\sum_{k\in\boldsymbol{I}'_a} k^2$. In addition, $\sum_{k\in\boldsymbol{I}'^o_a} k = 0$. Therefore, the choice $\boldsymbol{I}_a = \boldsymbol{I}_a^o$ maximizes $|\boldsymbol{J}_\theta|$, leading to a maximum $|\boldsymbol{J}_\theta| = |\boldsymbol{J}_\theta|^o$. As with the acquisition case, it can also be shown that the same arrangement also minimizes V_{τ_m}, where $m=(N-1)/2$. In summary, for the system model considered here, the choice that minimizes the CRB for frequency estimation with acquisition alone minimizes the CRB for frequency estimation for joint acquisition and tracking case as well.

8.4. Minimizing the MSE. The MSE, defined by (68), evaluates to

$$MSE = \frac{1}{\frac{K}{\sigma_a^2} + \frac{N-K}{\sigma_t^2}}\left[1 + \frac{T_1+T_2}{|\boldsymbol{J}_\theta|}\right], \tag{97}$$

where

$$\begin{aligned}
T_1 &= \operatorname{var}(\boldsymbol{U})\left(\frac{K}{\sigma_a^2} + \frac{N-K}{\sigma_t^2}\right)^2, \\
T_2 &= \frac{(N-K)^2K^2}{N^2}\left(\frac{1}{\sigma_a^2} - \frac{1}{\sigma_t^2}\right)^2 (m_a - m_t)^2. \qquad (98)
\end{aligned}$$

The term T_1 is independent of the choice of the acquisition indices. The split-preamble arrangement has the property that $m_a = m_t$, and therefore, it minimizes the term T_2. In addition, the split-preamble arrangement also maximizes the determinant $|\boldsymbol{J}_\theta|$. Therefore, using these properties, it is evident that the split-preamble arrangement minimizes the MSE for joint acquisition and tracking with the linear observation model.

9. Conclusion

The Cramér-Rao bound on timing estimation error variance was derived for ISI channels for the random walk model, and also for a general model consisting of a random walk and frequency offset. The CRB is a lower bound on the estimation error variance of any unbiased estimator, and hence serves as a benchmark to evaluate competing timing recovery algorithms. In addition, in this paper, the CRB is used as a tool to arrive at the optimal training symbol placement strategy for channels that suffer from ISI and frequency offset. The strategy that minimizes the CRB on frequency estimation error variance and also the mean-squared timing estimation error (MSE) is the split-preamble strategy, where the available training symbols are split into two halves, and placed at the start and the end of the sector. This strategy is shown to greatly reduce the training overhead requirement for the same MSE performance, when compared to the conventional strategy of placing all the known symbols at the start of the sector.

References

[1] H. L. Van Trees, *Detection, estimation and modulation theory: vol. 1*, New York: John Wiley and Sons, first edition, 1968.

[2] C. Berrou, A. Glavieux, and P. Thitimajshima, "Near Shannon limit error-correcting coding and decoding: Turbo codes", in *Proc. IEEE International Conf. Commun. 1993*, vol. 2, pp. 1064–1070, May 1993.

[3] R. Gallager, "Low-density parity-check codes", *IRE Trans. Inform. Theory*, vol. IT-8, pp. 21–28, Jan. 1962.

[4] D. Raphaeli and Y. Zarai, "Combined turbo equalization and turbo decoding", in *Proc. IEEE Global Telecommun. Conf. 1997*, vol. 2, pp. 639–643, Nov. 1997.

[5] T. Souvignier, A. Friedmann, M. Oberg, P. Siegel, R. Swanson, and J. Wolf, "Turbo decoding for PR4: parallel vs. serial concatenation", in *Proc. IEEE International Conf. Commun.*, vol. 3, pp. 1638–1642, Jun. 1999.

[6] H. Meyr, M. Moeneclaey, and S. A. Fechtel, *Digital communication receivers: synchronization, channel estimation and signal processing*, New York: John Wiley and Sons, 1997.

[7] D. C. Rife and R. R. Boorstyn, "Single tone parameter observation from discrete-time observations", *IEEE Trans. Inform. Theory*, vol. 20, no. 5, pp. 591–598, Sep. 1974.

[8] A. N. D'Andrea, U. Mengali, and R. Reggiannini, "The modified Cramer-Rao bound and its application to synchronization problems", *IEEE Trans. Commun.*, vol. 42, no. 2, pp. 1391–1399, Feb. 1994.

[9] L. L. Scharf and L. McWhorter, "Geometry of the Cramér-Rao bound", *Signal Processing*, vol. 31, no. 3, pp. 1–11, Apr. 1993.

[10] L. L. Scharf, *Statistical signal processing: detection, estimation, and time series analysis*, New York: Addison-Wesley, 1990.

[11] H. L. Van Trees, *Detection, estimation and modulation theory: vol. 2*, New York: John Wiley and Sons, first edition, 1971.

[12] A. Nayak, *Iterative timing recovery for magnetic recording channels with low signal-to-noise ratio*, PhD Dissertation, Georgia Institute of Technology, Aug. 2004.

Aravind Nayak, LSI Corp., 1811 Pike Rd, Suite 2C, Longmont, Colorado 80501
E-mail address: aravind.nayak@lsi.com

John Barry, School of Electrical and Computer Engineering, Georgia Institute of Technology, Atlanta, Georgia 30332
E-mail address: barry@ece.gatech.edu

Steven McLaughlin, School of Electrical and Computer Engineering, Georgia Institute of Technology, Atlanta, Georgia 30332
E-mail address: swm@ece.gatech.edu

DIMACS Series in Discrete Mathematics
and Theoretical Computer Science
Volume **73**, 2008

Macro-Molecular Data Storage With Petabyte/cm^3 Density, Highly Parallel Read/Write Operations, and Genuine 3D Storage Capability

Masud Mansuripur and Pramod Khulbe

ABSTRACT. Digital information can be encoded in the building-block sequence of macromolecules, such as RNA and single-stranded DNA. Methods of "writing" and "reading" macromolecular strands are currently available, but they are slow and expensive. In an ideal molecular data storage system, routine operations such as write, read, erase, store, and transfer must be done reliably and at high speed within an integrated chip. As a first step toward demonstrating the feasibility of this concept, we report preliminary results of DNA readout experiments conducted in miniaturized chambers that are scalable to even smaller dimensions. We show that translocation of a single-stranded DNA molecule (consisting of 50 adenosine bases followed by 100 cytosine bases) through an ion-channel yields a characteristic signal that is attributable to the 2-segment structure of the molecule. We also examine the dependence of the rate and speed of molecular translocation on the adjustable parameters of the experiment.

1. Introduction

Many of the traditional problems in disk and tape data storage can be overcome if data-blocks were to be released from the confines of a disk (or tape) and allowed to float freely between read/write stations (i.e., heads) and permanent "parking spots." The heads and parking spots thus become fixed structures within an integrated chip, while the macro-molecular data blocks themselves become the (mobile) storage media. In this scheme, a large number of read/write heads could operate in parallel, the heads and parking spots would be constructed (layer upon layer) in a truly 3-dimensional fashion, and individual nanometer-sized molecules – strung together in a flexible macromolecular chain – would be used to represent the 0's and 1's of binary information. In this paper we discuss the potential advantages of this alternative scheme for (secondary) data storage and, to demonstrate the feasibility of the concept, we present results of experiments based on DNA molecules that travel within micro-fluidic chambers.

2000 *Mathematics Subject Classification.* 68P20, 68P30, 92D20.

Key words and phrases. Information storage, macromolecules, storage media, nano-pore.

This work has been supported by the Office of Naval Research MURI grant No. N00014-03-1-0793 and by the National Science Foundation STC Program, under Agreement No. DMR-0120967.

©2008 American Mathematical Society

In principle, the four nucleotides of DNA can be used to represent a 2-bit sequence (A = 00, C = 01, G = 10, T = 11), although practical considerations may impose certain restrictions on the specific sequences that can be used to encode the information. A data storage device built around this concept must have the ability to (*i*) create macromolecules with any desired sequence of building blocks, i.e., *write* or encode the digital information into macromolecular strands; (*ii*) analyze and decode the sequence of a previously created macromolecule, i.e., *read* the recorded information; (*iii*) provide an automated and reliable mechanism for transferring the macromolecules between the read station, the write station, and designated locations (parking spots) for storing each such macro-molecule. Although methods of writing and reading macromolecular strands are currently available (e.g., arbitrary sequences of oligonucleotides can be synthesized, and DNA sequences can be deciphered), these methods require large machines and are slow and expensive. In an ideal molecular data storage system, routine operations such as write, read, erase, store, and transfer must be carried out within an integrated chip, reliably and at high speed.

2. Device Architecture

As a possible alternative to present-day mass data storage devices (e.g., magnetic and optical disks and tapes), we envision a system in which data blocks are encoded into macromolecules constructed from two or more distinct bases, say, x and y; the bases can be strung together in arbitrary order such as $xxyxyyxy\ldots xyx$ to represent binary sequences of user-data ($x = 0, y = 1$) (see [**1**, **2**]). The macromolecular data blocks must be created in a *write station*, transferred to parking spots for temporary storage, and brought to a *read station* for decoding and readout. The erase operation is as simple as discarding a data block and allocating its *parking spot* to another macromolecule. In principle, discarded molecules can be recycled after being broken down to their constituent elements. The parking spots and read/write stations depicted in Fig. 1, for example, are μ-fluidic chambers connected via μ-channels and μ-valves (not shown) that enable automatic access through an electronic addressing scheme [**2**]. With the dimensions of the various chambers indicated in Fig. 1, one can readily incorporate, on a 1.0 cm^2 surface area, a total of 10^6 parking spots (~ 0.25 cm^2), 1000 read/write stations ($\sim 0.1cm^2$), and necessary plumbing (e.g., 1 μm-wide connecting routes, $1 \times 1\,\mu m^2$ binary valves or switches), which would occupy an area $\sim 0.65\,cm^2$. Assuming megabyte-long data-blocks, the storage capacity of the 10^6 parking spots in this scheme will be 10^{12} bytes/cm^2. In a three-dimensional design based on 10 μm-thick layers, the capacity of the proposed molecular storage system would exceed 10^{15} bytes/cm^3. For a comparison with a current state-of-the-art technology, note that storing 10^{15} bytes of data on Digital Versatile Disks requires a 128 meter-tall stack of 12 cm-diameter DVD platters.

One may also envision packaging the molecular data blocks in microscopic spherical vesicles known as liposomes (see Fig. 2). This would provide a robust environment for the transfer of data blocks between the parking spots and the read/write stations. Moreover, by planting specific antibody molecules on the vesicle surfaces, it becomes possible to direct these "addressed" packages to desired locations tagged with antibody-specific antigens (i.e., receptors).

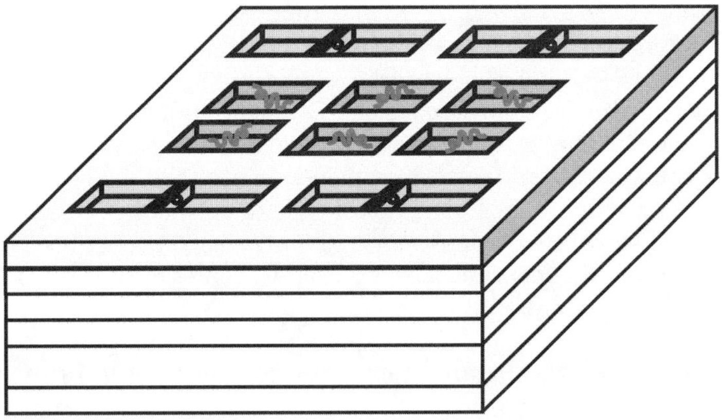

FIGURE 1. Chip surface utilization showing four read/write stations ($100 \times 100 \times 5\ \mu m^3$ each) and six parking spots ($5 \times 5 \times 5\ \mu m^3$ each). Each parking spot contains a 1 MB macromolecular data block (length $\sim$ 1 cm, diameter $\sim$ 1 nm). The thickness of each of the layers is $10\,\mu$m. The same arrangement of read, write stations and parking spots is repeated in stacked layers.

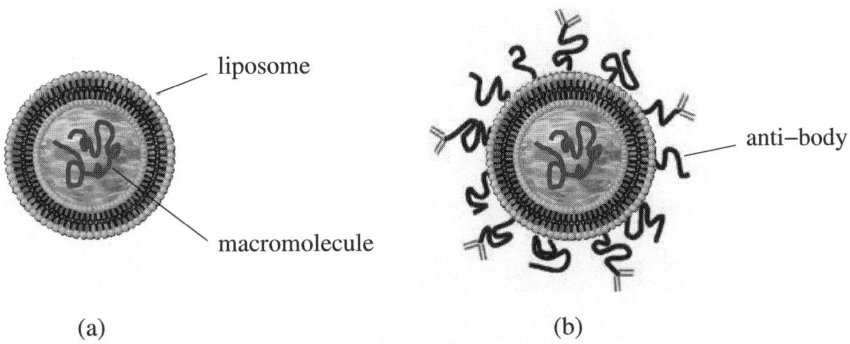

FIGURE 2. Liposomes are microscopic spherical vesicles that form when phospholipids are hydrated. When mixed in water under low shear conditions, the phospholipids arrange themselves in sheets, the molecules aligning side by side with heads up and tails down. The sheets then join tails-to-tails to form a bilayer membrane. Phospholipid bilayer spheres enclosing water and one or more macromolecules can be produced with uniform size (diameter $\sim$ 200 nm or smaller). Antibodies inserted in the outer surface of the liposome can target specific locations within the device tagged with antibody-specific antigens.

In an effort to demonstrate the feasibility of the proposed molecular storage scheme, we have built miniaturized read stations for DNA strands [**2**,**3**]. The idea is to translocate single-stranded DNA molecules through a nano-pore while monitoring the variations of the electrolytic current through the pore, as has been described elsewhere in the context of gene analysis and sequencing [**4**–**11**]. Whereas in decoding a genome the DNA sequence could be arbitrary, in the proposed data storage application it is possible to tailor the sequence to the characteristics of the read station. For instance, if the electrical signals corresponding to individual bases turn out to be indistinguishable (due to insufficient signal-to-noise ratio, SNR, or because the ion-channel is too long compared to the dimensions of single nucleotides), one might instead associate the information bits with strings of identical bases; for example, a string of 20 adenosines can be used to represent a 0, while a string of 30 cytosines could represent a 1.

3. Conventional Modes of Mass Storage and Their Limitations

The hallmarks of traditional secondary (i.e., disk, tape) data storage may be summarized as follows: (*i*) mechanical motion of the storage medium; (*ii*) mechanical motion of the read/write head; (*iii*) confinement of data to two-dimensional surfaces; (*iv*) data organization in sectors or blocks (as opposed to words); (*v*) difficulty of achieving parallel access to multiple sectors; (*vi*) dependence of achievable data density on the read/write/servo mechanism (as opposed to the physical properties of the storage medium). By releasing the data-blocks from the confines of the storage medium and giving them an independent physical identity, as depicted in Fig. 3, one could solve many of the traditional problems associated with disk/tape data storage. The released data sectors must still represent large blocks of data (item iv above); they also continue to require mechanical motion for moving around the storage device (item *i* above). However, the free-floating data blocks can now operate with stationary read/write heads, and will no longer be confined to a two-dimensional surface. The read/write heads will be permanently fixed within the storage system (i.e., no need for flying heads, track-following, auto-focusing, or scanning the storage medium to access various sectors). Therefore, the number of read/write stations that can be integrated into the storage system can increase dramatically compared to what is achievable in present-day devices. Parallel access to data thus becomes a natural mode of operation for a system that has hundreds or thousands of independent read/write stations.

4. Miniature Read Station

In previous publications we have described a method of reading molecular data blocks by translocation through nano-pores [**2**]. We have also reported methods of fabrication of the requisite fluidic chambers [**2**, **3**]. Our current research is focused on miniaturizing the read/write stations and integrating them with parking spots, μ-fluidic channels, and μ-valves. Our read stations, complete with electrodes and access ports, were molded from polydimethylsiloxane (PDMS), cast in a machined Teflon block. This design, which is scalable to even smaller dimensions, allows easy integration with multiple parking spots on the same chip. In the read station depicted in Fig. 4, the needle-like end of the tube that connects the cis and trans chambers was covered with a Teflon cap (aperture diameter $\sim 20\,\mu$m) to promote the formation of a lipid membrane over the aperture. The nano-pore, self-assembled in the lipid membrane from seven sub-units of α-haemolysin (αHL) protein, is a 10 nm-long ion-channel, whose cap (length $\sim$ 5 nm) resides in the cis chamber,

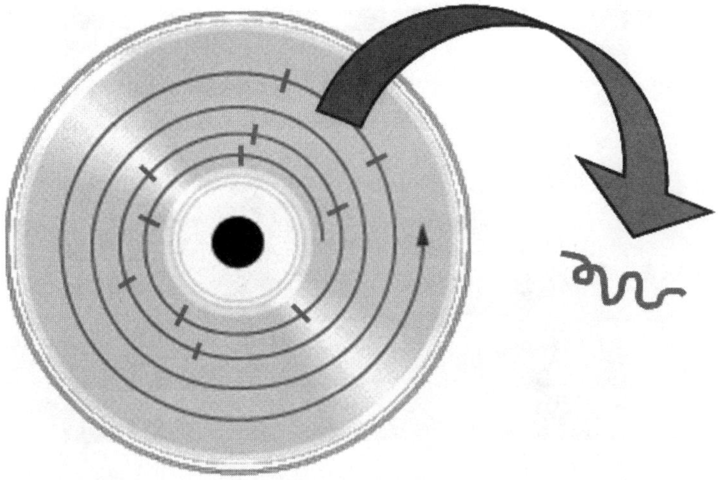

FIGURE 3. Releasing the data blocks from the storage medium can, in principle, solve many of the problems associated with conventional data storage schemes.

while its 5nm-long stem spans the lipid membrane. The ion-channel has an opening diameter of 2.6 nm at the entrance to the cap, 1.5 nm in the constricted region in the middle, and 2.2 nm at the far end of the stem located in the trans chamber [**4**, **5**].

In the read station of Fig. 4, the cis chamber is accessed (under microscope control) with a micro-pipette from the right-hand side, and the trans chamber from the left-hand side. The micro-pipette is used for filling the chambers with buffer, adding αHL or DNA to the cis chamber, and removing the additives by perfusion. At 50 μL volume (partial filling), the chambers are small enough to yield a low-noise electrolytic current signal, yet large enough to avoid problems associated with the evaporation of the liquids. If the device dimensions were to shrink further, both chambers would have to be capped to prevent evaporation.

Our goal was to improve the signal-to-noise ratio (SNR) of readout by increasing both the KCl concentration in the buffer and the applied voltage. The increased salt concentration, however, resulted in ion-channel gating, which is unacceptable behavior for observation of DNA translocation events. The higher voltage, on the other hand, helped raise the SNR by enhancing the signal without causing much increase in the noise.

5. Gating Behavior of α-haemolysin Nano-Pore at High KCl Concentration

The top, bottom, and middle traces in Fig. 5 show the electrical current through a single nano-pore with 1 molar KCl concentration at applied voltage levels of +210 mV, -210 mV, and 0 mV, respectively. The channel is always open at this KCl concentration, and the forward current is just over 250 pA, while the reverse current is about -200 pA. The width of the trace in each case is a good measure of

(a)

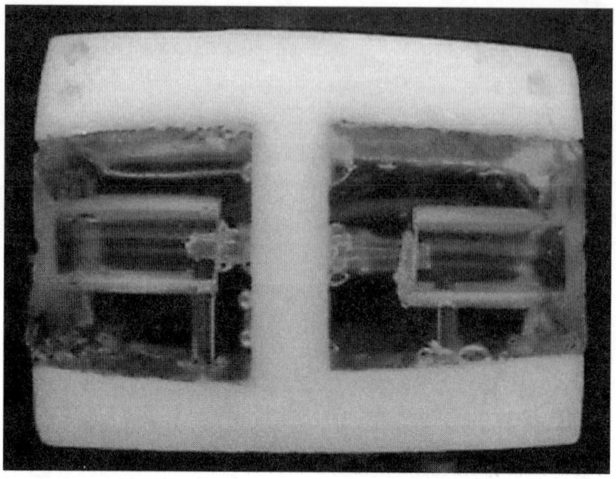

(b)

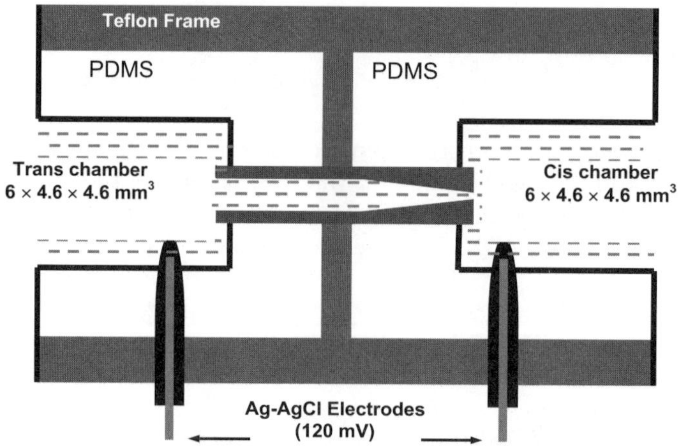

FIGURE 4. (a) Photograph and (b) diagram of a read station built inside a 10 mm-thick H-shaped Teflon frame. A Teflon tube, shrunk at one end to a 20 μm diameter aperture, goes through the central wall and forms a tight seal between the *cis* and *trans* chambers. The 6 mm-long, 4.6 mm diameter cylindrical chambers are large enough to hold the buffer solution for several hours; evaporation reduces the buffer by 50 % in 24 hours. The chambers are connected to an Axopatch 200B amplifier via Ag-AgCl electrodes. The 20 μm diameter aperture holds a (vertical) lipid bilayer, into which one or more αHL ion-channels are implanted. Single-stranded DNA molecules are driven through the channel by an applied voltage in the range 90–210 mV, positive at the trans side.

the noise level present during the measurement. (The KCl concentration was 1M on both cis and trans sides; in other words, there was no transmembrane gradient.)

When the KCl concentration is raised to 2M, the ion-channel exhibits a "gating" behavior, namely, it opens and closes randomly, as can be seen in the oscillating trace in Fig. 5. The applied voltage was reduced in this case to +120 mV to make the forward current (in the open state of the ion-channel) nearly equal to the forward current in the case of 1M KCl concentration. (At 2M KCl, gating behavior was also observed at higher voltages, up to 200 mV, and also when a reverse voltage, $V = -120\,\text{mV}$, was applied.) Apparently, at some KCl concentration between 1M and 2M, the nano-pore exhibits gating, irrespective of the level or polarity of the applied voltage.

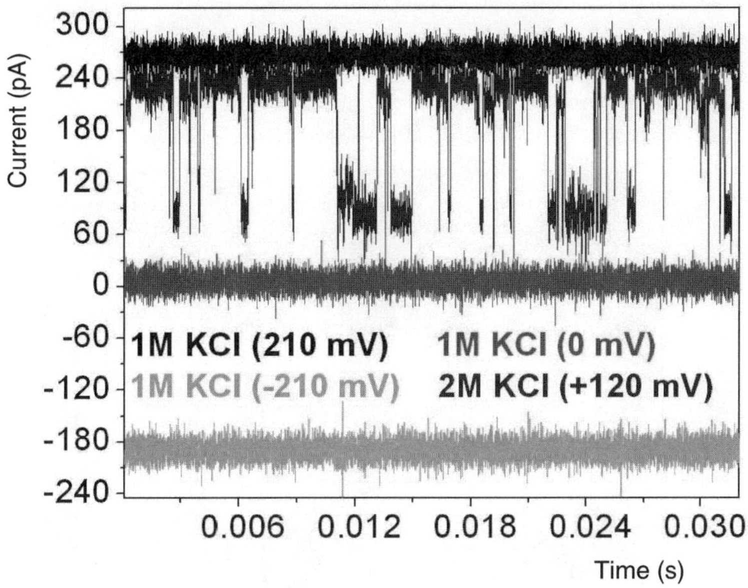

FIGURE 5. Current traces obtained from an αHL channel incorporated into a bilayer. The middle trace shows the channel in the non-conducting state, when there is no potential difference across the bilayer. The top and bottom traces show the channel in the conducting (open) state in response to a trans-bilayer applied voltage of +210 mV and -210 mV, respectively (in the presence of 1M KCl on both sides of the bilayer). Note the difference in the current level between the top and bottom traces, which indicates the channel's asymmetric response to a polarity reversal of the applied voltage. In the presence of 2M KCl, and in response to an applied voltage of +120 mV (oscillating trace), the channel fluctuates spontaneously between open and closed states (gating).

6. Translocation of $5'A_{50}C_{100}3'$ Single-Stranded DNA

The ssDNA molecules traversed the ion-channel under $V = 210\,\text{mV}$ at 1M KCl buffer concentration, and were observed with the amplifier bandwidth set to

100 kHz. In one trial, of the 171 translocation events monitored, 49 events, or nearly 29%, showed bi-level behavior. (Not every event is expected to exhibit a bi-level signal, either due to the large fluctuations of the blockade current, or because of incomplete translocation, in which the molecule is trapped in the vestibular region of the αHL cap for a certain length of time, then returned to the cis chamber without traversing the ion-channel.) The bi-level behavior is seen in three of the four events in Fig. 6. Translocation duration for the entire molecule is typically $\sim$150 μs. In some instances, such as the first event in Fig. 6, the molecule appears to get stuck in the midst of translocation, which results in a longer-than-average transition time. The fourth event in Fig. 6 is typical of the remaining 71% of events in which either the molecule entered the pore but did not complete translocation, or the bi-level signal was not clearly visible due to a lack of sufficient SNR. It is worth mentioning that, in our experiments, bi-level signals were not observed for $V = 120$ mV, 150 mV, or 180 mV; the higher applied voltage of 210 mV, was somehow necessary to obtain these signals. (Although a bi-level translocation signal from 2-segment RNA molecules has been reported in the literature [**6**], we are not aware of any such results in the published record for ssDNA.)

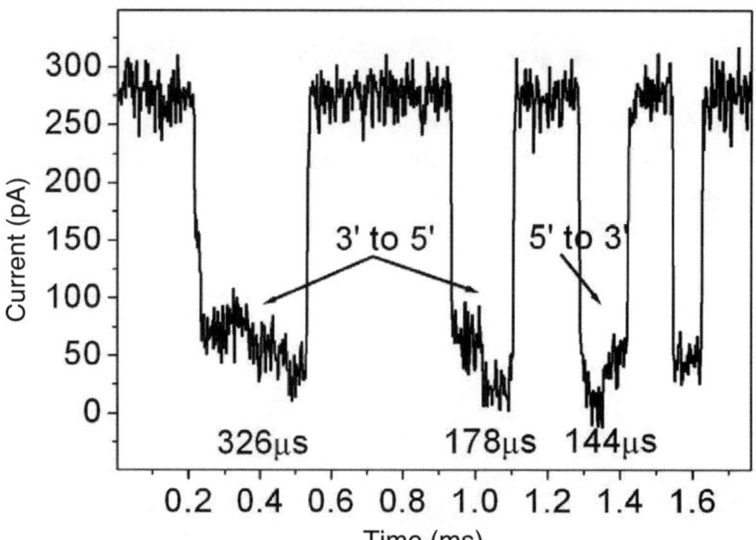

FIGURE 6. Effect on current flow of ssDNA passage through an αHLchannel. $5'A_{50}C_{100}3'$ ssDNA was introduced into the *cis* chamber (where the cap of the ion-channel is located). Buffer concentration = 1M KCl, applied voltage = +210 mV, amplifier bandwidth = 100 kHz. The channel's open state is interrupted by four brief closures (translocation events). The first and second events show two closure substates indicating the translocation of ssDNA from the 3' to the 5' end. The third event also shows two substates which, however, are reversed, indicating passage from the 5' to the 3' end. In the fourth event, the A_{50} and C_{100} sections of the molecule are indistinguishable.

It has been shown by several research groups that, for a given polynucleotide, translocation events generally fall into two categories, with one group of events showing less current blockade than the other. This grouping has been suggested to arise from translocation of the molecule in either of two orientations, namely, $3' \rightarrow 5'$ or $5' \rightarrow 3'$, or it might represent the translocation of the polymer in one of two different structural conformations [**5**–**9**]. An asymmetric interaction between the polynucleotide and the internal pore structure has been suggested as the cause of the observed grouping in those occasions where the entry of the molecule into the pore from its 5' end produces a larger current blockade than when the 3' end enters the pore first [**12**].

In our $5'A_{50}C_{100}3'$ ssDNA sample, keeping in mind that the C-nucleotide is smaller than the A-nucleotide, the 100-base-long C-segment is expected to drop the ionic current somewhat less than the 50 base-long A-segment does. The order in which the high and low portions of the bi-level signal occur during each translocation event depends on whether the 3'- or the 5'-end of the molecule enters the nano-pore first. Of the 29% bi-level events observed in the aforementioned experiment, nearly three-quarters were associated with the C-segment entering first, during which events the average normalized current, $\langle I_{blocked}/I_{open} \rangle$, was 0.37 ± 0.09 for the C-segment and 0.17 ± 0.04 for the A-segment. In the remaining quarter of the bi-level events (associated with the A-segment entering first) the average normalized current was 0.20 ± 0.03 for the C- and 0.12 ± 0.04 for the A-segment. These results are consistent with the aforementioned suggestion that the entry of polynucleotides into the pore from the 5'-end causes a larger current blockage than entry from the 3'-end.

7. Effect of Increased Voltage

Both the capture rate of the DNA molecules and the translocation speed through a single ion-channel were found to be strong functions of the applied voltage V, as has been reported by other researchers as well [**5**]. The three frames in Fig. 7 represent the translocation of 120-base-long $5'(AC)_{60}3'$ DNA molecules under the influence of three different voltages. At $V = 150\,\text{mV}$, the average open-channel current is $\langle I_{open} \rangle \sim 160\,\text{pA}$, and many translocation events are seen to occur. At $V = 120\,\text{mV}$ and $\langle I_{open} \rangle \sim 130\,\text{pA}$, the translocation rate has declined, and at $V = 90\,\text{mV}$, $\langle I_{open} \rangle \sim 90\,\text{pA}$, the events are relatively rare.

The observed behavior may indicate that the increased voltage has somehow directed a large number of DNA molecules (that would otherwise drift away from the vicinity of the pore) toward the ion-channel. This, in turn, is a clue concerning the transport mechanism of DNA molecules toward the pore, namely, that the drift of the molecule is not entirely controlled by thermal diffusion, and that the chamber geometry and placement of the electrodes can influence (and perhaps even control) the motion of DNA strands toward the ion-channel. When considering this particular method of molecular readout in the context of data storage, it must be remembered that controlled molecular transport is of utmost significance, as individual macromolecules are required to travel between their parking spots and the read/write stations.

Figure 8 shows some statistics of the translocation experiment depicted in Fig. 7. Figure 8(a) shows that at lower applied voltages the ion-channel is open (i.e., not clogged by a passing molecule) for a larger fraction of time than at higher

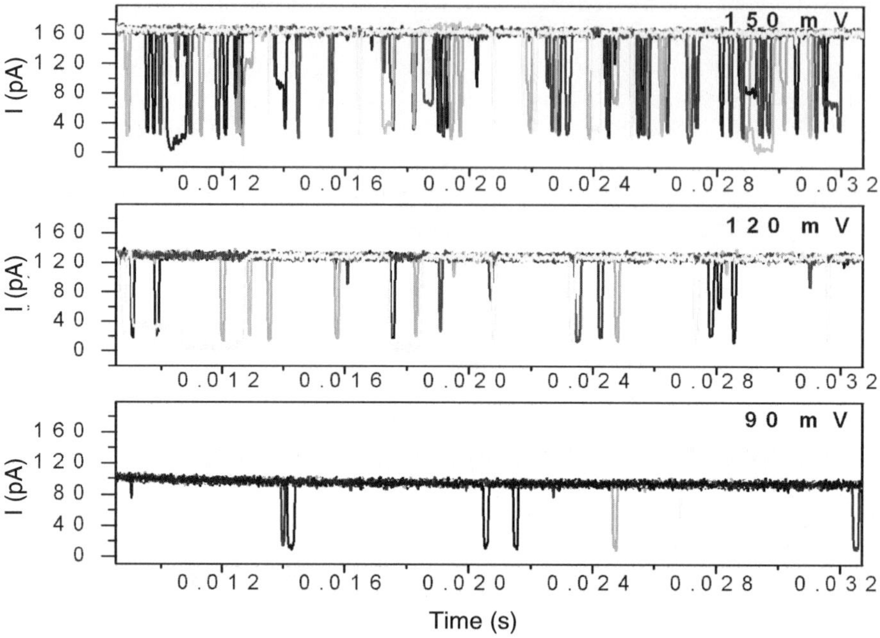

FIGURE 7. Translocation of 120-base-long $5'(\mathrm{AC})_{60}3'$ DNA molecules under different applied voltages. At $V = 150\,\mathrm{mV}$, $\langle \mathrm{I_{open}} \rangle \sim 160\,\mathrm{pA}$ and translocation events are frequent. At $V = 120\,\mathrm{mV}$, $\langle \mathrm{I_{open}} \rangle \sim 130\,\mathrm{pA}$ and translocation rate has declined. At $V = 90\,\mathrm{mV}$, $\langle \mathrm{I_{open}} \rangle \sim 90\,\mathrm{pA}$ and translocation events are rare.

voltages. According to Fig. 8(b), the translocation rate (i.e., number of events per second), whether complete (solid square) or incomplete (solid circle), is an increasing function of the applied voltage. The total translocation rate (solid triangle), which is the sum of complete and incomplete translocations per second, increases nearly three-fold in going from $V = 120\,\mathrm{mV}$ to $150\,\mathrm{mV}$.

Figure 9 shows the distribution of the event duration ΔT versus the current blockage in the experiment of Fig. 7. These data indicate that, at higher applied voltages, there is less current blockage, perhaps because the molecules are likely to be linearized, thus presenting a smaller cross-section to the pore. Also, at higher applied voltages the translocation duration is reduced, meaning that the molecules travel faster through the ion-channel. The speed of the molecules passing through the nano-pore is seen to be roughly proportional to the applied voltage, as has been reported by other research groups [**5**,**9**]. Faster translocation, of course, is desirable in data storage applications as it results in a greater data-transfer rate, so long as the SNR remains reasonably high at the correspondingly larger bandwidth.

8. Experiments with Multiple Nano-Pores

In a typical nano-pore experiment, αHL proteins are removed (by perfusion) from the cis chamber immediately after the formation of a single nano-pore. Given sufficient time, however, additional ion-channels reconstitute themselves in the same

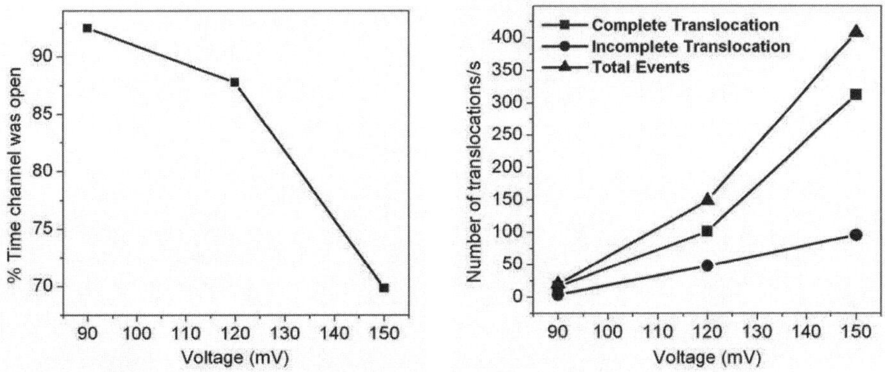

FIGURE 8. Characteristics of translocation events in the experiment depicted in Fig. 7. (Left) Fraction of time during which the ion-channel is open (i.e., not clogged) as function of the applied voltage V. (Right) Translocation rate versus the applied voltage.

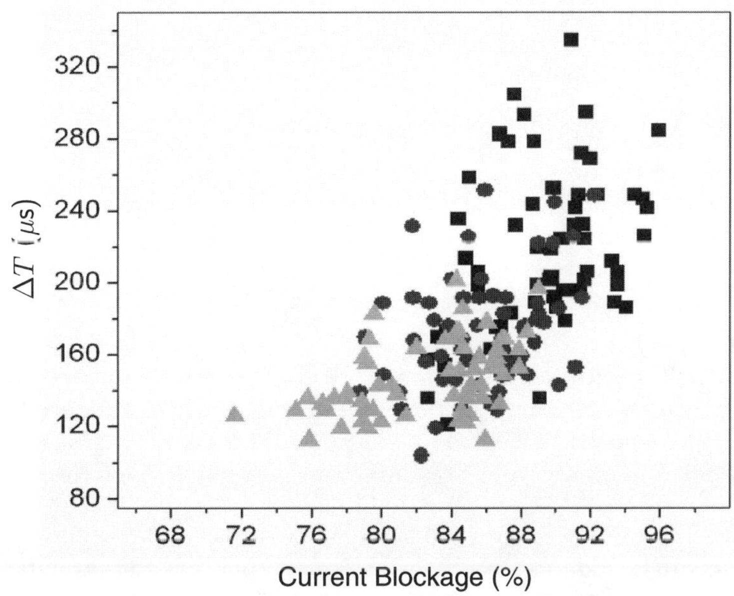

FIGURE 9. Translocation statistics in the experiment depicted in Fig. 7. The percentage current blockage is shown on the horizontal axis, while the event duration appears on the vertical axis. The cluster of triangles represents the case of $V = 150\,\text{mV}$, circles correspond to $V = 120\,\text{mV}$, and squares represent the case of $V = 90\,\text{mV}$.

lipid membrane. In one experiment, the lipid bilayer had a diameter of $20\,\mu\text{m}$, resulting in a pair wise separation of at most $20\,\mu\text{m}$ between nano-pores. Figure 10 shows a typical trace of the electrolytic current across the membrane where, initially,

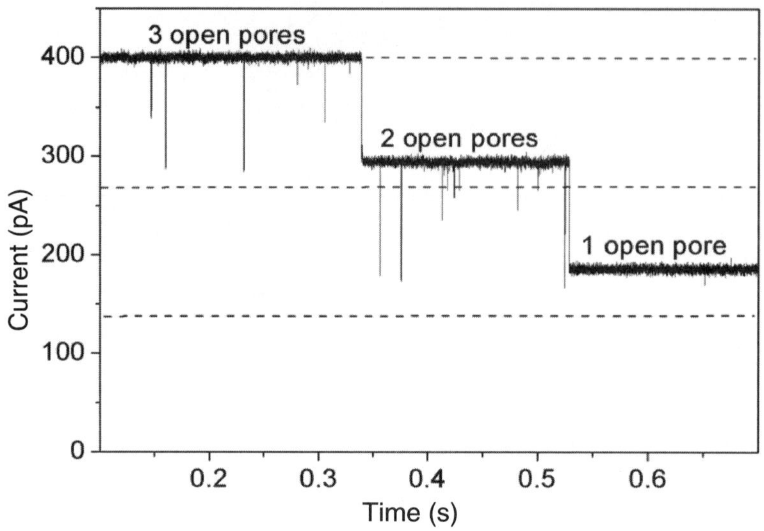

FIGURE 10. A typical trace of the electrolytic current obtained when three ion-channels (reconstituted in the same lipid membrane) operate simultaneously and independently of each other. When a DNA molecule is stuck in one of the nano-pores, the current drops to ~190 pA. With two nano-pores similarly clogged, the total current across the membrane is ~190 pA. The complete translocation events are found to have average rates of 12.6, 6.2, and 3.3 events per second, with zero, one, or two nano-pores clogged, respectively. The corresponding rate for partial events in these three cases are 19.2, 13.5, and 7.0 events/second, leading to total event rates of 31.8, 19.7 and 10.3 per second.

the total current is ~400 pA, indicating the presence of three open nano-pores. With all three channels open, the rate of capture and/or translocation is relatively high (31.8 events per second). When one of the pores is temporarily clogged, the current drops to ~290 pA, and the rate of capture/translocation through the two remaining open pores drops to ~19.7 per second. Similarly, when two of the nano-pores are clogged, the current drops to ~190 pA and the event rate declines to ~10.3 per second. This data indicates that, for each nano-pore, the electrolytic current is ~130 pA in the open-channel state and ~30 pA in the clogged state. The observed capture and/or translocation rate ratio of nearly 3 : 2 : 1 confirms that the three ion-channels operate independently of one another on drifting DNA molecules. We have observed the same behavior repeatedly: the event rate increased after reversing the applied voltage to clear the clogged channel(s), only to drop again with the next clogging.

9. Concluding Remarks

As a first step toward constructing a macromolecular data storage system, we have demonstrated the feasibility of conducting experiments with fairly short strands of DNA in a miniature read station. We showed that the A- and C-segments of a $5'A_{50}C_{100}3'$ ssDNA molecule can be distinguished during translocation through an αHL ion-channel. Needless to say, many hurdles must be overcome before this system can be implemented as an alternative to existing storage technologies.

The ultrahigh capacity is an obvious advantage of such molecular storage devices, but the data-rates require substantial improvement. If the $5'A_{50}C_{100}3'$ molecules, which represent 2-bit sequences of binary information, take $\sim 150\,\mu s$ to pass through a nano-pore, the corresponding data-transfer rate of only 12 kbit/s would leave a lot to be desired. On the other hand, if the technology could improve to the point that individual bases could be detected during translocation (perhaps through a shorter, more robust, solid-state nano-pore) [**13**], then the achievable rate of ~1 Mbit/s would not be out of bounds. Moreover, if thousands of read stations could be made to operate in parallel within the same chip, the overall data-transfer rate could approach the respectable value of several Gbits/s.

Access to data is another issue that requires extensive research. Our preliminary calculations show that a 1 Mbyte-long macromolecule, enclosed in a 200 nm diameter spherical shell (e.g., a liposome), can move electrophoretically across a 1.0 cm^2 chip in ~1.0 millisecond under a 10 V potential difference. Whether such molecules could be written and packaged on demand, within an integrated microchip, at high speed, and on a large scale, are questions to which only future research can provide satisfactory answers. Stability of the molecules over extended periods of time should obviously be a matter of concern. The lipid membrane and the proteinaceous ion-channel, both being of organic origin, are ill-suited for practical data storage systems; they must eventually be replaced with robust, solid-state equivalents [**13**]. Despite all the difficulties, it is our hope that the proposed scheme will encourage debate in the pursuit of an alternative path to conventional approaches to data storage.

Acknowledgments

The authors are grateful to Professors Raphael Gruener, Michael Hogan, and Nasser Peyghambarian of the University of Arizona, and Joseph Perry and Seth Marder of the Georgia Institute of Technology, for many helpful discussions.

Appendix

Experimental conditions. The buffer used in our experiments was 1M KCl, 10 mM HEPES (pH ~ 8.0), pH balanced by KOH, and the lipid was diphytanoyl phosphatidycholine (DPC). The Ag-AgCl electrodes were made by dipping a silver wire in Clorox. The patch-clamp amplifier was Axon Instrument's Axopatch 200B. Two different oligodeoxynucleotide samples were used in our experiments: the $5'A_{50}C_{100}3'$, with a total of 150 base-units per molecule, was used in the experiment described in Fig. 6. All other experiments (reported in Figs. 7–10) used $5'(AC)_{60}3'$, with a total of 120 bases per molecule. Both custom-synthesized, PAGE (Poly Acrylic Gel Electrophoresis) grade samples were purchased from Midland Certified Reagent Company (Midland, Texas). The samples were suspended in TE buffer (10 mM Tris / 1 mM EDTA) at pH 8.0, before being released into the cis chamber, where the final concentration of $5'A_{50}C_{100}3'$ was 7.15 nM/ml, while that of $5'(AC)_{60}3'$ was 14.3 nM/ml.

Prior to filling the chambers with buffer, 2 μL of a lipid solution in hexane (1.5 mg/mL) is released in the vicinity of the 20 μm aperture between the cis and trans chambers. The chambers are then dried under a mild stream of nitrogen, thus allowing a thin layer of lipid to coat the surrounding walls without clogging the aperture. Care must be taken to completely evaporate the hexane, as even trace amounts in the aperture area can ruin the bilayer. We found the bilayer that must cover the aperture between the two chambers does not form properly when applied to a PDMS surface. Although PDMS is hydrophobic – a requirement for this application – its porosity ultimately destroys the lipid membrane a few minutes after the formation of a bilayer. In the read station depicted in Fig. 4, the needle-like end of the tube connecting *cis* and *trans* chambers had to be covered with a Teflon cap (aperture diameter $\sim 20\ \mu$m) to promote the proper formation of a lipid membrane.

The cis and trans chambers (as well as the tube that connects them) are subsequently filled with buffer. We soaked 1.5 mg of lipid in $5\,\mu$L of hexadecane in a test tube for 60–90 seconds; the left-over hexadecane was then completely drained, leaving a viscous lipid at the bottom of the tube. A micro-capillary tube (length ~ 1 mm, inner diameter $\sim 300\,\mu$m) was filled with this viscous lipid in such a way as to form a convex meniscus at the tip of the capillary. Using a micro-manipulator, this lipid meniscus was brushed across the $20\,\mu$m aperture with a slight pressure. A 60 Hz, 5 mV square wave was then applied between the Ag-AgCl electrodes across the bilayer (the so-called seal test) to verify that the bilayer is adequate. The above procedure succeeds in creating a proper bilayer across the aperture in about 90% of the trials.

Once a stable bilayer was obtained, 40 ng of α-haemolysin (αHL protein) was dissolved in $2\,\mu$L of buffer and added to the cis chamber. By applying a potential ($V = 120\,\text{mV}$) across the bilayer enables one to observe the reconstruction of an ion-channel into the bilayer, an event which is indicated by an abrupt jump of the current from 0 to ~ 120 pA. The observed voltage to current ratio of ~ 1.0 GΩ is consistent with the single-channel conductance of αHL nano-pores under similar conditions, as reported in the literature [**5**]. Self-assembly of a single ion-channel within the lipid membrane typically takes 20–30 minutes, after which the excess αHL is removed by perfusion of 10 mL of fresh buffer.

References

[1] M. Mansuripur, "DNA, human memory, and the storage technology of the 21st century," keynote address, Optical Data Storage Conference, Santa Fe, New Mexico, April 2001; in *Proc. SPIE 2001 Optical Data Storage Conf.*, vol. 4342, pp. 1–29, Jan. 2002.

[2] M. Mansuripur, P.K. Khulbe, S.M. Kuebler, J.W. Perry, M.S. Giridhar, and N. Peyghambarian, "Information storage and retrieval using macromolecules as storage media," Optical Data Storage Conference, Vancouver, Canada, May 2003; in *Proc. SPIE 2003 Optical Data Storage Conf.*, vol. 5069, pp. 231–243, Sept. 2003.

[3] M.S. Giridhar, K.B. Seong, A. Schülzgen, P.K. Khulbe, N. Peyghambarian, and M. Mansuripur, "Femtosecond pulsed laser micromachining of glass substrates with application to microfluidic devices," Applied Optics, vol. 43, no. 23, pp. 4584-4589, Aug. 2004.

[4] D. W. Deamer and D. Branton, "Characterization of nucleic acids by nanopore analysis," Acc. Chem. Res., vol. 35, no. 10, pp. 817–825, Oct. 2002.

[5] A. Meller, "Dynamics of polynucleotide transport through nanometre-scale pores," J. Phys. Condens. Matter, vol. 15, R581-R607, 2003.

[6] M. Akeson, D. Branton, J. J. Kasianowicz, E. Brandin, and D. Deamer, "Microsecond time-scale discrimination among polycytidylic acid, polyadenylic acid, and

polyuridylic acid as homopolymers or as segments within single RNA molecules," Biophysical Journal, vol. 77, pp. 3227–3233, 1999.

[7] A. Meller, L. Nivon, E. Brandin, J. Golovchenko, and D. Branton, "Rapid nanopore discrimination between single polynucleotide molecules," Proc. Natl. Acad. Sci., vol. 97, no. 3, pp. 1079–1084, Feb. 2000.

[8] J. J. Kasianowicz, E. Brandin, D. Branton, and D. W. Deamer, "Characterization of individual polynucleotide molecules using a membrane channel," Proc. Natl. Acad. Sci., vol. 93, no. 24, pp. 13770–13773, Nov. 1996.

[9] A. Meller, L. Nivon, and D. Branton, "Voltage-driven DNA translocations through a nanopore," Phys. Rev. Lett., vol. 86, no. 15, pp. 3435–3438, Apr. 2001.

[10] S. Howorka, S. Cheley, and H. Bayley, "Sequence-specific detection of individual DNA strands using engineered nanopores," Nature Biotechnology, vol. 19, pp. 636–639, Jul. 2001.

[11] H. Bayley and P.S. Cremer, "Stochastic sensors inspired by biology," Nature, vol. 413, pp. 226–230, Sept. 2001.

[12] T. A. Pologruto, private communication.

[13] J. Li, M. Gershow, D. Stein, E. Brandin, and J. A. Golovchenko, "DNA molecules and configurations in a solid-state nanopore microscope," Nature Materials, vol. 2, pp. 611–615, Sept. 2003.

Optical Sciences Center, University of Arizona, Tucson, Arizona 85721
E-mail address: `masud@u.arizona.edu`

Optical Sciences Center, University of Arizona, Tucson, Arizona 85721
E-mail address: `pkkhulbe@u.arizona.edu`

DIMACS Series in Discrete Mathematics
and Theoretical Computer Science
Volume **73**, 2008

Can We Explain the Faithful Communication of Genetic Information?

Gérard Battail

ABSTRACT. Genomes are conserved with astonishing faithfulness through geological ages. To explain this fact, we made the hypothesis that the genetic message borne by DNA involves powerful error-correction means, consisting of 'nested codes' which provide a stronger protection to the most basic (and oldest) parts of the genomic message. It turns out that, assuming very long codes and performance close to that promised by the channel coding theorem of information theory, many basic features of the living world and of biological evolution can be explained: the existence of discrete species, the possibility of their taxonomy, and the trend of evolution towards complexity. Moreover, answers to controversial points are proposed, e.g., that evolution proceeds by jumps, which suggests a non-Darwinian mechanism for the origin of species. We assume that the hypothesized error-correction means use 'soft codes', a soft code being defined as a set of constraints which link symbols together. Not only deterministic constraints expressed by operations in mathematical structures like finite fields are considered, but also probabilistic constraints, or rules stating incompatibilities. We only require that these constraints modify the conditional probability of any symbol given subsets of other ones. Then, decoding (or, more precisely, regeneration) consists of reassessing the symbol probabilities so as to take account of all their mutual constraints. We examine how soft codes can arise from mechanical, geometrical and chemical constraints obeyed by the DNA molecule as well as, inside a gene, by the protein that DNA specifies by means of the 'genetic code'. Moreover, the genome being a 'blueprint' for the development and maintenance of a living thing, it must use some kind of language, implying morphologic and syntactic constraints which can be interpreted as soft codes. Although the paper is mainly speculative, we show that experimental works agree with the hypotheses made. Some decoding (regeneration) principles are outlined but the detailed mechanisms for their implementation, which involve chemical means, remain to be discovered.

1. Introduction

The support of genetic information is the deoxiribonucleic acid (DNA), a long unidimensional polymer bearing nucleic bases, which are small molecules of only

2000 *Mathematics Subject Classification.* 68P30, 92D20, 94B60.

Key words and phrases. Biological evolution, error-correcting codes, genome conservation, soft codes.

©2008 American Mathematical Society

four different types, denoted A (adenine), T (thymine), G (guanine) and C (cytosine). Each nucleic base acts as a symbol of the quaternary alphabet {A,T,G,C}, and the genetic message consists of a sequence of such molecules. DNA is thus a *molecular* memory, at variance with *all* man-made memory devices where the bearers of the alphabet symbols have a much larger physical size (although the progress of technologies makes it decrease as the years pass, as exemplified by [**1, 2, 3**]). The genetic message could thus be expected to be especially fragile as subject to quantum effects, thermal noise and radiations of various origins. In sharp contrast, however, its longevity widely outperforms that of man-made memories since the genome of extant living things faithfully bears information dating back to hundreds of million years and even more. As a striking example, *HOX* genes which determine features of a living being as fundamental as its organization plan are common to a large number of animal species, including humans and flies.

Only the hypothesis that the mechanisms of DNA replication involve powerful error-correcting codes which make it resilient to errors can conciliate the seeming weakness of DNA and the astonishing longevity of the message it bears. Being products of evolution, these codes are assumed to be almost optimized and they must be very long so as to make the error probability low enough. This hypothesis was formulated in [**4, 5**] and [**6**], together with the auxiliary one that the hypothesized error-correcting means consist of nested codes. Then it was shown that it could explain biological facts as basic as, for instance, the existence of distinct species, the possibility of their taxonomy and the trend of evolution towards complexity. The existence of some kind of error correcting codes in the genome, at the molecular level or involving short codes, was also suggested in [**7, 8, 9, 10**]. The interesting idea that introns are made of check symbols associated with the message borne by the exons was formulated in [**11**]. However, the search for a simple linear code described in [**12**] was unsuccessful[1]. On the other hand, biological error-correcting mechanisms foreign to the genome replication were discovered (see, e.g., [**13**]). The role of codes in biology, although not explicitly seen as error-correcting ones, has been emphasized in [**14**]. The references given above are not exhaustive, but it is clear nevertheless that comparatively few works have been done on biological coding systems. This paucity is surprising. Since the discovery by Avery, McCarty and MacLeod [**15**] that DNA is the bearer of hereditary information, and the subsequent discovery of its double-helix structure by Franklin, Watson and Crick [**16, 17**], it has been recognized that the genetic message consists of the sequence of nucleic bases in DNA. Since the science of digital sequences is an important part of information theory, it should have become a major tool in molecular biology, but it has not been so. The parochialism in sciences has to be blamed for that, and the difficulties of communicating results from a scientific discipline to another one should not be overlooked. It seems especially difficult to let results from an engineering discipline be known by the upholders of a fundamental one.

The need for genomic error-correcting means will be reviewed in Section 3, as well as the consequences of their hypothesized existence. In Section 4, we shall introduce the concept of *soft code*, which weakens but extends the engineering concept of error-correcting code so as to better fit the biological context. Then, we shall look for possible genomic soft codes in Section 5. Before dealing with these topics, we shall consider in Section 2 why a mutual benefit should result from a

[1]This negative result is very questionable; see Sec. 5.1.

collaboration of biology and engineering. A short glossary of molecular genetics is given as an appendix.

2. Biology and Engineering, a Needed Collaboration

Having produced all living beings, with their incredible variety of forms and functions although the basic components are shared by all, nature appears as an engineer of extremely broad competence. It thus seems that human engineers should be deeply interested in nature's achievements, and understanding the engineering aspects of life should be a major concern for biologists. However, even though nature's achievements very often outperform those of human engineers, the methods used by nature on the one hand, and human engineers on the other hand, exhibit a sharp contrast.

At variance with human engineers, nature does not perform purposeful design, but 'tinkering', exhaustive search and natural selection. It ignores time limitation. Continuity of life is its sole (but tough) major constraint. There is also a broad difference between nature and engineers as regards spatial and temporal scales: engineers design and build objects of large physical size within a short time, and these objects have short lifetimes. The most basic properties of living things depend on objects at the molecular scale, and the time scale of nature extends to that of geology, i.e., up to billion years.

As regards the difference in performance, nature's achievements are outstanding. In almost any case, they are understood only insofar as human engineers invented similar solutions to problems that nature solved aeons ago. Nature achievements very often outperform what human engineers can do, and even appeared until recently as far beyond their reach (think of the autonomous motion and spontaneous behavior of animals). Having genuine self-repair capabilities, living beings are moreover much more flexible and resisting degradation than the products of human engineering. No wonder if during millenia humans could account for these differences only by the existence of supernatural entities.

The progresses of science and technology however reduced to some extent the gap between nature's and engineers' achievements. It became increasingly clear that the mechanisms of life do not rely on mystic properties like a 'vital force' but just obey the laws of physics and chemistry. As regards the time scale, the deep past is better and better understood, first thanks to Darwin's theory of evolution, and nowadays due to the availability of physical means to estimate the ages of rocks and fossils, and to the possibility of establishing the phyletic trees of living species based on genome comparisons. As regards the physical size, objects at the molecular level can now be 'seen' and 'handled', and even 'manufactured' as nanotechnologies are becoming a reality. Again, [**1, 2, 3**]) are impressive examples of this trend. The main distinctive features of the living beings are their extreme complexity, which is unmatched in the nonliving world, and (not independently) the rather obvious but still overlooked fact that, besides matter and energy, they receive and transmit information, and they heavily rely on its transfer and conservation. This last point too has no equivalent outside the living world and appears as the specific mark which radically differentiates the living world from the nonliving one. It makes biology especially relevant to information theory, thus challenging information engineers and prompting biologists to use information theory as a main tool.

3. Hypothesizing Genomic Error Correction

3.1. The Need for Genomic Error Correction. Perhaps the most convincing argument for the need of genomic error-correcting means is the fact that mutations, i.e., errors in the genome replication due to chemical agents or radiations, are responsible for aging and certain diseases like cancers. If the error rate in communicating genomic information has noticeable effects at the scale of the lifetime of an individual, then the accumulation of errors during periods million times longer would simply make genetic communication impossible.

Moreover, if we look at the literature on chromosomes and cellular division, on the one hand, and that on the performance of DNA replication on the other hand, the former appears as describing messy, involved and unreliable mechanisms; however, outstanding faithfulness of DNA replication is reported in the latter. This sharp contrast strongly suggests that error-correction mechanisms needed in order to correct replication errors actually exist. Many 'proof-reading' mechanisms[2] are known, but true error-correcting codes are necessary to reach the needed performance level since proof-reading can just ensure that the copy is faithful to the original, i.e., can only correct the errors due to the replication process itself, not the errors of external origin that affect the original. As a molecule, DNA is subject to mechanical, chemical and radiative aggressions. It is shielded against mechanical and chemical aggressions by membranes (the cellular membrane for all living beings, and furthermore the nucleic membrane in the case of eukaryotes whose genome thus benefits from a two-level protection). However, only error-correcting codes can efficiently protect against errors arising from radiations. These are of solar and cosmic origin, or due to natural radioactivity.

Although it is difficult to understand what such a figure really means, the error rate of DNA replication is reported to be of about 10^{-9} per nucleic base and per replication for higher animals. It is far greater (10^{-3} and even more) for some genes of viruses and bacteria. This difference between more or less complex living beings is itself difficult to understand without hypothesizing that more efficient error-correcting means exist in higher living beings than in bacteria and viruses. In turn, this assumption is consistent with the difference of the corresponding genome sizes and the proven result of information theory that the longer the encoded message, the more efficient can be the correction of errors.

To summarize, the outstanding performance of the genetic communication process cannot be accounted for unless assuming the existence of highly efficient error-correction means making genomes resilient to errors. They should thus go far beyond elementary encoding means and short codes, and we believe that error correction is not only possible but *necessary.* It is a *major* factor in genetics, not a dispensable one. This opinion is corroborated by the fact that, as will be reviewed in Sec. 3.2, very fundamental properties of evolution and of the living world can be derived from the mere hypothesis that the genome includes an error correction system with performance close to the information-theoretic limit, i.e., the channel capacity.

---

[2]Based on the duplication, in complementary form, of the sequence of nucleotides in the double-helix structure and the assumption that damages on one string can be corrected in terms of the other one.

Not only errors resulting from substitution of a wrong nucleic base to another one have to be considered, but possibly those due to erasures, deletions and insertions. We shall nevertheless limit ourselves to the errors due to substitutions because this case has been extensively studied by engineers, although the deletions and insertions are at least equally important.

It would be naïve to expect that the hypothesized natural error-correction means closely resemble those the engineers design. This paper is intended to outline what such natural error-correcting means may look like. A key concept will be that of *soft code*, which weakens but extends the engineering concept of code, and we will moreover try to outline the concept of *nested* soft codes. It will become clear that, in search for genomic error correction means, looking for soft codes is interesting in that any constraint that affects the sequence of nucleic bases in DNA (either mechanical, geometrical, chemical, physiological, ...) can be thought of as contributing somehow to the genomic message regeneration. Another interesting point will be that such codes are met also in linguistics, although to the best of our knowledge the potential error correcting capabilities of languages has not been scientifically studied. That natural languages have such capabilities is nevertheless an obvious lesson of daily experience. Some kind of language is needed for communicating hereditary information, which as a soft code implies error-correction capabilities.

3.2. Consequences of the Hypothesized Existence of Genomic Error Correction. We briefly review consequences of the hypothesized existence of genomic error-correcting means, which were already stated in [**4, 5**] and [**6**]. These consequences are in agreement with biological facts, or suggest answers to still controversial questions.

1 - Existence of discrete species. According to our viewpoint, it is a direct consequence of the distance structure of an error-correcting code. The existence of discrete species is generally considered as a fact, although precisely defining the concept of species is difficult and still controversial.

1' - Taxonomy is possible. It is a consequence of the auxiliary hypothesis that the genome error-correcting means consist of nested codes. This is generally considered as a fact, or at least as an essential working hypothesis in biology.

2 - Evolution proceeds by jumps (is 'saltationist'). This is a still controversial issue. According to our viewpoint, it is again a direct consequence of the distance structure of an error-correcting code. It implies that natural selection does not act on close variants of existing beings, but on mutants with a genome at a distance from the original one equal at least to the minimum distance of the code, which depends itself on the code level in the assumed system of nested codes. It results in a non-Darwinian mechanism for the origin of species, reminiscent of the 'hopeful monster' hypothesized by Goldschmidt.

3 - There exists a trend of evolution towards complexity. If understood as implying that species having a larger genome than the previously existing ones appeared in many instances during the process of evolution, it may be considered as an experimental fact, although a larger genome does not imply an increase in complexity but only makes it possible (see Sec. 5.5). It can be interpreted as a consequence of the hypothesis that error-correcting means exist in the genome. Indeed, a longer genome is an evolutive burden as regards the speed of replication but is advantageous as enabling a more efficient error correction, according to the

channel coding theorem of information theory, so its net effect may be to increase the genome *permanency* (as defined in [**5**]) and therefore to provide an evolutive benefit.

4. Soft Codes: Definition and Properties

4.1. Soft Codes vs Conventional Codes. Let us first consider a linear binary block code $\mathcal{C}(n,k)$ of length n and dimension k as a typical example of a conventional error-correcting code. It has two possible equivalent definitions:

i) as a subset of the set of vectors $\mathbb{F}_2^n$ over the binary field $\mathbb{F}_2$ such that any codeword $c \in \mathcal{C}(n,k)$ belongs to a list of 2^k words, $k < n$, which can be obtained by giving the information vector $\underline{u} \in \mathbb{F}_2^k$ all possible values and computing $\underline{c}$ according to

$$\underline{c} = \underline{u}\mathrm{G}, \tag{1}$$

where G, an $n \times k$ binary matrix, is the generator matrix of the code. Vectors $\underline{u}$ and $\underline{c}$ are represented as row matrices. Any binary vector $\underline{v} \in \mathbb{F}_2^n$ thus belongs or not to $\mathcal{C}$.

ii) as a subset of $\mathbb{F}_2^n$ such that any binary vector $\underline{c} \in \mathbb{F}_2^n$ belongs to $\mathcal{C}(n,k)$ if and only if it obeys the check equation

$$\underline{c}\mathrm{H}^{\mathrm{t}} = \underline{0}, \tag{2}$$

where H, an $n \times (n-k)$ binary matrix, is the parity-check matrix of the code. Superscript t denotes matrix transposition and $\underline{0}$ is an $(n-k)$ row matrix all the entries of which are 0. Given a binary vector $\underline{v} \in \mathbb{F}_2^n$, it belongs or not to $\mathcal{C}$ depending on $\underline{v}\mathrm{H}^{\mathrm{t}}$ being zero or nonzero: a codeword $\underline{c} \in \mathcal{C}(n,k)$ is thus characterized by the fact it obeys the constraint expressed by (2).

Then, the matrix equality (1) describes the encoding process, while (2) is useful for detecting errors, which is often the first step of an error-correction process. The two matrices G and H are closely related to each other since, when G is put in the systematic form

$$\mathrm{G} = [\mathrm{I}_k |\ \mathrm{P}]\,,$$

H reads

$$\mathrm{H} = \left[\mathrm{P}^{\mathrm{t}} \middle|\ \mathrm{I}_{n-k}\right]$$

where I_k denotes the unity matrix of order k and P is some $(n-k) \times k$ matrix. This close relationship makes definitions i) and ii) of $\mathcal{C}$ not so different.

If one wants to extend the concept of error-correcting code, however, definition ii) is most convenient since other constraints than those expressed by deterministic mathematical equalities can be used. For instance, probabilistic constraints can be contemplated, as well as constraints expressed by incompatibilities or forbidding rules. Such extensions of error-correcting codes will be referred to as 'soft codes'.

Of course, the dichotomic property that any binary vector $\underline{v} \in \mathbb{F}_2^n$ belongs or not to $\mathcal{C}$ is lost if $\mathcal{C}$ is a soft code. One can only assign a probability distribution to any $v \in \mathbb{F}_2^n$ as induced by the constraints which define the soft code. The concept of 'information message' vanishes (hence the encoding operation becomes meaningless[3]) and there is no longer a simple encoding rule like (1). As compared

[3]That purposeful encoding is not needed answers some criticisms against the use of Shannon's paradigm made in [**9**] so as to model the process of synthesis of a protein in terms of the DNA message borne by a gene.

with an ordinary error-correcting code, the usual parameters like the dimension k, the distribution of distances and the minimum distance are no longer defined or become random variables. The function of decoding can no longer be thought of as intended to recover an information message and we shall instead define as more appropriate the function of 'regeneration', to be introduced later. Before we deal with the function of regeneration, let us illustrate the concept of soft code by a few examples.

4.2. Some Examples. We shall only consider two examples which are mainly intended to show some connection between the concept of soft code and the conventional one.

Our first example is the set of words of an error-correcting code seen through a noisy channel. As a very simple error-correcting code, let us consider the (6,3) binary systematic linear code (it is the (7,4) Hamming code shortened so as to become 'threshold decodable') having as generator matrix

$$\mathrm{G} = \begin{bmatrix} 1 & 0 & 0 & 1 & 0 & 1 \\ 0 & 1 & 0 & 1 & 1 & 0 \\ 0 & 0 & 1 & 0 & 1 & 1 \end{bmatrix}, \tag{3}$$

and thus as parity-check matrix

$$\mathrm{H} = \begin{bmatrix} 1 & 1 & 0 & 1 & 0 & 0 \\ 0 & 1 & 1 & 0 & 1 & 0 \\ 1 & 0 & 1 & 0 & 0 & 1 \end{bmatrix}. \tag{4}$$

Assume that this code is seen through a noisy channel, say a binary symmetric channel with error probability $p < 1/2$. Let $e_1, \ldots, e_6$ denote the binary errors which affect the code symbols $c_1, \ldots, c_6$. We may think of the set of words $\{c'_1 = c_1 \oplus e_1, \ldots, c'_6 = c_6 \oplus e_6\}$ as a soft code which, instead of the deterministic parity-check equations that the codewords of $\mathcal{C}$ verify, namely

$$\left.\begin{array}{rcl} c_1 \oplus c_2 \oplus c_4 & = & 0, \\ c_2 \oplus c_3 \oplus c_5 & = & 0, \\ c_1 \oplus c_3 \oplus c_6 & = & 0, \end{array}\right\} \tag{5}$$

can be characterized by the probabilistic constraint

$$\Pr(h_1 = 0, h_2 = 0, h_3 = 0) = q, \tag{6}$$

where

$$\begin{array}{rcl} h_1 & \triangleq & c'_1 \oplus c'_2 \oplus c'_4, \\ h_2 & \triangleq & c'_2 \oplus c'_3 \oplus c'_5, \\ h_3 & \triangleq & c'_1 \oplus c'_3 \oplus c'_6, \end{array}$$

and where $q = (1-p)^2(1-4p+6p^2)$ has been calculated in terms of the channel error probability p using the trellis associated with code $\mathcal{C}$. Note that we must consider the joint probability since the parity checks h_1, h_2 and h_3 are not independent, as having symbols in common.

As another example linking soft and conventional codes, we shall consider soft output decoding of, say, a binary code of length n. Soft output decoding means that the decoding role has been extended to reassess the probability of all the codewords [**18**]. In this case, the result of decoding is (ideally) the list of all codewords, each affected with its reassessed probability. This may be thought of as a soft code where the probability of an n-tuple is 0 if this n-tuple is not a codeword, but is nonzero for each codeword and specific to it and a function of the received codeword.

4.3. Decoding and Regeneration.

4.3.1. *A Convenient Formalism.* We now look at the problems of decoding. We shall restrict ourselves in the following to the binary alphabet, which will enable us to use the simple formalism which associates with any binary random variable b its *algebraic value*, i.e. the real number a defined as:

$$a \triangleq \ln \frac{\Pr(b=0)}{\Pr(b=1)}. \tag{7}$$

When the probabilities in (7) are conditional probabilities, for instance when b is the output of a noisy channel, a is itself a random variable. According to (7) its mean is

$$\mathrm{E}[\mathrm{sign}(a)] = \mathrm{E}[(-1)^b] = 1 - 2\Pr(b=1) = t(a),$$

where:

$$\mathrm{t}(\cdot) \triangleq \tanh(\cdot/2) = \frac{\exp(\cdot)-1}{\exp(\cdot)+1}. \tag{8}$$

The algebraic value a of a random binary variable b is a real number. Its sign represents the most probable decision $\hat{b}$ according to

$$\mathrm{sign}(a) = (-1)^{\hat{b}}$$

and its magnitude measures the reliability of this decision, since

$$|a| = \ln \frac{b=\hat{b}}{b \neq \hat{b}}.$$

If the probabilities in (7) are just those of a channel output, the algebraic value a is referred to as an *a priori* algebraic value. If these probabilities are computed in terms of *a priori* algebraic values so as to take account of the constraints of a code, the resulting algebraic value is referred to as an *a posteriori* algebraic value and denoted by a capital letter (at variance with the usual notation where capital letters denote random variables and lower case ones realizations; here, both a and A are random variables, but the former is a channel output while the latter is that of a decoder). Computing an *a posteriori* algebraic value is referred to as a *soft decision.* Keeping only its sign is referred to as a *hard decision.* The soft decision thus involves, besides a mere binary decision, an assessment of its reliability which is lost in a hard decision.

Extension of this formalism to larger-size alphabets endowed with the finite field structure is rather straightforward and has been used for decoding nonbinary linear codes [**19, 20**], but will not be dealt with here.

4.3.2. *The Case of Mere Repetition.* The usefulness of this formalism is clear if we consider the simple case of a mere n-fold *repetition.* Let us consider an equiprobable binary symbol u which is repeated, for instance, $n = 3$ times. A codeword (c_1, c_2, c_3) thus obeys the coding constraint $c_1 = c_2 = c_3 = u$. If c_1, c_2 and c_3 are transmitted using independent binary symmetric channels[4] having p_i

[4]Or when c_1, c_2 and c_3 are successive outputs of a memoryless channel the individual reliabilities of which are separately measured.

($0 < p_i \le 1/2,\ i \in \{1, 2, 3\}$) as error probabilities, then the optimum decision rule consists of computing:

$$A = \sum_{i=1}^{n} a_i = a_1 + a_2 + a_3, \tag{9}$$

where $a_i = (-1)^u \ln \frac{1-p_i}{p_i}$ is the *a priori* algebraic value associated with the i-th channel output. Then the quantity A computed by (9) is the *a posteriori* algebraic value of the optimum (maximum likelihood) binary decision U on u so we have:

$$A = (-1)^U \ln \frac{1-P}{P}, \tag{10}$$

where P is the probability that this decision is wrong [**21, 19**]. The quantities a_1, a_2 and a_3 are available as the outputs of ideal(matched filter) binary demodulators. The decoder which implements (9) is of the soft-input soft-output (SISO) type i.e., its inputs as well as its output are real numbers which represent both a binary decision (borne by the sign) and the estimate of its reliability (the magnitude).

4.3.3. *Threshold Decodable Code.* This decision rule can be extended to more complicated cases, for instance, the still very simple (6,3) code considered above. We can solve the parity-check relations (5) in terms of c_1, which results in $c_1 = c_2 \oplus c_4$ and $c_1 = c_3 \oplus c_6$. This means that $c_2 \oplus c_4$ and $c_3 \oplus c_6$ repeat c_1 so it is possible to apply the above decision rules to the 3 received *replicas* of c_1: c'_1, $c'_2 \oplus c'_4$ and $c'_3 \oplus c'_6$, where the prime denotes the received symbols. The situation is not very different from the three-fold repetition of a single bit considered above, except that the code rate is now 1/2 instead of 1/3. We shall refer to the first replica as the 'trivial' one (it is the symbol to be decoded itself) and the other two as 'compound replicas', made of a combination of other symbols.

The 'soft decision' rule consists of applying (9) to the corresponding *a priori* algebraic values, namely a_1 which is associated with c_1, and the *a priori* algebraic values associated with the sums modulo 2 $c'_2 \oplus c'_4$ and $c'_3 \oplus c'_6$. Let a_2, a_4, a_3 and a_6 denote the *a priori* algebraic values of c'_2, c'_4, c'_3 and c'_6, respectively. One easily shows that the algebraic value a associated with the sum modulo 2 of two received binary symbols of algebraic values a_i and a_j is such that

$$t(a) = t(a_i)t(a_j) \tag{11}$$

where $t(a)$ has been defined in (8). Then (11) results in

$$a = \ln \frac{1 + t(a_i)t(a_j)}{1 - t(a_i)t(a_j)} = \ln \frac{\exp(a_i + a_j) + 1}{\exp(a_i) + \exp(a_j)}. \tag{12}$$

Using this expression enables writing the *a posteriori* algebraic value A_1 associated with c_1 in terms of *a priori* algebraic values as

$$A_1 = a_1 + \ln \frac{1 + t(a_2)t(a_4)}{1 - t(a_2)t(a_4)} + \ln \frac{1 + t(a_3)t(a_6)}{1 - t(a_3)t(a_6)}, \tag{13}$$

where A_1 is the *a posteriori* algebraic value associated with c_1. Similar expressions for decoding c_2 and c_3 are easily derived.

This case is especially simple since the compound replicas of the information bits have no symbol in common. It is the soft-input soft-output version of Massey's threshold decoding [**22**].

4.3.4. *General Case.* For an arbitrary (n, k) conventional code $\mathcal{C}$, we may define the *a posteriori* algebraic value of the i-th binary symbol as the ratio of the probability that it belongs to the set of words of the code $\mathcal{C}$ having 0 as i-th symbol, to be denoted $\mathcal{C}_{i0}$, to that of belonging to $\mathcal{C}_{i1}$, the set of words of the code $\mathcal{C}$ having 1 as i-th symbol. Writing it in terms of the *a priori* algebraic values results in

$$\begin{aligned} A_i &= \ln \frac{\sum_{\underline{c}\in\mathcal{C}_{i0}} \exp(-\sum_j c_j a_j)}{\sum_{\underline{c}'\in\mathcal{C}_{i1}} \exp(-\sum_j c'_j a_j)}, \\ &= a_i + F_i(a_1,\, a_2,\, \ldots,\, a_n). \end{aligned} \tag{14}$$

$F_i(\cdot,\ \cdots,\ \cdot)$ does not depend on a_i and is complicated except for particular cases like (13); it expresses the *a posteriori* algebraic value of the replica of the i-th symbol which combines all the other symbols according to the code constraints. It thus represents the 'extrinsic information' in the vocabulary of turbo-codes [**23**]. Decoding algorithms which use a trellis to represent the code constraints may be thought of as means to compute this function [**24, 21, 25, 26**]. Notice that the *a posteriori* algebraic values involved in the decision rule (14) are those of the n encoded symbols, not only of the information symbols if the code is systematic, so this decision rule remains valid even if information symbols are no longer well defined, which is the case for soft codes, provided it is properly extended.

The decoding rule (14) deals separately with each symbol, and it turns out that the word consisting of the hard decisions on each *a posteriori* algebraic value is not necessarily a codeword. This decoding rule can be simplified by only keeping in the numerator and denominator of the fraction in (14) the largest of the exponential terms which results in

$$\begin{aligned} A'_i &= \min_{\underline{c}'\in\mathcal{C}_{i1}} (\sum_j c'_j a_j) - \min_{\underline{c}\in\mathcal{C}_{i0}} (\sum_j c_j a_j), \\ &= a_i + F'_i(a_1,\, a_2,\, \ldots,\, a_n) \end{aligned} \tag{15}$$

where $F'_i(a_1,\, a_2,\, \ldots,\, a_n)$ does not depend on a_i and, for a linear code, is a sum of *a priori* algebraic values. This highly simplified rule provides only an approximate *a posteriori* algebraic value of each symbol, but it turns out that taking hard decisions on each of the approximate *a posteriori* algebraic values A'_i in (15) results in the optimally decoded word [**21, 19**].

Let us now look at the case of a soft code. We may in principle extend the decoding rule (14) to a soft code characterized by the set of constraints K as

$$A_i = \ln \frac{\sum_{\underline{c}\in\mathcal{F}_2^n} \Pr(c_i = 0|\underline{c}, K)}{\sum_{\underline{c}\in\mathcal{F}_2^n} \Pr(c_i = 1|\underline{c}, K)}.$$

Let us redefine $\mathcal{C}_{i0}$ and $\mathcal{C}_{i1}$ as $\mathcal{C}_{i0} \triangleq \{\underline{c} \in \mathbb{F}_2^n | c_i = 0\}$ and $\mathcal{C}_{i1} \triangleq \{\underline{c} \in \mathbb{F}_2^n | c_i = 1\}$. Using Bayes rule and the algebraic value formalism then results in

$$\begin{aligned} A_i &= \ln \frac{\sum_{\underline{c}\in\mathcal{C}_{i0}} \Pr(\underline{c}|K)\Pr(c_i = 0)}{\sum_{\underline{c}'\in\mathcal{C}_{i1}} \Pr(\underline{c}'|K)\Pr(c'_i = 1)}, \\ &= a_i + F_i^K(a_1,\, a_2,\, \ldots,\, a_n) \end{aligned} \tag{16}$$

where, similarly to (14), $F_i^K(\cdots)$ does not depend on a_i and expresses the extrinsic information about the i-th symbol. Again, this function is in general very complicated but can be widely simplified by keeping only the largest of the terms in the numerator and denominator of the fraction in (16).

4.3.5. *The Regeneration Function.* We already noticed that decision rules (14), (15) and (16) can be used to reassess the probabilities of all the symbols of the word, not only the information symbols of a systematic code. They may thus be interpreted as performing *regeneration* rather than decoding. In the case of a soft code, this concept should be substituted for that of decoding since the notion of information symbols vanishes. However, this function is not specific to soft codes.

Let us assume that we have to communicate some redundantly encoded message through the successive use of two channels, as depicted in Fig. 1. At the output of the first channel, we may use a decoder so as to restore the information message, and if the encoding-decoding system is properly designed it will incur an arbitrarily small error probability. The decoder output, i.e., the restored information message, must then be encoded again before its transmission over the second channel. The combined operation of encoding and decoding may be thought of as a single regeneration operation, which succeeds with large probability in restoring the initial encoded sequence by means of exploiting the coding constraints. Although the operation of encoding loses almost any significance for soft codes, restoration of the transmitted sequence thanks to the coding constraints remains possible in a probabilistic sense, so the regeneration of the input sequence remains meaningful although decoding in its usual acceptation does not. The use of several successive channels typically depicts the successive genome replications, so regeneration is fully relevant to this case.

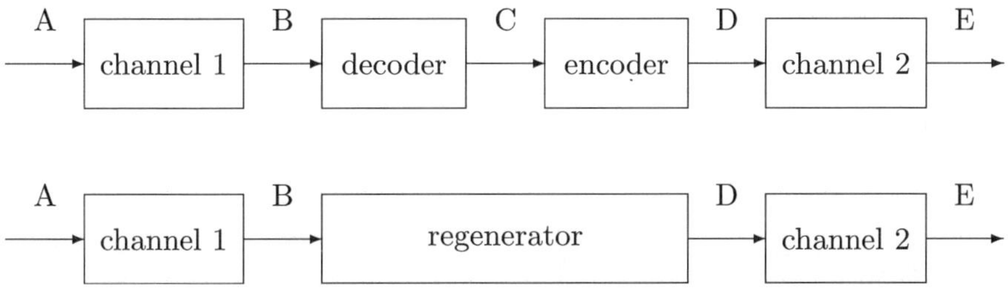

FIGURE 1. The regeneration function. Channels 1 and 2 have to be used successively. The upper picture is relevant to a conventional error-correcting code. The sequences found at the points designated by letters are: in A, an encoded sequence; in B and E, received sequences; in C, an information message; and in D, the sequence which results from the encoding of the decoded information message, hence restoring the initial sequence if no decoding error occurs. In the lower picture, the decoder and encoder have been merged into a single entity labeled 'regenerator'. The information message no longer appears in this scheme so it is valid for soft codes, too.

Moreover, we may think of decoding a conventional error-correcting code as a two-step process. Consider the space of all n-tuples endowed with the Hamming metric. For long enough words, the point which represents the received word is close to the surface of the sphere centered on the transmitted word and having as radius the expected number of errors as a mere consequence of the law of large numbers. Maximum likelihood decoding consists first of determining the point which represents the closest codeword to the point representing the received word, and then to output the information message which labels this point. The first step may be interpreted as regenerating the original codeword, and the second one is almost trivial due to the one-to-one correspondence between codewords and information messages.

Decoding error-correcting codes is based on the assumption that the constraints obeyed are known with certainty, while the received word not only can differ from the transmitted one due to the channel operation, but actually differs from it with high probability in conditions which make the encoding-decoding process efficient. The decoding process thus looks for a word which obeys the constraints, and the received word just *approximately* indicates where to look for. Thus, faithful reconstruction of the transmitted word is achieved through unconditionally relying on the constraints, the received word giving only an indication of proximity. The same can be done in the case of soft codes, except that now the constraints are no longer necessarily deterministic. (Exactly knowing a probabilistic constraint implies no contradiction.)

In the absence of a thorough study of soft codes, we may assume for convenience that, although the main parameters which determine the performance of a conventional code, for instance its distance distribution and especially its minimum distance, become random when transposed to a soft code, the main properties of error-correcting codes are not fundamentally altered so they remain approximately relevant to the biological soft codes. The consequences of using error-correcting means made of soft codes will thus not be significantly different from those of conventional codes, which leaves the conclusions of Sec. 3.2 essentially valid. Besides a convenient assumption, it may be fairly close to reality if both the code lengths considered are large and the soft code is specified by many independent constraints, as a consequence of the law of large numbers.

4.4. Nested Soft Codes. Nested codes can be more easily described in the case of conventional binary systematic codes. We assume that a first information message I_0 of length k_0 is encoded according to a code $\mathcal{C}(n_0, k_0)$. Then, a second message I_1 of length k_1 is appended to the codeword which resulted from the first encoding, and it is encoded again by a code $\mathcal{C}(n_1, n_0+k_1)$. This process is repeated t times. The last information message I_t is left uncoded. This process is depicted in Fig. 2 using the fortress metaphor where each code is depicted as a wall which encloses its encoded information message, for $t = 3$.

The case of nonsystematic codes is less simple but any linear code can be put in systematic form without loss of generality. Another mean for obtaining nested codes consists of using different alphabets of size increasing in terms of the encoding level. Many variants are possible.

Defining *nested soft codes* is more difficult since then the concept of information message vanishes. We may think of the nested code concept in general terms: the i-th encoding creates dependency between the results of $i-1$ previous encodings, regardless of the codes and the alphabets which are used. Similarly to the case of conventional codes, the alphabet may differ from an encoding to another one.

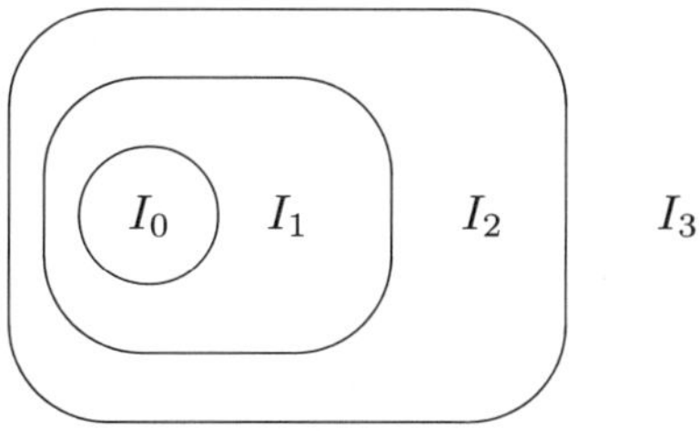

FIGURE 2. The fortress metaphor. A code is represented as a closed wall which protects what is inside it. I_0, I_1, I_2 and I_3 are successive information messages. I_0 is protected by 3 codes, I_1 by 2 codes, I_2 by a single code and I_3 is left uncoded.

5. Looking for Genomic Soft Codes

Thanks to the concept of soft code, any constraint that affects the sequence of nucleic bases in DNA (either mechanical, geometrical, chemical, physiological, ...) can be thought of as contributing somehow to its regeneration. The biological literature is rich in descriptions of such constraints. Each of them implies a peculiar soft code in the assumed nested coding system. We shall review some of such constraints and their hypothesized or experimentally observed consequences as regards regeneration of the DNA message. Prior to doing so, we must look at the problem of identifying the alphabet.

5.1. Identification of the Alphabet. In engineering problems, the alphabet is almost always unambiguously defined, being given as a parameter. This is not the case for the hypothesized error-correcting codes of DNA where the alphabets themselves have to be determined. We put here 'alphabets' to the plural since we consider nested soft codes, and we already noticed that the successive encodings involved can use different alphabets.

An apparently obvious choice is that of the quaternary alphabet {A, T, G, C}, but it should be endowed with some mathematical structure. This approach was used by Liebovitch et al. [**12**], who assumed that this structure was $\mathbb{Z}/4\mathbb{Z}$, the ring of integers modulo 4. This choice is arbitrary and the negative result of [**12**] just means that no error-correcting code using this alphabet was found. A proper linear code would have been searched for if the Galois field $\mathbb{F}_4$, defined as an extension of the binary field based on the primitive polynomial $1 + x$, were used instead.

It is not sure that such an approach is good, even if $\mathbb{F}_4$ is used rather than $\mathbb{Z}/4\mathbb{Z}$. The connection which the concept of soft code establishes between the physical and chemical constraints and the error-correcting properties suggests to look at alphabets having a physico-chemical significance. In this respect, it is much more relevant to consider that any quaternary symbol in DNA simultaneous belongs to two binary alphabets. First, the alphabet {R,Y} where the symbols are the chemical structure of the corresponding nucleic base, namely purine (2-cycle molecule, A or G), denoted R, or pyrimidine (single-cycle molecule, T and C), denoted Y. Second, the alphabet {2H,3H} where 2H represents the couple of complementary nucleotides A–T which are tied together by two hydrogen bonds (H-bonds), and 3H the other couple, namely G–C, where the nucleotides are tied together by three H-bonds. The alphabet {R,Y} corresponds to nucleic bases of different physical size, while the second one, {2H,3H}, indicates how strongly a nucleic base is tied with the complementary one. Then, Forsdyke interpreted a sequence of quaternary symbols as simultaneously bearing two independent binary codes, one over the alphabet {R,Y} and the other one over {2H,3H} [**27**]. According to the 'second Chargaff parity rule', the first code is balanced, i.e., the two symbols R and Y have the same frequency, like almost all codes designed by human engineers. On the contrary, the code over the alphabet {2H,3H} is not balanced since the frequency of its symbols varies from a species to another one and, for long and inhomogeneous genomes like the human one, from a region to another one inside the genome. It could be interpreted as a kind of 'density modulation' which maybe is read at several scales. The different number of hydrogen bonds of the two symbols implies that this density modulation results in a variation of the bonding energy between the two DNA strands.

Other constraints are naturally expressed in terms of other alphabets. For instance, constraints induced on DNA by the structural properties of the proteins for which it 'codes' are likely to involve triplets of nucleic bases, i.e., the codons of the genetic 'code'. Genes themselves can even be considered as the symbols of an alphabet [**28, 29**]. The successive use of alphabets of different size is a mean of implementing nested codes, as mentioned in Sec. 4.4.

Closely related to the alphabet identification is the problem of source coding, or compression, of a DNA sequence. The attempts to apply standard source coding algorithms to DNA sequences have been yet quite unsuccessful [**29**], maybe because they can only deal with short-term dependence. A full understanding of the hypothesized nested codes system would be necessary for performing efficient source coding of DNA sequences, then consisting of 'undoing' the channel-coding process. Such source coding is thus likely to imply several levels and alphabets. Could a source coding system perform efficiently on a DNA sequence, then it would be possible to restore the concept of an information message associated with it.

5.2. Constraints from the Spatial Structure of DNA. The alphabet which is relevant here is more likely to be {R,Y} as introduced in the previous section, but the alphabet {2H,3H} may also be relevant since the ease of separating the two DNA strands is an important factor during the replication process.

Among the constraints which affect the message borne by a DNA molecule, we may first think of mechanical and chemical constraints due to the spatial structure of the DNA molecule, its bonding with proteins like histones and especially its packing in nucleosomes and higher-order structures (when such structures exist, i.e., in eukaryotes).

The experimental analysis of DNA sequences has shown they exhibit long-range dependence. First of all, their power spectral density has been found to behave as $1/f^{\beta}$, asymptotically for small f, where f denotes the frequency and β is a constant which depends on the species: roughly speaking, β is the smaller, the higher the species is in the scale of evolution; it is very close to 1 for bacteria and significantly less for animals and plants [**31**].

Another study of DNA sequences first restricted the quaternary alphabet of nucleic bases {A, T, G, C} to the binary one {R,Y} by retaining only their chemical structure, purine or pyrimidine. An appropriate wavelet transform was used to cancel the trend and its first derivative. Then the autocorrelation function of the binary string thus obtained has been shown to decrease according to a power law [**32**]. This implies long-range dependence at variance with, e.g., Markovian processes which exhibit an exponential decrease. Moreover, in eukaryotic DNA the long-range dependence thus demonstrated has been related to structural constraints [**32**]: the double-strand DNA is actually wrapped around histone molecules acting as a spool (making up together a 'nucleosome'), which implies bending constraints along the two turns (more precisely, the 165 base-pair-long) DNA sequence in each nucleosome.

The $1/f^{\beta}$ behavior of the spectrum and the long-range dependence of the DNA sequence restricted to the purine/pyrimidine alphabet are of course compatible with each other. Moreover, they both denote (at least if further conditions are fulfilled) the existence of a fractal structure, meaning that the DNA sequence is in some sense self-similar. In other words, a basic motif is more or less faithfully repeated at any observation scale. We may therefore think of the message borne by the DNA strand as resulting from 'multiple unfaithful repetition' which could in principle enable the use for decoding of many low-reliability replicas of the basic motif symbols, hence to reliable decisions on these symbols based on many unreliable replicas. This implies a very large redundancy, indeed an obvious property of the DNA message. The existence of such a decoding process, possibly approximated by majority voting, is as yet a conjecture. It remains to determine if, and how, nature implements a decoding process based on long range dependence at some stage of the DNA replication process [**30**].

One may wonder why the regeneration process does not turn this unfaithful repetition into a faithful one by correcting the 'wrong' symbols. We may explain why it is not so by assuming that other soft codes also exist with independent constraints. Then, an actual symbol of the DNA message results from a compromise between the constraints of the several soft codes in which it is involved.

5.3. Constraints Induced on DNA Inside the Genes by the Structure of Proteins. Physiologically active proteins do not reduce to the polypeptidic chain that the sequence of codons of a gene specifies. They are made of a number of 3-dimensional substructures (α helices, β sheets, which are themselves included into higher order structures named 'domains') which impose strong constraints on proteins. Moreover, proteins owe their functional properties to their folding according to a unique pattern, which implies many chemical bonds between amino-acids which are separated along the polypeptidic chain but close together in the 3-dimensional space when the protein is properly folded. For instance, many proteins having enzymatic function fold into a globular shape. Despite their weakening through the inverse genetic 'code', i.e., the one-to-many correspondence between the amino-acids and the codons (triples of nucleic bases), the constraints of steric and chemical character obeyed by proteins induce constraints on the corresponding DNA. Due to the central role of genes in directing the synthesis of proteins, these constraints must be present in the genome of any living being, whether it is a prokaryote or a eukaryote.

5.4. Is a Gene Involving Exons and Introns a Kind of Systematic Codeword? The interesting idea that introns are made of check symbols associated with the message borne by the exons was formulated by Forsdyke in 1981 [**11**]. The literature generally states that introns are more variable than exons. A counter-example was however provided in 1995 by Forsdyke, who experimentally found that the exons are more variable than introns in genes which 'code' for snake venoms [**33**].

It turns out that both the generally observed greater variability of introns and Forsdyke's counter-example can be explained by the assumption that the system of exons and introns actually acts as a systematic error-correcting code where exons constitute the information message (which directs the synthesis of a protein) and introns are made of the associated check symbols. Interpreted as a decoding error, a mutation occurs with large probability in favor of a codeword at a Hamming distance from the original word equal to the minimum distance of the code or slightly larger. If the exons 'code' for a protein of physiological importance, which is by far the most usual case, it may be expected that only mutations with a few errors within the exons, hence having no or little incidence on the protein, will survive natural selection. Few errors being located in the exons, most of them will affect the introns since the total number of errors is at least equal to the minimum distance of the code.

The situation is completely different in the case of genes which 'code' for snake venoms. The typical preys of snakes are rodents. Snakes and rodents are involved in an 'arms race': some rodents incur mutations which provide an immunity to snake venom, the population of rodents with such mutations increases as they escape their main predators, and the snakes are threatened with starvation unless mutations in their own genes make their venom able to kill mutated rodents [**33**]. The genes which 'code' for snake venoms are thus under 'high evolutive pressure': natural selection favors mutated genes producing proteins as different as possible from the original one. In terms of the Hamming distance, much of the difference should thus be located in the exons. The total number of errors in exons and introns being roughly constant for a given code (equal to the minimum distance or slightly larger), introns are much less variable.

5.5. Linguistic Constraints. In the absence of redundancy, the number of different genomes of size 3×10^9 (the approximate length of the human genome) would be $4^{(3\times 10^9)}$, a number which defies imagination. A genome of a few hundred base pairs would be enough to uniquely characterize not only all past and extant species, but all individuals having once belonged or presently belonging to them. Even the shortest genomes are thus highly redundant.

The contrast between the comparative brevity of the message which is needed for unambiguously identifying a biological species and an individual inside it on the one hand, and the length of actual genomes on the other hand, has rather obvious reasons. The genome role is by no means restricted to identify a living being since modern biology interprets it as a *blueprint* for its construction. The genome of any living being actually contains the *recipe* for its development and its maintenance. Besides those parts of the genome which direct the synthesis of proteins, i.e., the genes in a restricted sense, and the associated *regulatory* sequences which switch on or off their expression (i.e., make the gene direct or not the synthesis of the protein it specifies), the genome must somehow *describe* the succession of operations which results in the development and the maintenance of a living thing. This demands some kind of *language*. Biologists do not yet know this language although some of them claim in newspapers that they 'decipher' or 'decrypt' genomes. In a sense, many of them deny its existence when they dub 'junk DNA' every part of the DNA outside the genes and their regulatory sequences: they declare useless what they do not understand. But, on the other hand, they consistently use the metaphor of a written text to explain the role of the genetic message, at least in popular science books like [**34**] and many others. This metaphor is quite convincing, but the consequences it can have on the genome conservation are overlooked: indeed, it turns out that a language involves many morphological and syntactic constraints which may be interpreted as soft codes having error-correcting capabilities. Moreover, the linguistic constraints appear at several different levels, so a written text assumes the structure of 'nested soft codes' which we were led to hypothesize for the genetic message. Of course, it remains to understand how these error-correcting capabilities are exploited. Indeed, recent researches use tools of formal linguistics in order to describe the genomes and proteins [**35, 36**] but ignore the error correction problem. Moreover, the concept of dependence is actually shared by information and coding theory on the one hand, and formal linguistics applied to genomes and proteins on the other hand. As another interesting analogy, natural languages have undergone evolution, and the same kind of methods as used for studying biological evolution have been applied to that of languages.

The connection just outlined between semantics and error-correcting capabilities implies that a longer genome is not only useful to decrease the error probability, but also provides room for 'more semantics' and thus enables specifying more complex beings. An important and useful tenet of information theory is the separation between information and semantics. However, the hypothesized error-correction mechanisms based on linguistic constraints heavily rely on the genome being a blueprint for the construction and maintenance of a living being, so one could consider the error-correction property of the genetic message as, at least partially, a by-product of its semantics. But this is only a facet of the question. One can equally well argue that the error-correction property is the main feature of this message, since without it no transmission of hereditary characters would be possible and life could not have developed. Then, the construction and maintenance of living things would be a mere projection in the physico-chemical world of the abstract properties of the genetic message which enable error correction. This is a hen-and-egg problem, as often met in biology.

5.6. Further Comments on Regeneration and Copying. The genome replication process results in a new genome. As such, it is subjected to all the constraints that a genome should obey. On the other hand, it should replicate the old genome which presumably suffered errors, so these conflicting requirements must be solved in favor of the *constraints*. But we likened the constraints of biological origin with soft codes, so obeying constraints is equivalent to correcting errors. Replacing the word 'genome' by 'codeword' in the above statement just describes the technical function of regeneration, defined above as the first and more important step of any decoding process. We may thus think of the replication process as necessarily performing regeneration by *providing the approximate copy of the old genome which best fits the genomic constraints.*

The assumption that the error-control system in DNA is a by-product of prior biological constraints matches a characteristic of nature's method, namely, the use of some preexisting hardware to perform a function other than the initial one, which can be referred to as tinkering.

6. Conclusion

We think that information theory can answer the question asked in the title of this paper. The concept of soft code may be helpful to understand how the many constraints of biological character which affect the genome also involve error-correcting capabilities. Of course, the precise underlying mechanisms at work remain to be identified. Progresses along this line cannot be expected unless information and coding theorists collaborate not only with biologists and especially with molecular geneticists, but also with chemists and linguists. Clearly, a broad interdisciplinary effort is needed if the ideas outlined above are to be developed.

Erwin Chargaff wrote in 1979 a paper entitled "How genetics got a chemical education" [**37**], where he complained that geneticists were so reluctant to accept the consequences of the discovery that DNA was the actual bearer of genetic information (by Avery et al. [**15**], 35 years earlier) that a more appropriate title of his paper could have been "How genetics refused to get a chemical education". We hope that the title "How genetics got an information-theoretic education", paraphrasing Chargaff, will eventually match reality.

Appendix A. A Short Glossary of Molecular Genetics

The reader should be warned that the content of this glossary is highly simplified and that many statements incur exceptions or other restrictions to their validity. Italic words inside a definition refer to another entry of the glossary.

amino-acids. Any amino-acid is made of a carbon atom (referred to as C_α) to which are attached a hydrogen atom, an amino group (NH_2), a carboxy group (COOH) and a radical named 'side chain' specific to it, which may assume a variety of forms. A *polypeptidic chain* is a unidimensional polymer made of a sequence of amino-acids linked together by 'peptide bonds' formed by eliminating a water molecule OH_2 from the COOH group of an amino-acid and the NH_2 group of another one. Such a polypeptidic chain is thus characterized by the sequence of side chains of its constituent amino-acids. When properly folded, it makes up a *protein.*

Proteins contain only 20 amino-acids which are listed in the following table.

acr.	name	class	#	acr.	name	class	#
Met	methionine	h-phobic	1	Tyr	tyrosine	h-philic	2
Trp	triptophan	h-phobic	1	Ile	isoleucine	h-phobic	3
Asp	aspartic acid	acid	2	Ala	alanine	h-phobic	4
Glu	glutamic acid	acid	2	Gly	glycine	h-phobic	4
Asn	asparagine	h-philic	2	Pro	proline	h-phobic	4
Cys	cysteine	h-phobic	2	Thr	threonine	h-philic	4
Phe	phenylalanine	h-phobic	2	Val	valine	h-phobic	4
Gln	glutamine	h-philic	2	Arg	arginine	base	6
His	histidine	base	2	Leu	leucine	h-phobic	6
Lys	lysine	base	2	Ser	serine	h-philic	6

The first column indicates the 3-letter acronym of the amino-acid, while the fourth column indicates the number of codons which correspond to it according to the *genetic 'code'*. The amino-acids have been put into 4 classes: hydrophobic (abbreviated as h-phobic), hydrophilic (h-philic), acid (bearing a negative electric charge), and base (bearing a positive charge). Their class is indicated in the third column of the table. Except for glycine which has a single hydrogen atom as side chain, they all are chiral molecules (i.e., they can assume two forms which are symmetric with respect to a plane in the three-dimensional space, like an object and its image in a mirror), but only their L-form occurs in proteins. There is no known reason why the amino-acids listed above were 'chosen' rather than others nor why the L-form has been 'preferred'. Cystein, whose side chain is the group SH, can form disulphide bridges with another cystein molecule close to it in the 3-dimensional space due to the protein folding.

chromosomes. See *genome.*

codon. See *genetic code.*

complementary base pairs. See *nucleic base.*

deoxiribonucleic acid (DNA). In its usual double-helix structure, the DNA polymer is made of two strands of a unidimensional polymer where a phosphate group regularly alternates with a sugar molecule, deoxyribose. These strands are referred to as the 'backbones' of DNA and they assume the double-helix pattern. Between the two backbones, *complementary base pairs* A–T and G–C are tied to two sugar molecules of the opposite backbones by covalent bonds. The complementary base pairs have a plane structure depicted in Fig. 4 in *nucleotide.* Their plane is orthogonal to the axis of the double helix. We thus may think of the double-stranded DNA as a twisted ladder, with the backbones as uprights and the complementary base pairs as steps. Its overall width is about 2 nanometers (a nanometer, abbreviated as nm, is 10^{-9} meter), the distance between two base pairs is 0.34 nm and a complete turn of the double helix corresponds to about 10 base pairs.

If the hydrogen bonds which tie together the complementary bases are broken, single stranded DNA results and takes the form of a string of nucleic bases attached to one of the backbones, which represents the genetic message within the quaternary alphabet A, T, G, C.

enzyme. See *protein.*

eukaryotes. As opposed to *prokaryotes*, they are living beings where the *genome* is contained inside a nucleus physically separated by a double-layer lipidic membrane from the remainder of their cell, and having many other distinctive features like the presence of *mitochondria.* They may be unicellular like yeasts or amiboeae, but all multicellular beings like plants and animals are eukaryotes. Moreover, *genes* organized according to the exons-introns model generally belong to eukaryotes, and only a fraction of the whole *genome* is made of genes, i.e., contributes to the synthesis of *proteins.* Again at variance with prokaryotes, the double stranded *DNA* is packed into nucleosomes, which consist of a histone octamer acting as a spool with almost two turns (165-nucleotide long) of double stranded DNA wrapped around it. (Histones are proteins associated with DNA in chromosomes.) Moreover, nucleosomes themselves are packed together in higher order structures generally referred to as 'fibers'. Another distinguishing feature of the eukaryotic cell is the presence of a 'cytoskeleton', i.e., a kind of molecular armature in a state of dynamic instability. The eukaryotic cell is much more complicated that the prokaryotic one and very probably younger by almost 2 billion years.

exons. See *gene.*

gene. Precisely defining a gene is not easy. At the very beginning of genetics, a gene was thought of as an 'atom' of Mendelian heredity but its nature was unknown. Since the discovery that the genetic message is borne by *DNA*, one may say that a gene is a sequence of nucleic bases which is transcribed into messenger *RNA*. Its most important function is the synthesis of a *protein* which results from the further *translation* of the messenger RNA into a sequence of amino-acids which directs the synthesis of a protein, through the *genetic 'code'*. However, some genes only generate specific RNA strands having other functions. In *eukaryotic* cells, the genes often comprise regions which actually direct the synthesis of a protein, named 'exons', which alternate with regions which do not, called 'introns', and are considered by many biologists as useless. When a gene has this structure, the RNA strand which results from the DNA *transcription* is 'spliced', i.e., the regions in it which correspond to the introns are cut out and the remaining RNA pieces are glued together, making up the messenger RNA which actually directs the protein synthesis. Sometimes, different alternative splicings may result in several proteins being synthesized from the same gene.

genetic 'code'. The genetic 'code' is a mapping from the triples of successive *nucleic bases* of messenger *RNA* (referred to as 'codons') into the set of 20 *amino-acids* which are the elementary components of *proteins*, plus the command which stops the protein synthesis. Figure 3 shows this mapping. Since there are $4^3 = 64$ codons for an output alphabet of size 21, an output symbol can be designated by several codons. Indeed, the number of codons which designate an amino-acid can be 1, 2, 3, 4 or 6, depending on this amino-acid. Due to this many-to-one correspondence, changes in the sequence of *nucleic bases* do not necessarily result in a change in the sequence of *amino-acids* of the protein. Since this mapping is definitely not a code in the engineering sense, we used quotes every time we referred to the genetic 'code'. The genetic 'code' is universal as being the same for all living beings (with very few exceptions, the most notable one being slight differences which concern *mitochondria*). It is the standard genetic 'code' which is shown in Fig. 3.

The genetic 'code' shows some regularities but seems to some extent arbitrary. Although it is far from being random, its emergence may have resulted, at least in part, from contingent events. Many authors tried to explain its regularities, often referring to coding theory, e.g., [**7, 10**].

genome. The total *DNA* that a living being possesses in (almost) each of its cells, generally organized in *chromosomes*. The genome is replicated every time the division of a cell occurs. The chromosomes are structures where DNA is packed together with *proteins*, especially histones. *Prokaryotes* generally possess a single circular chromosome, at variance with *eukaryotes* which have several rod-shaped chromosomes which appear as pairs of homologous chromosomes in somatic (non-sex) cells. In eukaryotic cells, the word 'genome' generally refers to the nucleic *DNA*, but the *mitochondria* also possess their own *DNA* which is independently replicated.

introns. See *gene.*

mitochondria. A *eukaryotic* cell possesses a number of organelles named mitochondria which provide it with ATP (adenosine triphosphate) molecules, the energy source of the cells. There are strong reasons why mitochondria are probably

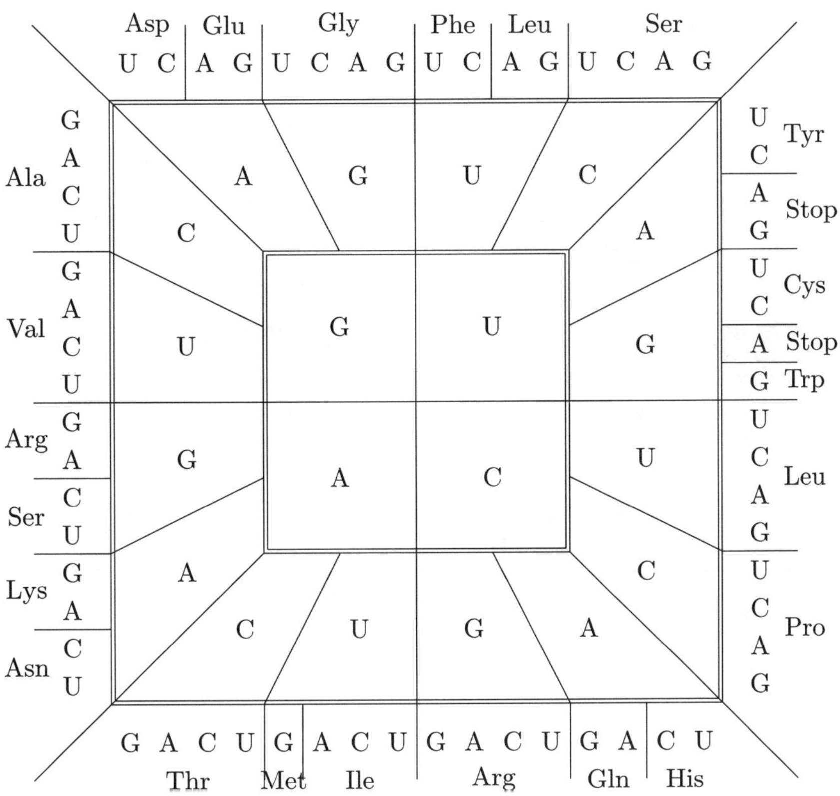

FIGURE 3. The genetic 'code'. This chart indicates how the codons of messenger RNA specify amino-acids or stop the synthesis of a polypeptidic chain. The letters A, C, G, U denote the nucleic bases. Any codon is a 3-nucleic-base word read from center to periphery. The 3-letter acronyms at the periphery indicate the amino-acids which correspond to codons or to the 'stop' command. For instance, UAC 'codes' for the amino-acid tyrosine (Tyr), while UAA stops the process. AUG both starts the synthesis process when it is preceded by a proper control message referred to as 'promoter' and 'codes' for the amino-acid methionine (Met).

former *prokaryotes* which became symbiotic with other cells so as to make up the eukaryotic cell, about 1,500 million years ago. They still have their own genome which is replicated independently of the host cell. They use a version of the genetic 'code' slightly different from the standard one.

nucleotides or **nucleic bases.** The molecular elements which act as information bearing symbols in *DNA* and *RNA*. Three nucleic bases are common to DNA and RNA: adenine, abbreviated as A, guanine (G) and cytosine (C). The fourth nucleic base is thymine (T) in DNA and uracil (U) in RNA. T and U have similar structure (a methyl group CH_3 of T is merely substituted for a hydrogen atom in U). As regards the chemical structure, A and G are purines, i.e., 2-cycle molecules denoted R, while C, T, and U are pyrimidines, single-cycle molecules denoted Y. A purine and a pyrimidine together can constitute a complementary base pair where the two molecules are tied together by two hydrogen bonds for the pairs A–T or A–U, by three hydrogen bonds for the pair G–C. The complementary base pairs A–T and G–C have geometric dimensions and angles of their bonds to the DNA 'backbones' which are close enough to enable their location anywhere in the double helix structure of DNA. Their chemical structure is shown in Fig. 4.

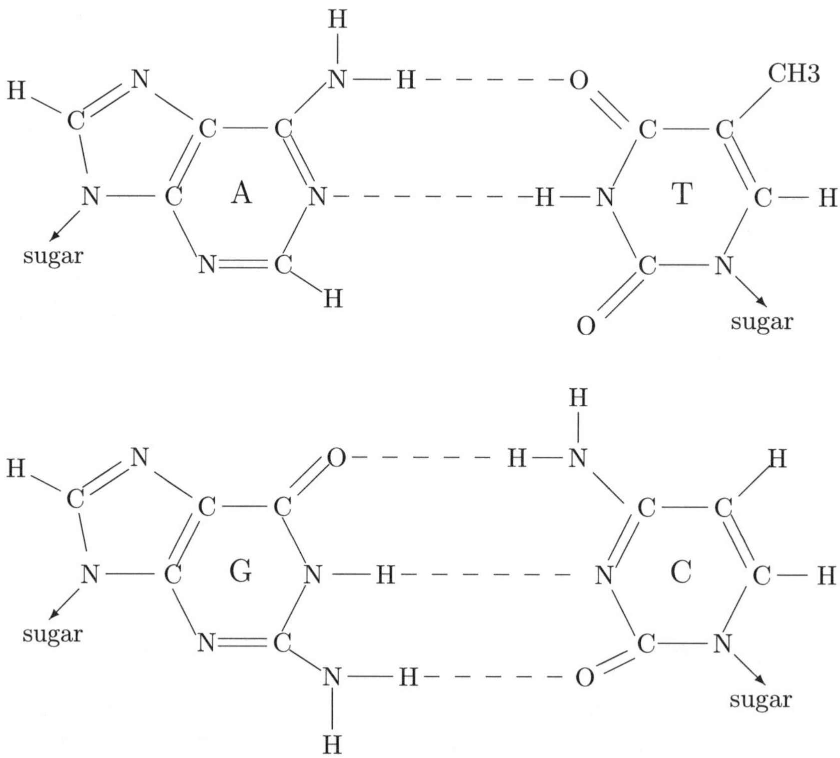

FIGURE 4. Chemical structure of the complementary base pairs A–T(top) and G–C (bottom). The purines (A and G) are at left and the pyrimidines (T and C) at right. In RNA, the uracil molecule (U) replaces thymine (T), which is identical to it except that the methyl group CH_3 at top right is replaced by a hydrogen atom H. Dashed lines represent hydrogen bonds. The mutual distances of the atoms are roughly respected, which shows that the two complementary base pairs have almost equal lengths. Moreover, the angles of the covalent bonds with the sugar molecules of the backbones are also almost the same, so any of these complementary base pairs can occur everywhere in the double-helix structure.

The reason why precisely these molecules are used for bearing information in DNA and RNA is unknown. The words 'nucleic base' or 'nucleotide' may be thought of as misnomers since the DNA of a *prokaryotic* cell is made of nucleotides although it has no nucleus. These words have merely a historical origin since these bases were discovered in a cell nucleus.

nucleosome. See *eukaryotes.*

prokaryotes. Living beings where the *genome* is not physically separated from the remainder of the cell. They all are unicellular beings: bacteria or archaea. Almost the full length of their genome contributes to the synthesis of proteins. They have most often a single circular chromosome. There is evidence that they predated the much more complicated *eukaryotes* by about 2 billion years.

polypeptidic chain. See *amino-acids.*

protein. A protein results from a *polypeptidic chain* by an appropriate folding which gives it a unique three-dimensional shape. A typical protein is made of a few hundreds of *amino-acids.* It combines several substructures like α-helices and β-sheets, which themselves are combined into higher order structures named 'domains'. Disulphur bridges between cystein molecules, as well as the attraction of electric charges borne by polar molecules, help maintaining the protein spatial structure.

Proteins are the most important constituents of the living matter, having both a structural and catalytic role. When they act as catalysts, they are referred to as *enzymes.* Especially, *DNA* replication as well as DNA *transcription* and *translation* are catalyzed by proteins. Therefore, proteins catalyze their own synthesis.

replication (of DNA). Replication of double-stranded DNA first results from separating its two strands, then providing the complementary nucleic bases and a second 'backbone' to each of them so as to eventually get two identical double-stranded DNA polymers. Proof-reading mechanisms ensure the copying fidelity. These highly complex processes are catalyzed by many specific proteins.

Every time a cell divides itself, its genome is replicated so that each of the daughter cells possesses its own copy of the genome. In *eukaryotic* cells, this process takes two forms: 'mitosis' in the case of a somatic cell and 'meiosis' when the cell division results in sex cells. For somatic cells of higher beings like animals and plants with sexual reproduction, which contain pairs of chromosomes of each type, mitosis keeps the number of chromosomes constant in the daughter cells, but this number is halved when meiosis occurs so a sex cell contains a single chromosome of each type.

ribonucleic acid (RNA). The ribonucleic acid is similar to *DNA* except that the sugar molecule of its backbone is ribose instead of deoxiribose, and that the nucleic base uracil (U) replaces thymine (T) (see Fig. 4 in *nucleotides*). Its double-helix structure is less stable than that of DNA so it is most often found in the single-stranded form. RNA assumes many functions: the most important are 'messenger RNA' which copies in complementary form the genetic message borne by a DNA strand (see *transcription*), 'transfer RNA' which associates the proper *amino-acid* with each codon of the messenger RNA in the process of protein synthesis, and 'ribosomic RNA' as part of the ribosome machinery (see *translation*). RNA has moreover some catalytic activity.

ribosome. It is the part of the cell, made of a large complex of *RNA* and *proteins,* which recognizes the transfer RNA associated with a codon and puts the corresponding *amino-acid* at its place in the *polypeptidic chain* during the process of *translation.*

transcription. The process of copying, in complementary form, one of the strands of *DNA* of a *gene* into a messenger *RNA* molecule. In the case of a gene made of exons and introns, the transcription results in a 'pre-messenger' RNA molecule which has to be spliced to result in the proper messenger RNA which is actually used in the *translation* process.

translation. The process of synthesis of a *polypeptidic chain* which, properly folded, becomes a *protein*. The polypeptidic chain derives from the sequence of *nucleic bases* of a messenger RNA according to the *genetic 'code'*. The messenger RNA itself resulted from the *transcription* of the genetic message borne by the DNA of a gene. It involves a transfer RNA associated with each *codon* and the operation of the *ribosome*.

References

[1] M. Mansuripur, "Macro-molecular data storage with petabyte/cm^3 density, highly parallel read/write operations, and genuine 3D storage capability", DIMACS working group on theoretical advances in information recording, Mar. 22–24, 2004.

[2] W. Coene, "Coding and signal processing for two-dimensional optical storage", DIMACS working group on theoretical advances in information recording, Mar. 22–24, 2004.

[3] G. Cherubini, "A nanotechnology-based approach for highly-parallel, ultra-dense data storage", DIMACS working group on theoretical advances in information recording, Mar. 22–24, 2004.

[4] G. Battail, "Does information theory explain biological evolution?," *Europhysics Letters*, vol. 40, no. 3, pp. 343–348, Nov. 1, 1997.

[5] G. Battail, "Is biological evolution relevant to information theory and coding?", *Proc. ISCTA '01*, Ambleside, UK, pp. 343–351, July 2001.

[6] G. Battail, "An engineer's view on genetic information and biological evolution", *Pre-proceedings, 5-th International Workshop on Information Processing in Cells and Tissues*, Lausanne, Switzerland, Sept. 2003, pp. 431–448. *Biosystems*, vol. 76, pp. 279–290, 2004.

[7] G. Cullmann and J.-M. Labouygues, "The logic of the genetic code", 1983, *Biosystems*, vol. 16, pp. 9–29, 1983.

[8] J. Rzeszowska-Wolny, "Is genetic code error-correcting?", *J. Theor. Biol.*, vol. 104, pp. 701–702, 1983.

[9] H. P. Yockey, *Information theory and molecular biology*, Cambridge University Press, 1992.

[10] D.A. Mac Dónaill, "A parity code interpretation of nucleotide alphabet composition", *Chem. Communic.*, vol. 18, pp. 2062–2063, 2002.

[11] D.R. Forsdyke, "Are introns in-series error-detecting sequences?", *J. Theor. Biol.*, vol. 93, pp. 861–866, 1981.

[12] L.S. Liebovitch, Y. Tao, A.T. Todorov, and L. Levine, "Is there an Error Correcting Code in the Base Sequence in DNA?", *Biophysical Journal*, vol. 71, pp. 1539–1544, 1996.

[13] E.E. May, M.A. Vouk, D.L. Bitzer, and D.I. Rosnick, "Coding theory based models for protein translation initiation in prokaryotic organisms", *Pre-proceedings, 5th International Workshop on Information Processing in Cells and Tissues*, Lausanne, Switzerland, Sept. 2003, pp. 371–389. *Biosystems*, vol. 76, pp. 249–260, 2004.

[14] M. Barbieri, *The Organic Codes*, Cambridge University Press, 2003.

[15] O. Avery, M. McCarty, and C. MacLeod, "Studies of the chemical nature of the substance inducing the transformation of pneumococcal types. Induction of transformation by a desoxyribonucleic acid fraction isolated from Pneumococcus Type III", *J. Exp. Med.*, vol. 79, pp. 137–158, 1944.

[16] R.E. Franklin and R.G. Gosling, "Molecular configuration in sodium thymonucleate", *Nature*, vol. 171, no. 4356, pp. 740–741, 25 Apr. 1953. Reprinted in *Nature*, vol. 421, no. 6921, pp. 400–401, Jan. 23, 2003.

[17] J.D. Watson and F.H.C. Crick, "Molecular structure of nucleic acids", *Nature*, vol. 171, no. 4356, Apr. 25, 1953, pp. 737–738. Reprinted in *Nature*, vol. 421, no. 6921, pp. 397–398, Jan. 23, 2003.
[18] G. Battail, "Le décodage pondéré en tant que procédé de réévaluation d'une distribution de probabilité," *Annales Télécommunic.*, vol. 42, no. 9–10, pp. 499–509, Sep.-Oct. 1987.
[19] G. Battail, M. Decouvelaere and P. Godlewski, "Replication decoding", *IEEE Trans. Inf. Th.*, vol. IT-25, no. 3, pp. 332–345, May 1979.
[20] G. Battail, "Décodage pondéré par résolution d'un système d'équations implicites analogiques", *Annales Télécommunic.*, vol. 45, no. 7–8, pp. 393–409, Jul.-Aug. 1990.
[21] G. Battail and M. Decouvelaere, "Décodage par répliques", *Annales Télécommunic.*, vol. 31, no. 11–12, pp. 387-404, Nov.-Dec. 1976.
[22] J.L. Massey, *Threshold decoding*, MIT Press, 1963.
[23] C. Berrou, A. Glavieux and P. Thitimajshima, "Near Shannon limit error-correcting coding and decoding: turbo-codes", *Proc. ICC'93*, Geneva, Switzerland, pp. 1064–1070, May 1993.
[24] L.R. Bahl, J. Cocke, F. Jelinek and J. Raviv, "Optimal decoding of linear codes for minimizing symbol error rate", *IEEE Trans. Inf. Th.*, vol. IT-20, Mar. 1974, pp. 284–287.
[25] G. Battail, "Pondération des symboles décodés par l'algorithme de Viterbi," *Annales Télécommunic.*, vol. 42, no. 1–2, pp. 31–38, Jan.-Feb. 1987.
[26] J. Hagenauer and P. Hoeher, "A Viterbi algorithm with soft-decision outputs and its applications", *Proc. GLOBECOM'89*, Dallas, Texas, pp. 1680–1686, Nov. 1989.
[27] D.R. Forsdyke, http://post.queensu.ca/ forsdyke/
[28] S.A. Kauffman, *The origins of order*, Oxford University Press, 1993.
[29] O. Milenkovic, "The information processing mechanism of DNA and efficient DNA storage", DIMACS working group on theoretical advances in information recording, Mar. 22–24, 2004.
[30] G. Battail, "Replication decoding revisited", *Proc. Information Theory Workshop 2003*, Paris, France, pp. 1–5, Mar.– Apr. 2003.
[31] R.F. Voss, "Evolution of long-range fractal correlation and $1/f$ noise in DNA base sequences", *Phys. Rev. Lett.*, vol. 68, pp. 3805–3808, June 1992.
[32] B. Audit, C. Vaillant, A. Arneodo, Y. d'Aubenton-Carafa, and C. Thermes, "Long-range correlation between DNA bending sites: relation to the structure and dynamics of nucleosomes", *J. Mol. Biol.*, vol. 316, pp. 903–918, 2002.
[33] D.R. Forsdyke, "Conservation of stem-loop potential in introns of snake venom phospholipase A_2 genes. An application of FORS-D analysis", *Mol. Biol. and Evol.*, vol. 12, pp. 1157–1165, 1995.
[34] R. Dawkins, *The Blind Watchmaker*, Longman, 1986.
[35] R.N. Mantegna, S.V. Buldyrev, A.L. Goldberger, S. Havlin, C.-K. Peng, S. Simons, and H.E. Stanley, "Linguistic features of noncoding DNA sequences", *Phys. Rev. Lettr.*, vol. 73, pp. 3169–3172, 1994.
[36] D.B. Searls, "The language of genes", *Nature*, vol. 420, no. 6912, pp. 211–217, Nov. 14, 2002.
[37] E. Chargaff, "How genetics got a chemical education", *Ann. New York Acad. of Sc.*, vol. 325, pp. 345–360, 1979.

E.N.S.T., 75013 Paris, France (retired)
Current address: "La Chanatte", Le Guimand, F-26120 Chabeuil, France
E-mail address: gbattail@club-internet.fr

DIMACS Series in Discrete Mathematics
and Theoretical Computer Science
Volume **73**, 2008

Data Storage and Processing in Cells: An Information Theoretic Approach

Olgica Milenkovic

Abstract. The vast information stored in the genetic code of living organisms, responsible for regulating and dynamically changing the characteristics of cells, is still poorly understood. We describe three mechanisms for storage of genetic information, arising at the level of DNA sequences, RNA and protein two- and tree-dimensional folds, and gene regulatory networks. We propose a novel approach for studying these complex functionalities based on techniques from information and coding theory.

1. Introduction

In the last decades, it became apparent that it is impossible to explain many phenomena in life sciences without combining the attributes of *information* with those of matter and energy [**32**]. The current understanding is that, without information, a living organism cannot perform complex tasks and exhibit sophisticated self-organizing properties.

The quest for finding the source of information responsible for governing the life cycle of living organisms has reached a point where many answers, and many more questions, are at hand. It is known that the source of genetic information is a molecule known as Deoxyribonucleic Acid (DNA). DNA sequences, and some closely related bio-chemical entities, appear in every higher-level life form and are responsible for maintaining and regulating the structural and functional properties of a cell. Nevertheless, many processes of the cell cycle, and their relationship to the genetic DNA code itself are not well understood. Most importantly, the myriad of pathways for converting information in DNA sequences into cell actions and structures are still largely unknown.

We propose to investigate the various means by which information is stored in a cell. To this end, we focus on information stored in sequences, in two-dimensional shapes, and in dynamically changing networks. The information stored in a sequence can be determined by applying appropriate data compression techniques, while the information of a shape can be assessed through the grammatical rules used for generating it. In the latter setting, it is possible to consider shapes as biologically

Key words and phrases. Central Dogma of Genetics, DNA Compression, Information Storage, Coding Theory.

The author was supported in part by NSF Grant CCF-0514921.

©2008 American Mathematical Society

constrained structures described by context-free languages. The most complex form of information storage occurs at the level of gene regulatory networks, responsible for controlling the exchange of genetic information. The analysis of control systems with information processing features is tightly connected to the well-studied process of message passing in communication networks.

The goal of this work is twofold. The first objective is to provide a self-contained review of the most important concepts of molecular biology [**69**]. The second objective is to introduce a set of challenging new problems in information theory and coding that arise in the study of the information content of genetic data.

The paper is organized as follows. Section 2 provides a brief introduction to the Central Dogma of Genetics, and the notion of genetic information. Section 3 contains an overview of the statistical properties of DNA sequences and mutation mechanisms responsible for altering their statistical properties. Section 4 describes state-of-the art compression algorithms for analyzing DNA sequences, and a collection of new approaches for addressing the problem of lossless DNA sequence representation. Section 5 discusses the problem of determining the information content of a shape, through the notion of the derivational entropy of a grammar. Section 6 introduces gene regulatory and Boolean networks, and the concept of attractor entropy. Concluding remarks are given in Section 7.

2. Information Storage in Cells

2.1. An Overview of Basic Cellular Processes. The hereditary information of almost all living organisms is stored in chemical compounds known as DNA molecules. DNA consists of three types of building blocks: phosphate groups (PH_3), five-carbon Deoxyribose sugars, and bases of four different types. Bases are grouped into two structurally similar families: Purines and Pyramidines. The former class contains Adenine (henceforth, **A**) and Guanine (henceforth, **G**), while the latter contains Cytosine (henceforth, **C**) and Thymine (henceforth, **T**). A DNA polymer is a chain of alternating sugar and phosphate molecules, with bases attached to the sugar molecules. A structural unit that consists of one phosphate group and one sugar molecule with its corresponding base is called a *nucleotide*.

The alternating sugar and phosphate groups of DNA form a deterministic structure known as the *sugar-phosphate backbone*. This backbone has an orientation, due to the asymmetry of the sugar molecule. The two terminal ends of the backbone are known as the $3'$ and $5'$ ends, indicating the label of the free carbon atom in the corresponding sugar atom.

The chemical structure of the bases and the sugar-phosphate backbone are shown in Figure 1. Each vertex in the ring of the sugar molecule contains a carbon atom, and the phosphate groups are attached to the carbon atoms labeled by $3'$ and $5'$.

Genetic information is encoded in the sequence of bases of the sugar-phosphate backbone: bases are strung at an approximate distance of 0.35 nm from each other, giving DNA a data density of nearly 9 Mb/inch. Two sugar-phosphate backbones are interleaved in a double-helix formation, stabilized through chemical bonds between DNA bases on opposite strands.

In the double-helix, one strand runs in the $3' \rightarrow 5'$ direction, while the other (complementary) strand has the opposite orientation. With very high probability,

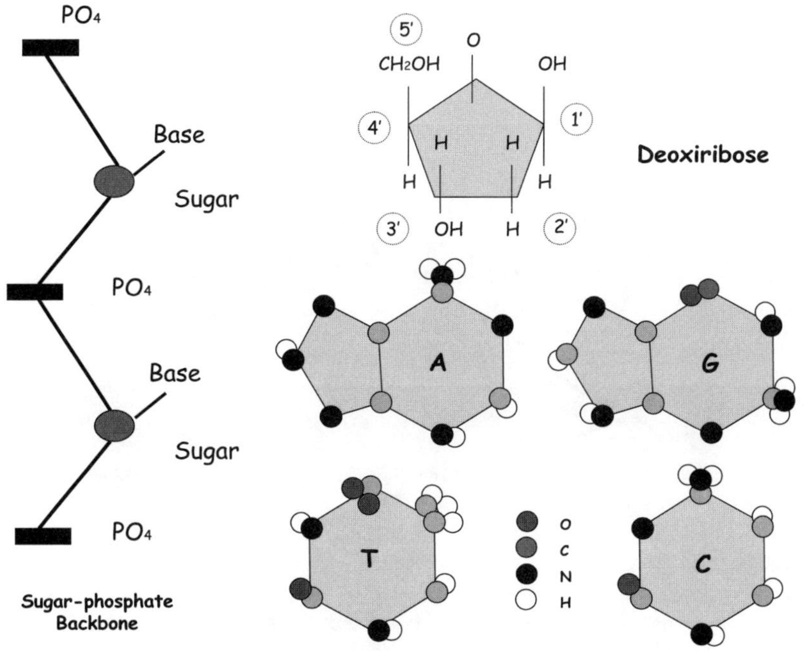

FIGURE 1. Chemical structure of DNA.

a base **A** on one strand shares two hydrogen bonds with a base **T** on the complementary strand, and vice versa. Similar chemical bonds exist between the bases **G** and **C**, in this case established through three hydrogen atoms. These selective pairing properties are known as the Watson-Crick (WC) rules, summarized below.

$$\overline{\mathbf{A}} = \mathbf{T}, \quad \overline{\mathbf{G}} = \mathbf{C}, \quad \overline{\mathbf{C}} = \mathbf{G}, \quad \overline{\mathbf{T}} = \mathbf{A}.$$

The structural stability of the double-helix is a consequence of the stacking effects of long stretches of bases obeying the WC rule. The process of WC bonding between pairs of bases on complementary strands is usually referred to as DNA *hybridization*. A perfectly hybridized double-helix DNA structure is depicted in Figure 2.

The higher levels of organization of the genetic material depend on the cell containing a special organelle known as the cell nucleus. Organisms without a nucleus are called *prokaryotes*, while organisms that contain a nucleus are called *eukaryotes*. In eukaryotes, a double-stranded DNA helix is organized in *chromatin complexes*. A chromatin complex consists of five different proteins, named histones, long DNA chains, and a large collection of diverse proteins. The five types of histones create two structures: one, the histone-octamer, which serves as a bead on which DNA strands are wrapped, and another, which links different beads. The aforementioned concepts are illustrated in Figure 2.

Each histone-octamer coil contains either 146 or 147 base pairs (bps), while the number of bases between two linkers is approximately 50. The histone-octamers, along with the linker histones and inter-histone DNA strands, can be visualized as a beaded necklace. This type of DNA coiling is necessary for storing extremely long DNA chains within a compact cell nucleus.

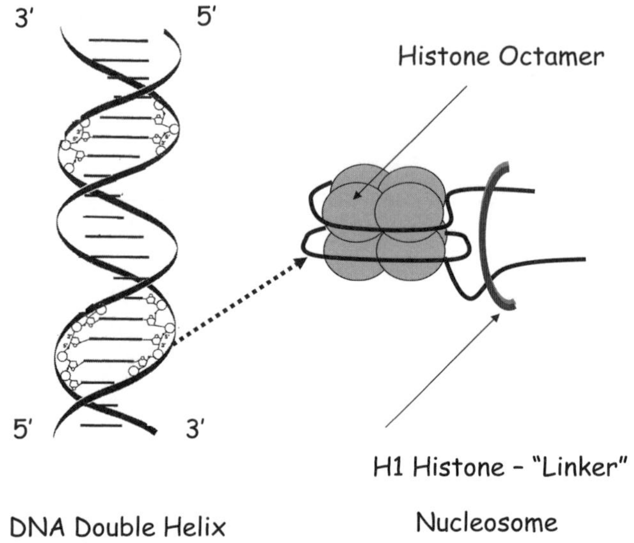

FIGURE 2. The DNA double helix and the nucleosome.

Chromatin has two distinguishable forms, *euchromatin* and *heterochromatin*. Euchromatin is a loosely packed structure, since it contains DNA strands that are frequently used by the cell. Heterochromatin, on the other hand, is a more tightly packed chromatin complex, containing less frequently used DNA strands. During a special stage in the cell cycle (more precisely, during cell division), chromatin forms tightly condensed and characteristically shaped structures known as *chromosomes*. Chromosomes can have a size as large as 20 μm, and are visible under a light microscope. Each chromosome consists of two sister *chromatides*, and very often, both chromosomes and chromatides are referred to as chromosomes. The two chromatides form a pair of *arms*, the short p and long q arms, held together through the *centromere* (see Figure 3). The terminal ends of the arms are known as *telomeres*.

The collection of chromosomes in an organism represents its *karyotype*. The human karyotype comprises twenty-two pairs of autosome chromosomes, and two additional sex chromosomes. In males, the two sex-chromosomes are structurally and genetically distinguishable, and known as the X and the Y chromosome. In females, both sex-chromosomes are X chromosomes. In contrast, prokaryotes usually have a single chromosome with a circular structure.

Besides this structural composition, the genetic material stored in DNA sequences also exhibits higher degrees of statistical and functional organization. This organization is apparent only in the context of the basic processes of the *central dogma of genetics*. The central dogma asserts that transfer of genetic information can be achieved in three (apparently) unidirectional ways: from DNA to Ribonucleic Acids (RNA), from RNA to proteins, and from DNA to DNA. This transfer model is depicted in Figure 4.

RNA has a chemical structure similar to that of DNA, with two notable exceptions: the sugar Deoxyribose is replaced by the sugar Ribose, and the base Thymine

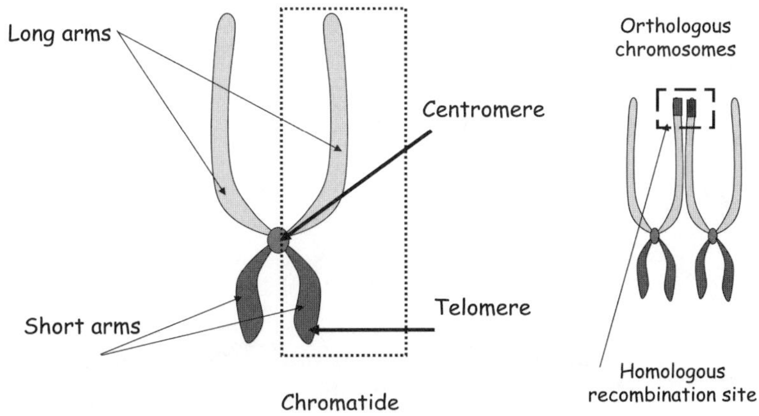

FIGURE 3. Chromosome structure.

is replaced by the base Uracil (henceforth, **U**). In addition, RNA molecules are inherently single-stranded, although they tend to fold back on themselves through *self-hybridization.* A folded two-dimensional RNA strand is shown in Figure 5.

Proteins are macromolecules composed of *amino-acids.*

All amino-acids consist of one α amino group NH_3, a carbon/hydrogen group, and a carboxyl group, as shown below.

$$\begin{array}{cccc} & \mathbf{R} & & \\ & | & & \\ \mathbf{H_3\,N} - & \mathbf{CH} & \mathbf{C} & \mathbf{O} \\ & & | & \\ & & \mathbf{O}. & \end{array} \tag{1}$$

Amino-acids differ in their R-groups, or side chains. The side chain can be as simple as one atom (for example, hydrogen) or a significantly more complex chemical structure. A protein is a linear chain of amino acids, and similar to RNA strands, protein strands fold into characteristic three-dimensional shapes. One such structure is shown in Figure 6.

The three information transfer processes in the Central Dogma are known as *transcription*, *translation*, and *replication*, respectively.

Transcription is a process during which the content of a DNA strand is converted into its WC complement in the form of a single RNA strand, termed *pre-messenger* RNA (pre-mRNA). The mechanism of DNA transcription is extremely complicated, and only understood in part. For successful transcription, a complex of more than 50 proteins, known as *transcription factors*, has to be placed in and around so-called DNA *promoter* and *enhancer* regions, in order to aggregate the required transcription *enzymes*[1]. Transcription enzymes include *helicases*, responsible for unwinding the double helix and enzymes known as RNA *polymerases* that perform the synthesis of an RNA copy of one chosen DNA strand. A polymerase can perform synthesis only in the $3' \to 5'$ direction of the template strand, and at

[1]Enzymes are functional proteins capable of catalyzing biochemical processes.

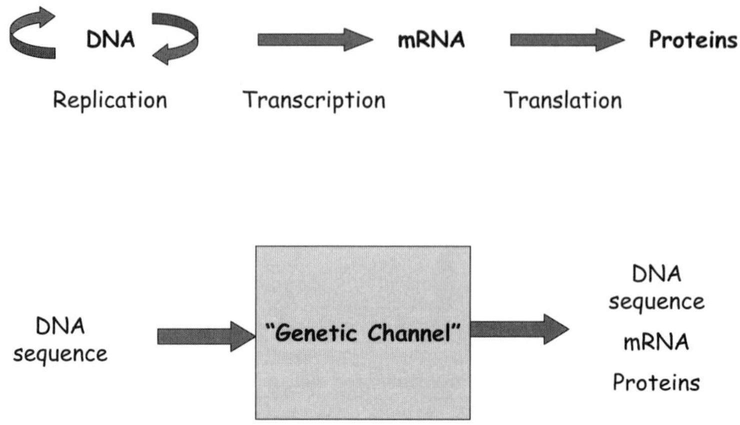

FIGURE 4. Central dogma of genetics.

a given position in the DNA molecule, either strand may serve as the transcription template. In certain rare cases, both strands of the same segment of DNA can be transcribed. Nevertheless, even in this case, the RNA polymerase is allowed to proceed in the $3' \rightarrow 5'$ direction only. The process of transcription is depicted in Figure 7.

If the final product of a transcribed DNA strand represents a protein, the transcribed DNA region is known as a (protein) gene. A gene represents a collection of subsequences known as *exons* and *introns*. Exons are sometimes called *coding regions*, while introns and other inter-genic regions are termed *non-coding*, or "junk DNA". If the final product of the copied DNA strand is an RNA molecule, the corresponding DNA region is sometimes called an *RNA gene.*

The average size of a protein gene is $10 - 15$ Kbp, although large deviations from this value are frequently encountered. Genes can contain one exon, or more than 70 exons. As an illustrative example, the dystrophin gene is approximately 2.4 Mbp long, and it contains around 80 exons. Usually, exons are quite short (several hundred bp), while introns are orders of magnitude longer than exons.

Although both exons and introns are initially transcribed to pre-mRNA strands, introns are subsequently spliced out of the string. The resulting strand is known as *mature* mRNA, or mRNA. Splicing is a process performed by the *spliceosome* complex that contains a large number of RNA molecules and more than 140 different proteins. The spliceosome can perform splicing in several alternative ways, thereby leading to increased diversity of the transcriptional products. More than 50% of human genes are alternatively spliced, so that with less than 25 thousand genes, human cells can produce at least ten times as many different proteins.

Pre-mRNA and mRNA are inherently single-stranded, but they inevitably undergo the process of folding. Folding ensures an increased stability of mRNA molecules, and sometimes also represents a means for signaling other molecules to attach themselves to a self-hybridized strand.

Translation is the process of synthesizing proteins based on the content of mRNA sequences. For this purpose, specialized structural proteins, enzymes, and

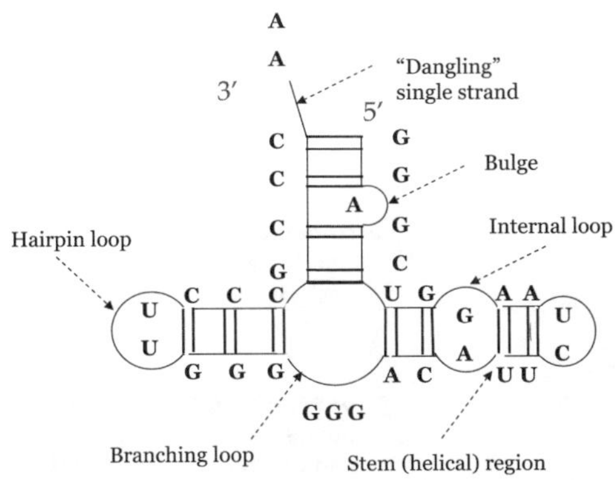

3′- ΔΔ ΛΛΛΛ ΛΛΛ ΔΔ Υ Υ Υ ΔΔΔ ΛΛ Δ ΛΛ ΔΔ ΥΥ Δ ΥΥ ΥΥ Δ ΥΥ – 5′

FIGURE 5. An RNA fold and its ternary representation.

RNA molecules create the *ribosomal complex*, inside of which the process of translation takes place. The sequence of bases in the RNA strand is converted into a sequence of amino-acids according to a mapping rule known as the *genetic code.* The genetic code is depicted in Figure 8. According to the genetic code, a triplet of bases encodes one amino acid. In human cells, twenty amino-acids are used, and encoded by a total of $4^3 = 64$ triplets. As a consequence, the genetic code is degenerate and more than one codon encodes the same amino-acid. The only two amino-acids that have a unique codon are Methionine and Tryptophan. Most triplets encoding for the same amino-acid share the same first two bases, and differ only in the third position. Different genomes and different genomic subsequences often display strong biases with respect to codon usage: one codon is used more frequently than the other codons representing the same amino-acid.

The triplets used in encoding are read in a synchronous and non-overlapping manner, beginning with a triplet that represents the start codon (**AUG**), and ending with one out of three triplets representing a stop codon (**UAA**, **UAG**, or **UGA**). A DNA fragment between a START and STOP codon is known as an *open reading frame* (ORF).

A triplet of bases is translated into an amino-acid through the aid of *transfer* RNA. This is achieved in terms of hybridization between the RNA codon and its WC complement (i.e., its anticodon) that constitutes one arm of the transfer RNA molecule. The transfer RNA molecule has a characteristic clover-leaf shape, with two out of the three arms "carrying" the anticodon and its corresponding amino-acid.

In humans, only ten out of the twenty amino-acids used in transfer RNA are synthesized by the cell itself, and there exists no enzymatic mechanisms that support complete amino-acid production. The remaining amino acids are supplied through food. Plants, on the other hand, are capable of synthesizing their full spectrum of amino-acids.

Replication of DNA strands is one of the most important processes in the life cycle of a cell. The cell cycle is an ordered collection of tasks, known as *stages*, that

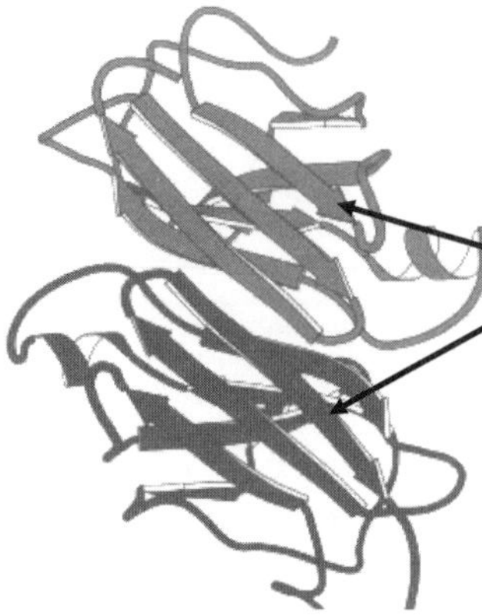

FIGURE 6. Protein folds.

proceed in the following direction:

$$\mathbf{G}_1 \rightarrow \mathbf{S} \rightarrow \mathbf{G}_2 \rightarrow \mathbf{M} \rightarrow \mathbf{G}_1. \tag{2}$$

In the $\mathbf{G}_1$ – Gap 1 – stage, the cell grows, accepts and responds to signals governing its preparation for the division process. During the **S** stage, the genetic material of the cell is doubled through the process of DNA replication. Upon completion of the **S** stage, the cell performs a variety of control and proofreading functions in the $\mathbf{G}_2$ – Gap 2 – stage, in order to ensure that the cell is ready to proliferate. The physical process of nuclear division occurs during the **M** – Mitosis – stage. This stage is divided into several phases, including *prophase*, *metaphase*, *anaphase*, and *telophase*. During these stages, the replicated DNA strings aggregate into chromosomes, the nuclear membrane disintegrates, the chromosomes split through the centromer, and the chromatides move with the aid of the division spindle to opposite sides of the cell. Upon completion of the **M** stage, the cell returns to its $\mathbf{G}_1$ resting stage. Embryonic cells usually do not go through the two gap stages, while gamete cells perform the process of *meiosis*, rather than mitosis.

The central process of the **S** stage of the cell cycle is DNA replication. During DNA replication, the double helix is first unwound by helicases. This unwinding occurs at selected positions on the DNA strands, termed *replication initiation sites* (origins of replication), leading to the creation of replication *forks* and replication *bubbles*. In bacteria, only one replication site is formed. In human cells, multiple initiation sites appear at the same time, and at each site a *replication primer* is inserted. The primer is a short sequence complementary to the initial fragment of the DNA sequence to be replicated. The process of replicating each of the two DNA strands is performed by polymerases, which operate only starting from a primer and proceeding in the $3' \rightarrow 5'$ direction. Consequently, replication of one strand is performed continuously, while replication of the other strand is performed fragment-by-fragment. These fragments, termed *Okazaki's fragments*, are subsequently linked together through the action of *ligase* enzymes.

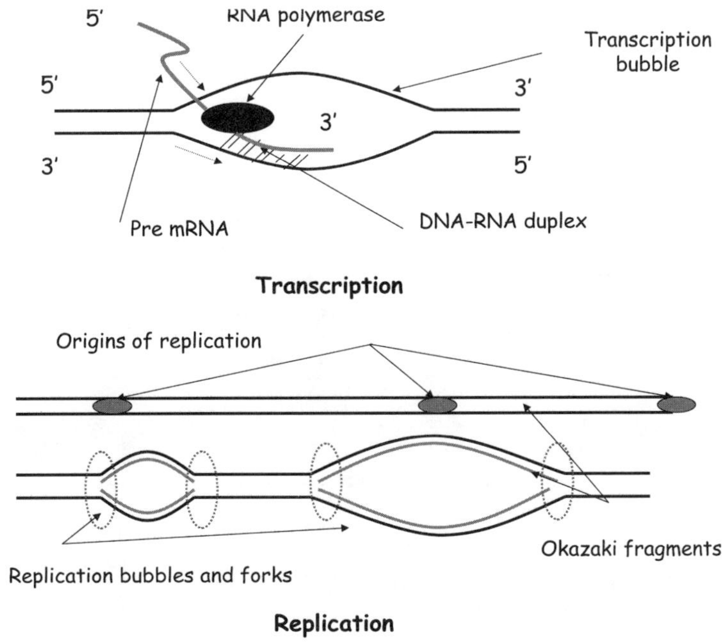

FIGURE 7. Transcription and replication.

The process of replication is a fairly time consuming task: it usually lasts around an hour, and in human cells only 50 bases are copied in a second. DNA replication is depicted in Figure 7, along with the process of DNA transcription, which shares many properties with DNA replication.

2.2. Genetic Information Storage Hierarchy. The brief description of the processes of the central dogma, provided in the previous section, reveals that information in a living cell is stored hierarchically.

At the first level, information is stored in a one-dimensional sequence over a four-letter alphabet, $\{\mathbf{A}, \mathbf{T}, \mathbf{C}, \mathbf{G}\}$, i.e., the DNA sequence[2]. Although DNA sequences are responsible for controlling almost every aspect of a cell's life cycle, their information content cannot be fully understood at this level. This is due to the fact that living organisms are three-dimensional entities, in which information is represented by *shapes*, rather than sequences. This implies that at the second level of the hierarchy, information is represented by the shape of RNA and proteins. Shapes have the ability to lock onto each other, creating a cascade of reactions that result in cell action. Although each shape has its own information content, it is the overall combination of shapes of molecules and their interaction patterns that represents the most significant biological information. At this level, information can be seen as being embedded in a network of interacting patterns.

In the next three sections, we describe these three aspects of information storage in more detail, and outline techniques from coding and information theory useful for studying these biological mechanisms. We begin with an overview of the statistical properties of DNA sequences, which will be used throughout the paper.

[2]Along with its derivatives, RNA and protein sequences.

The Genetic Code/Mapping										
		Second Base								
		U		C		A		G		
First Base	U	UUU	Phe	UCU	Ser	UAU	Tyr	UGU	Cys	U
		UUC		UCC		UAC		UGC		C
		UUA	Leu	UCA		UAA	Stop	UGA	Stop	A
		UUG		UCG		UAG	Stop	UGG	Trp	G
	C	CUA	Leu	CCU	Pro	CAU	His	CGU	Arg	U
		CUC		CCC		CAC		CGC		C
		CUA		CCA		CAA	Gln	CGA		A
		CUG		CCG		CAG		CGG		G
	A	AUU	Ile	ACU	Thr	AAU	Asn	AGU	Ser	U
		AUC		ACC		AAC		AGC		C
		AUA		ACA		AAA	Lys	AGA	Arg	A
		AUG	Met	ACG		AAG		AGG		G
	G	GUU	Val	GCU	Ala	GAU	Asp	GGU	Gly	U
		GUC		GCC		GAC		GGC		C
		GUA		GCA		GAA	Glu	GGA		A
		GUG		GCG		GAG		GGG		G
										Third Base

Abbreviations			
Ala (A) = Alanine	Gln (Q) = Glutamine	Leu (L) = Leucine	Ser (S) = Serine
Arg (R) = Arginine	Glu (E) = Glutamate	Lys (K) = Lysine	Thr (T) = Threonine
Asn (N) = Aspartamine	Gly (G) = Glycine	Met (M) = Methionine	Trp (W) = Tryptophan
Asp (D) = Aspartate	His (H) = Histidine	Phy (F) = Phenylalanine	Tyr (Y) = Tyrosine
Cys (C) = Cysteine	Ile (I) = Isoleucine	Pro (P) = Proline	Val (V) = Valine

FIGURE 8. The genetic code.

3. Compositions of DNA Sequences

Less than 5% of the human genome represents coding regions, and the vast majority of a DNA string is used either for RNA coding or has, at this point, an unknown function. Similar properties are shared by the genomes of other eukaryotes, while most prokaryotes have almost no non-coding regions. It is widely believed that the length and structure of a genome and its coding regions strongly correlates with the size of the underlying host cell, although interesting counterexamples are known[3].

The genetic sequence in the nucleus of a human cell consists of a large number of highly repetitive DNA subsequences. Most families of repeats appear in non-coding regions, and they are usually considered remnants of viral infections and the process of *reverse transcription.* A virus, upon entering the cell, can insert parts of its genetic material into the host DNA sequence by using *reverse transcriptase* enzymes termed *RNA-dependent DNA polymerases.* These polymerases transcribe single-stranded RNA or DNA sequences into double-stranded DNA. For example, retroviruses, such as the HIV virus, have the ability to perform reverse transcription. Reverse transcription is an example of a biological process in violation of the central dogma of genetics.

It has long been hypothesized that the reason why non-coding repeats are very frequent is that these repeats are not subject to negative or purifying selection, which refers to the removal of inserts that are deleterious for the cell. Nevertheless, much of non-coding DNA exhibits both negative and positive selection, which indicates that at least part of the "junk DNA" may be of functional importance. For

[3]Most notably, in the case of cells with two nuclei [**80**], termed eukaryote-eukaryotic cells.

a comprehensive overview of the importance of introns in protein regulation and RNA editing, the interested reader is referred to [**43**].

Non-coding DNA repeats are organized in two groups: *tandem* and *interspersed* repeats [**40, 69**].

The first family of repeats is composed of a collection of nearly identical blocks of DNA subsequences, repeated in consecutive order. The *span* of a tandem repeat is its total length, and the repeated subsequence is sometimes referred to as the *basic repeat unit.* Tandem repeats appear in variable numbers in different genomes of the same species, and this variability is believed to arise during *unequal crossover.* Crossover, or *homologous recombination,* is a process that involves two homologous chromosomes (see Figure 3 for an illustration). Two sister chromatides on each of the two chromosomes form a bond known as the *chiasma.* The two homologs exchange the DNA segment from the chiasma to the end of chromosomes. Due to significant sequence homology, the repetitive sequences of one chromatid may not line up exactly with their corresponding regions in a homologous chromatid or sister chromatid. This creates a variable exchange of regions and variability in tandem repeat numbers.

As the name of the second class of repeats indicates, a member of this family consists of repetitive blocks that are not physically adjacent. The repeating blocks may be present at widely different locations, even including different chromosomes. Within certain species, interspersed repeats arise both as well conserved and highly variable units [**69**].

Tandem repeats are classified into four categories, according to the size of their span and basic repeat unit.

- *Micro-Satellite Repeats* have short basic repeat units and short spans. These repeats are present throughout the human genome. The basic repeat unit is up to four bases long, and it consists either of runs of one single base (most frequently, the base **A** or **T**), a triple of bases (trinucleotide repeats, with ten possible motifs), pairs of bases (like **CA** or **AG**), or simple patterns of bases **G** and **C**. Some pairs of bases are highly uncommon in micro-satellites, due to their susceptibility to deleterious mutations.

  Most micro-satellite repeats occur in non-coding regions, although some are also found in exons. Their function is still not well understood.
- *Mini-Satellite Repeats* have short basic repeat units and moderately long spans. Most mini-satellite repeats are found in the vicinity of, or within, telomeres of chromosomes. Two of the most prevalent types of these repeats are:
  (1) *Hypervariable mini-satellites,* with basic repeat unit

  $$\mathbf{GGGCAGGANG},$$

  where $\mathbf{N} \in \{\mathbf{A}, \mathbf{T}, \mathbf{G}, \mathbf{C}\}$ denotes an arbitrary base;
  (2) *Hexanucleotide repeats,* with basic repeat unit **TTAGGG**;

  The first class of repeats appears both in coding and non-coding regions, in the former case as a hotspot for homologous recombination, while in the latter case mainly within a specific gene, known as the *glycoprotein gene.* The second class of repeats plays a major role in maintaining proper functionality of DNA telomeres.

- *Satellite Repeats* have short basic repeat units and very long span. These repeats are usually found in the centromere region, with some repeats of length approximately 170 bps found in every centromere of human cells. These units, known as α-satellites, bind special classes of proteins. Another example of satellite repeats is the short basic repeat unit **ATTCC**.
- *Macro-Satellite Repeats* have long basic repeat units (measured in Kbps) and moderate to long span. A well know example includes the "RS447 mega-satellite" [**69**], with a basic repeat unit of size almost 5Kbps. Around 60 copies of this mega-satellite constitute an array which is speculated to include DNA coding sequences.

Interspersed repeats mainly fall within non-coding DNA regions, and can be grouped into two main families: short and long interspersed nuclear elements (SINEs and LINEs).

- *SINEs*: Most members of this family appear in mammalian or primate genomes only, and are believed to have originated from reverse transcription. Examples include Alu repeats, found exclusively in primates, and MIR repeats [**69**]. Alu repeats are characterized by their high **GC** content and their high frequency - over half a million Alu repeats are present in the human genome, accounting for 10% of its size. The repeat itself consists of two sequences of length approximately 120 bps, separated by an **A**-rich region. One of the two sequences also contains an additional subsequence of length 32 not present in its counterpart. Several Alu repeats can be found in transcriptionally active regions of the human genome.
- *LINEs*: The most frequently encountered members of this family are found in mammalian genomes, and they include the family of Kpn repeats. Kpn repeats are a very abundant family of repeats, with over 10^5 instances in the human genome. They are highly heterogeneous, and actively transposing – i.e., they represent few of the known "jumping genes". "Jumping genes" are self-replicating DNA sequences with the ability to create new copies of their content at different locations in the genome. Interestingly, many Kpn repeats appear in DNA regions in which Alu repeats are not common. One feature shared by both Alu and Kpn repeats is that very few of them are transcribed.

Besides repeats, DNA sequences also contain a large number of *palindromes* and *inverse repeats*. A DNA subsequence $\mathbf{p} = p_1 p_2 \ldots p_n$ is said to be a palindrome if $p_i = \overline{p}_{n+1-i}$, where the complement is taken in the WC sense. For example, the sequence **AGCCATGGCT** is a palindrome. If a palindromic sequence is interrupted by a non-empty insert at its center or close to it, the resulting sequence is known as an *inverse repeat*.

Palindromes are sites in the genome frequently recognized by restriction enzymes. These are enzymes that have the ability to "cut" the DNA strand at a certain location. DNA palindromes also frequently occur in human cancer cell lines [**56**]. In certain bacteria, palindromic sequences constitute as much as 3% of the genome, one example including the HRP1 (highly repeated palindrome 1) octamer **GCGATCGC** [**56**].

Inverse repeats usually serve as transcription factor binding sites. They also frequently appear in genomic regions coding for proteins and functional RNA. This can be attributed to the fact that, in order to fold, an RNA strand needs stretches of bases that are WC complementary to each other.

Although DNA sequences are used as templates for RNA and protein sequences, there exist certain repeats that arise only at the mRNA and protein sequence level. One example is the *exon repetition* phenomenon [**55**]. It manifests itself in terms of the presence of tandemly repeated exons, not accounted for in the transcribed DNA sequence. For a small class of genes, as much as 50% of the mRNA sequence is subjected to exon repetition.

Almost all DNA repeats were discovered using biochemical analysis of the test strings, and the question of identifying general functional attributes of repeats remains unresolved. In the next section, we describe how DNA compression algorithms can utilize the knowledge about approximate DNA sequence repeats to compress genetic data; alternatively, we outline how such algorithms can aid in the discovery of new classes of repeats or genetic sequence composition.

Before proceeding with this description, we briefly describe several mutation mechanisms responsible for dynamically changing the statistical properties of repeats and other subsequences in DNA strands.

3.1. DNA Mutations. Mutations in DNA strands arise internally (as chemical or functional mutations), or due to exogenous causes. In the first case, errors inherent to certain cellular processes or chemical compounds in the cell lead to irreversible changes in the DNA sequence, while in the latter case, such changes occur due to external mutagenic factors. A mutation starts in the form of a *pre-mutation* that is either corrected by specialized repair systems, or transformed into a stable mutation which then becomes an integral part of the genetic sequence. A detailed classification of DNA mutations and DNA repair processes can be found in [**40**]. We briefly describe the most common mutations found in DNA strands, since these have a bearing on the statistical properties of both coding and non-coding sequences. Clearly, mutations in coding regions are subjected to strong negative selection, and are expected to be less frequent than those in non-coding regions.

Chemical mutations arise due to the chemical structure of DNA building blocks. Despite the fact that the DNA molecules are very stable[4], there exist certain types of chemical reactions that can lead to changes in their structure. Two examples include *tautomeric shifts* (TS), and structural changes such as *deamination, oxidation and methylation* of Purine and Pyrimidine bases [**40**].

TS mutations arise due to the chemical structure of purine and pyrimidine bases. As one can see from Figure 1, **T**, **G**, and **C** all contain oxygen atoms that participate in the creation of hydrogen bonds between bases. Oxygen acts as an acceptor, while hydrogen acts as a donor of protons, but in certain cases protons can be supplied by neighboring nitrogen N atoms. Due to this "shift" of supplier, erroneous pairings of the form **T** − **G**, **A** − **C** appear. These pairings tend to preserve the type of bases (i.e. Purines are replaced by Purines), and are called transitions [**40**]. On the other hand, the process of deamination involves the NH_2 group in the base **C**, which can be replaced by an oxygen atom, followed by the release of an NH_3 group. Deamination leads to mutations involving mispairings of

[4]It is widely believed that RNA molecule were the first carriers of genetic information, only to be replaced during evolution by DNA polymers that are chemically more stable then RNA strands.

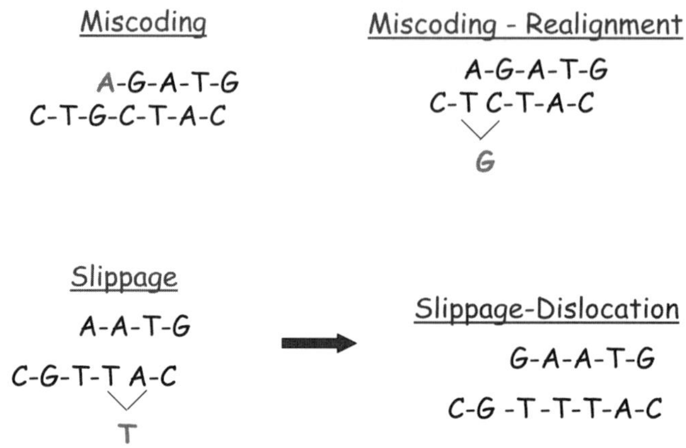

FIGURE 9. DNA mutations.

the type **U** − **G** and **T** − **G**. The process of oxidation tends to increase the affinity of bonding between **G** and **A** bases, while methylation usually affects **A** bases only.

In addition to the pairing modifications described above, one often encounters broken bonds between the carbon atom of the sugar and the nitrogen atom of a base, leading to so-called AP (Apurinic/Apyramidinic) sites. AP sites correspond to deletions of bases in the DNA sequence, and the correction of such pre-mutations usually involves extremely sophisticated error-correction mechanisms.

Damages of the form described above are tackled by several different repair mechanisms. Transitions from **C** to **U** are detected by repair enzymes known as *glycosylases*, while base-pair losses are fixed by arrays of *endonucleases*. Furthermore, since most deamination pre-mutations appear in repeated **CG** and **GC** bases, evolution itself seems to have addressed this issue by significantly reducing the frequency of such base pairs.

Functional mutations occur during various stages of the cell cycle, including DNA replication and homologous recombination. The latter problem was already described in the context of DNA replication. Errors during replication are due to polymerase misinsertions, and they occur with probability in the range of $10^{-3} - 10^{-5}$. These errors are corrected in terms of proofreading, by using the information in the "old" template strand. More than 100 different proofreading repair mechanisms are known, involving specialized enzymes such as *exonucleases* and several classes of *mismatch-specific post-replication* enzymes. These mechanisms reduce the error-probability of replication by two orders of magnitude, resulting in not more than, on average, one error per human DNA replication.

Exogenous mutations appear in the form of DNA strand breakage, loss of Purine and Pyrimidine bases due to radiation (on average, 5000 − 10000 Purines and 200 − 500 Pyramidines per day), and oxidative damage.

The aforementioned errors represent a combination of substitution, deletion, insertion, shift, and reversal errors (see Figure 9 for more examples of DNA mutation mechanisms). As a consequence, a DNA sequence can be see as undergoing "time-sensitive transmissions" over a noisy "genetic channel" that introduces errors of the forms described above. Errors appear at the level of a single base (like simple base substitutions), or they afflict a complete exon or intron. As such, they play an important role in changing the statistical properties of DNA sequences and their repeat composition adn organization.

4. DNA Compression

The entropy and entropy rate, as measures of the information content of sequences generated by stochastic processes, are often estimated through compression.

Many universal compression algorithms used in commercial software, such as gzip, pkzip, gif (based on the Ziv-Lempel (ZL), Burrows-Wheeler and general Grammar Based Transform Coding algorithms), were recently tested on DNA and protein sequences. An illustration of our findings for chromosome 2 of the specie Plasmodium Falciparum (PF) is shown in Table 1. PF is a single-celled eukaryote (a protozoa) responsible for more than 80% of cases of human malaria. Chromosome 2 of this organism consists of 947102 base pairs. The sequence itself shows a strong bias towards the bases **A** and **T** which is a feature shared with other eukaryotes. In the PF sequence, **A** and **T** equally contribute to 80.3% of the bases, while **G** and **C** each account for close to 9.9% of the sequence base pairs.

TABLE 1. Performance of Classical Compression Algorithms of the PF Sequence.

Algorithm	Description	Size (Bytes)
No compression	2b/bp	236 776
	Entropy	203 259
LZW	Winzip 8.0	245 076
	Windows XP	245 271
	Compress 4.2.4	212 858
LZ77	Zlib 1.2.2	237 684
	Gzip 1.3.3	237 608
BWT	Bzip 1.0.2	225 157

In the table, the acronyms LZ, LZW, and BWT stand for the Lempel-Ziv and Lempel-Ziv-Welch algorithms, and the Burrow-Wheeler transform, respectively [**59**]. For the faithful representation of a four-letter alphabet, at most two bits per symbol are needed[5]. With the exception of the BW and Compress algorithm, all compression schemes listed in the table lead to an expansion of the description length of a symbol beyond the two-bit value.

The PF sequence is a single chromosome, and it contains both coding and non-coding subsequences. Non-coding sequences, as described in the previous section, contain many classes of repeats that should allow for significant compression rates. As a result, the failure of the existing compression algorithms can be attributed to

[5]For an alphabet of size 20, this number equals 4.32.

their inherent inability to recognize such repeats, rather than to the incompressibility of the sequences themselves. One reason behind this apparent failure is that DNA sequences undergo random mutations, so that all sufficiently long repeats and palindromes are only *approximate.* This represents a major stumbling block for algorithms that use LZ parsings. LZ parsing schemes rely on identifying exact (deterministic) repeats. Another reason behind the failure of LZ compression schemes is the fact that they do not account for palindromes and inverse repeats.

These issues were addressed in several different DNA-oriented compression algorithms [**12, 24, 13, 70**], including:

- *BioCompress*: This algorithm detects inverted repeats and palindromes, but does not lead to compression rates significantly lower than 2 bits/bp. This is due to the fact that only exact repeats are accepted by the algorithm.
- *GenCompress*: This algorithm is capable of detecting *approximate repeats and palindromes.* It provides the best known compression rates for a large number of DNA sequences.
- *Grammar Based Compression* algorithms: The idea underlying this compression scheme is that a DNA sequence can be modelled by a context-free grammar, the rules of which can be efficiently compressed. Algorithms with this feature operate with mixed success, and usually have large complexity.
- *Maximum likelihood Compression* algorithms: In this setting, a normalized maximum likelihood (NML) model capable of handling approximate repeats is used. The algorithm compresses a DNA sequence based on a preset discrete regressor sequence, constructed from a parametric probability model. The universal NML probabilities are generated by normalizing the maximum likelihood estimates.

Compared to non-coding regions, coding regions are highly incompressible. This property is observed both on the level of a single protein sequences, and at the level of concatenation of all protein sequences (i.e., the proteome) of a given organism. In the latter case, it was shown in [**47**] that predictive compression algorithms cannot achieve compression rates above $1 : 1.1$ for the *H. Influenza* (influenza virus), *S. Cerevisiae* (baker's yeast), and *H. Sapiens* (human) proteoms. The algorithm in [**47**] is based on the PPM (prediction by partial matching) scheme that relies on a Markov chain model for DNA sequences, and estimates the probability of a given symbol from a number of previously observed symbols. More optimistic rates of $1 : 1.3$ were described in [**26**], while the best performing techniques [**2, 3**] that use sorted common prefixes lead to compression rates as high as $1 : 1.65$ (although only for the H. Influenza virus proteome). Universally good compression algorithms for protein sequences are still not known.

These findings raise a similar question as the one posed for non-coding regions: are protein sequences inherently incompressible, or are the known compression methods inadequate for performing this task? Despite the fact that coding regions contain far less repeats than non-coding regions, they contain many hidden regularities. For example, many paralogs[6] of a given gene exist in the human genome, which henceforth implies that tandem or interspersed approximate repeats have to exist in the proteome of an organism. Furthermore, proteins fold

[6]A paralog of a gene is a mutated copy of the gene within the same genome.

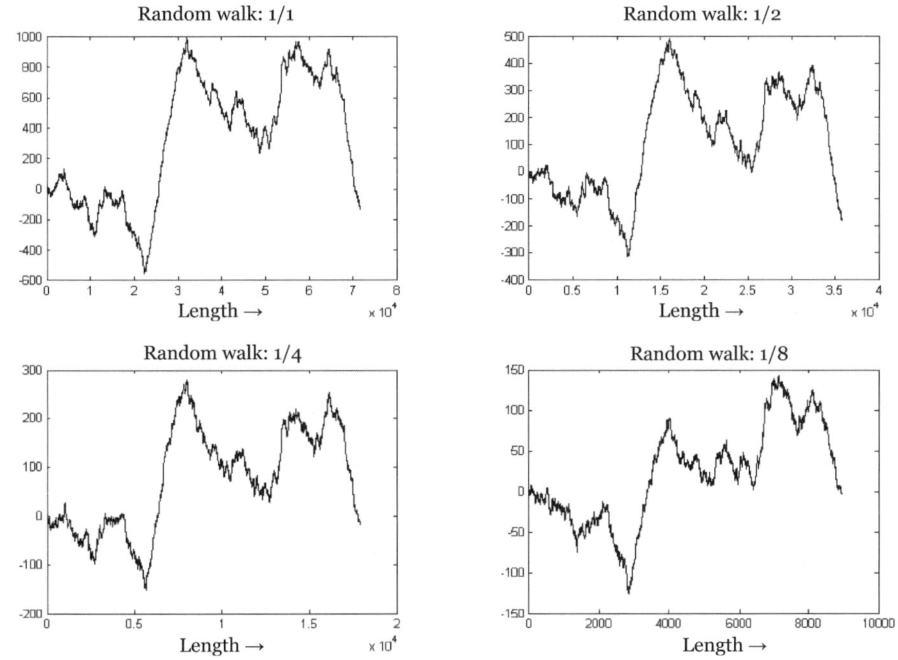

FIGURE 10. Binary random walk of the HUMHBB sequence.

into well defined α-helix and β-sheet formations, as illustrated in Figure 6. Parts of these sheets and helices have a fixed composition of amino acids. Consequently, the assumption that protein sequences are inherently random, and are therefore incompressible, is inappropriate.

This conclusion is supported even further by some obvious drawbacks of the compression schemes proposed so far. Although the PPM-based method in [**47**] is very simple, it is not suitable for sequences that do not follow Markovian probabilistic laws. Such is the case with protein sequences, which are neither Markovian[7] nor stationary. The fact that DNA and protein sequences are non-stationary is overlooked in a large body of work: as a result, statistical compression schemes relying on the notion of Shannon entropy and its implications are highly misleading. Achievable compression rates can in this case be measured via the entropy rate of the distribution producing a given sequence, but there exist no accurate methods for estimating this rate for DNA sequences. This is due to the highly varying statistical properties of subsequences of DNA strands and their finite length.

4.1. Long Range Correlation and Fractal Properties of DNA and Protein Sequences. Long range correlations in DNA and protein sequences can be attributed to the presence of repeats, palindromes and gene paralogs. Long range correlations arise both in the form of statistical and pattern correlations,

[7]The fact that proteins fold immediately rules out the possibility of a Markovian model for their underlying sequences, since a shape is maintained through specific long-range interactions of amino-acids.

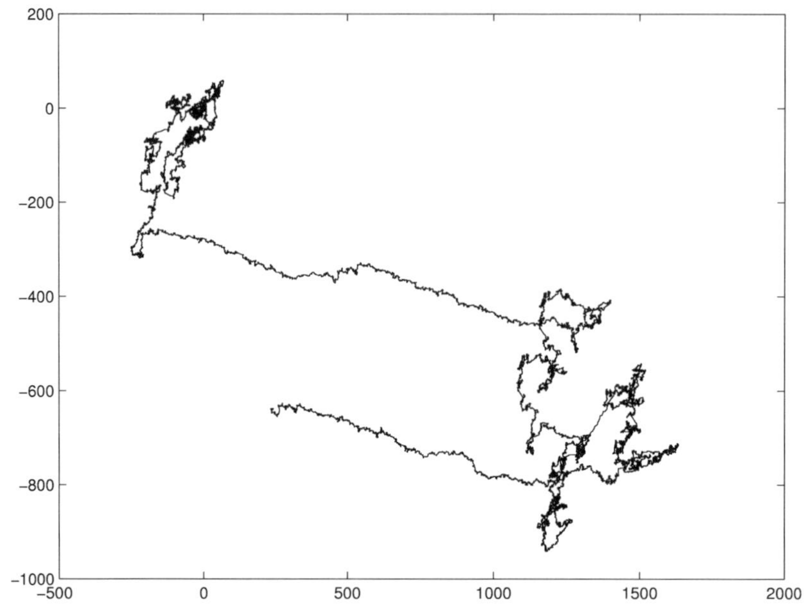

FIGURE 11. Quarternary Levy walk of the HUMHBB sequence.

the former manifesting itself as dependance between the distributions of symbols at a large distance from each other. The latter appears in the form of direct symbol correlation. Long range correlations in DNA sequences were first described in [**1, 52**], were different decay laws for the autocorrelation function of coding and non-coding regions were reported. Such a behavior is inherent to self-similar sequences which lack a typical distance scale.

A simple means for visualizing self-similarities in DNA and protein sequences is in terms of random (Levy) walks. These walks are usually depicted in two-dimensions, and in the case of DNA sequences they involve either two (binary walks) of four (quaternary walks) steps.

In a binary DNA walk, the four bases are grouped into Purines and Pyrimidines, and the step $(1,1)$ is assigned to the first pair, while the step $(1,-1)$ is assigned to the second pair. There exist several possible non-equivalent mappings between steps and bases in a quarternary walk; we restrict our attention to the following one:

$$\mathbf{A} := (-1,0),\ \mathbf{T} := (1,0),\ \mathbf{G} := (0,-1),\ \mathbf{C} := (0,1). \tag{3}$$

This mapping, first described in [**1**], has several desirable properties. First, it is unbiased, since the probabilities of up and down steps are almost identical, and the same is true of the probabilities of left and right steps. As already pointed out, in almost all known genomes, the bases **G** and **C** are far less common than the bases **A** and **T** [8].

[8]This may be attributed to the fact that the hydrogen bonds between **G** and **C** are stronger than those between **A** and **T**, and consequently more energetically costly to break during replication and transcription. On the other hand, these bases contribute more to the overall stability of both the DNA double-helix and RNA folds.

Examples of binary and quarternary DNA walks are shown in Figures 10 and 11. The sequence displayed is the *HUMHBB region*, the human β globin sequence on chromosome 11. This sequence is frequently used in DNA studies because of its fairly long length (73326 bases), and its mixture of exons, introns (a total of six globin genes), and Alu repeats (eight repeat families).

Two observations regarding the Levy walk of this sequence are in place. In the binary walk, we observe sequence self-similarities at the scales $2, 4$, and 8, provided that the amplitudes of the decimated walks are properly scaled. What this implies is that the family of random walks obtained from keeping only every second, or every fourth, or every eight, etc. base in the HUMHBB sequence has similar statistical properties. On the other hand, the filaments in the quarternary walk reveal the presence of long range correlations, and a mixture of biases in the sequence base composition.

DNA sequences, as well as other systems that exhibit scaling symmetry (symmetry preserved at various scales), can be characterized by their *fractal dimension*. There exist several related fractal dimension measures that describe objects with scaling symmetry, including the Hausdorff dimension and box counting dimensions. An example of the latter is *Kolmogorov's dimension*, defined as follows.

DEFINITION 4.1. Let F be a fractal object. Partition the object into equally sized cubes of dimension equal to the dimension of the space in which the object is embedded, and with edge length ϵ. If $N(\epsilon)$ is the smallest number of cubes in any such partition, the Kolmogorov dimension is defined as

$$D_k(F) = \lim_{\epsilon \to 0} \frac{\ln(N(\epsilon))}{\ln(1/\epsilon)}.$$

The box-counting dimensions of a number of genetic sequence random walks were studied in [**52, 1**]. These studies were performed in order to discriminate between exons and introns, since in a given organism, the fractal dimensions of these two regions usually differ. As an illustration, we plotted the number of boxes N needed to cover the quarternary random walk for the HUMHBB sequence, versus the size of the covering cubes R. The doubly-logarithmic representation of these numbers is shown in Figure 12. The solid curve is the result of box-counting, while the dashed line represents a reference line with slope 1.42. This slope represents the Kolmogorov dimension of the HUMHBB walk. The space-filling box count curve is shown in the same figure, illustrating the fact that different fractal dimensions exhibit very diverse behaviors.

There is substantial evidence that almost all DNA sequences exhibit fractal and multi-fractal nature. In the next section, we describe one of the best studied fractal sequences, the *Thue-Morse* (TM) sequence, and provide a straightforward analysis that shows why a truncated version of this sequence cannot be efficiently compressed by the LZ algorithm. We then proceed to explain how integer-to-integer wavelet (IIW) transforms can be used to accomplish this task. This motivates the study of IIW transforms for DNA sequence compression.

4.2. The Thue-Morse Sequence. The Thue-Morse (TM) sequence is a prototypical fractal sequence that appears in many areas of physics, theory of state matter, geometry, biology and acoustics [**61**]. It can be generated in many equivalent ways, and we focus on two such methods.

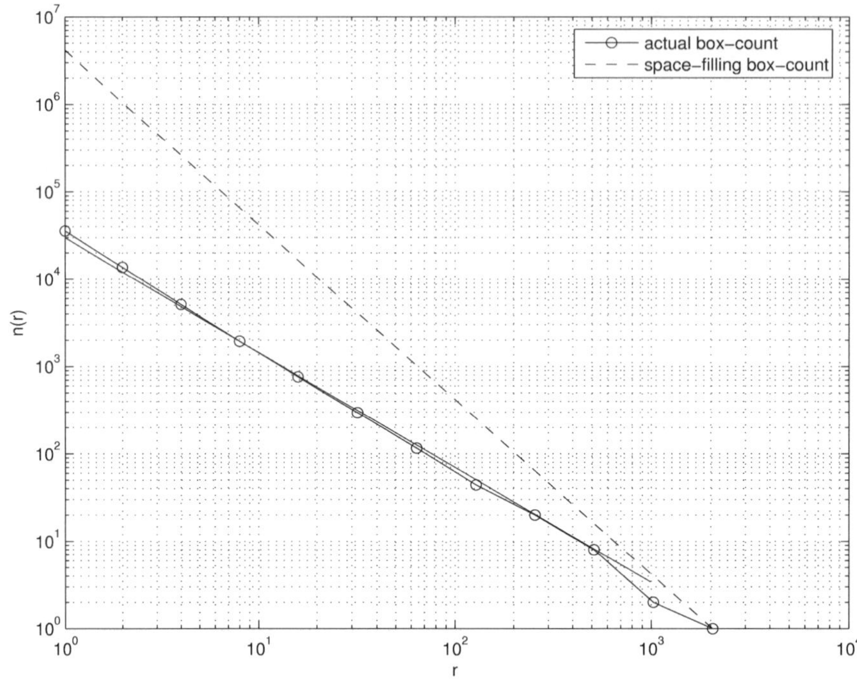

FIGURE 12. Box counting for the HUMHBB sequence.

DEFINITION 4.2. Let S be the sequence of non-negative integers, $0, 1, 2, 3, \ldots$. The TM sequence is the sequence of parities (modulo-two sums) of the standard binary representations of the integers in S.

Following this definition, we write the binary representations of the non-negative integers as 0, 1, 10, 11, 100, ... Taking the modulo-two sum of each binary representation produces the sequence $0, 1, 1, 0, 1, \ldots$ – the TM sequence.

The TM sequence has many remarkable properties: it is a deterministic, aperiodic sequence that exhibits perfect self-similarity. Self-similarity in this context refers to the fact that striking out every second symbol in the sequence reproduces the starting sequence. As a consequence, this sequence can also be constructed recursively, by starting from the symbol 0 and appending to each current subsequence its complement. This process leads to the following prefixes of the TM sequence 0, 01, 0110, 01101001, ... This rule can be formalized as

$$\Phi_{n+1} = \Phi_n \mid \overline{\Phi}_n, \quad \text{where} \quad \Phi_1 = 0, \tag{4}$$

and where $\mid$ denotes concatenation, while $\overline{P}$ denotes the complement of the sequence P.

Yet another method for generating the TM sequence is in terms of Lindenmayer (L) systems [**48, 36**]. L-systems were first introduced as mathematical abstractions for modelling biological development. The systems are described by an initial string and rewriting rules for each letter, applied iteratively and in parallel on a given initial string. The TM sequence is an L-system with initial string 0 and rewriting rules $0 \to 01$ and $1 \to 10$.

Although the TM sequence is defined over a binary alphabet and has the same average number of zeros and ones, there exist well-known generalizations of these sequences over arbitrary finite alphabets, which have a prescribed bias for the distribution of zeros [**56**]. The self-similarity of these sequences induces long-range correlations and leads to the formation of arbitrary long palindromes [**56**].

It is straightforward to see why a compression scheme like LZ coding fails to compress the TM sequence. The LZ parsing of a finite truncation of the TM sequence takes the form $0, 1, 10, 100, 11, 00, ...$, failing to capture the correct construction rule of the sequence. If C_n denotes the number of commas in the LZ parsing of a sequence, than a result in [**82**] asserts that

$$\frac{C_n \log(C_n)}{n} \to H, \quad \text{as} \quad n \to \infty, \tag{5}$$

where H is the Shannon entropy of the source producing the parsed stationary sequence. As a consequence, based on 73326 bits of the TM sequence (roughly the same length as the HUMHBB sequence), LZ parsing produces $C_n = 2562$ phrases and an estimate for the entropy of the underlying probability distribution equal to $H = 0.39$. This is obviously not an adequate measure of the achievable compression rate, since the sequence is deterministic.

On the other hand, a parsing rule which recognizes concatenations of sequences in a dynamically changing dictionary, along with their complements, produces $0, 1, 10, 1001, \ldots$. For a TM sequence truncated after 2^n bits, this parsing contains $n+1$ blocks. As a result, in order to efficiently compress fractal-like sequences, the rules for building a dictionary have to be changed, or a different approach to the problem has to be devised.

For this purpose, let us focus on the IIW transform. Compression algorithms based on this transform are known to lead to efficient lossless representations of fractal-like images or sequences [**10**]. Among the most simple such transforms is the integer version of the Haar ($\mathcal{H}$) transform, defined as follows. Let $\mathbf{s}=\{s_{0,j}\}$, $j = 1, 2, \ldots$, be a given sequence. The $\mathcal{H}$ transform consists of a low-pass $\{s_{1,j}\}$ and high-pass $\{d_{0,j}\}$ sequence of coefficients, obtained according to the rules

$$d_{1,l} = s_{0,2l+1} - s_{0,2l},$$
$$s_{1,l} = s_{0,2l} + \lfloor d_{1,l}/2 \rfloor.$$

Applying the $\mathcal{H}$ transform to the TM sequence, mapped according to the rules $0 \to -1$, $1 \to 1$, shows that all low pass coefficients are zero, while the high pass coefficients equal $2-2-22-222-2-222-22-2-2\ldots$. The high pass coefficients correspond to the TM sequence scaled by a factor of 2.

The TM sequence represents an idealized sequence with self-similarities on scales that equal perfect powers of two. This self-similarity exists even when the sequence undergoes random insertion, deletion, and substitution mutations during each steo of its iterative construction process described by 4. The Levy walk of one such mutated TM sequence is shown in Figure 13.

It is therefore of interest to test if other IIW transform are capable of detecting structural regularities in the HUMHBB DNA sequence. For this purpose, one can use the $\mathcal{H}$ and $S+P$ transforms [**10**], the latter defined as according to the following equations:

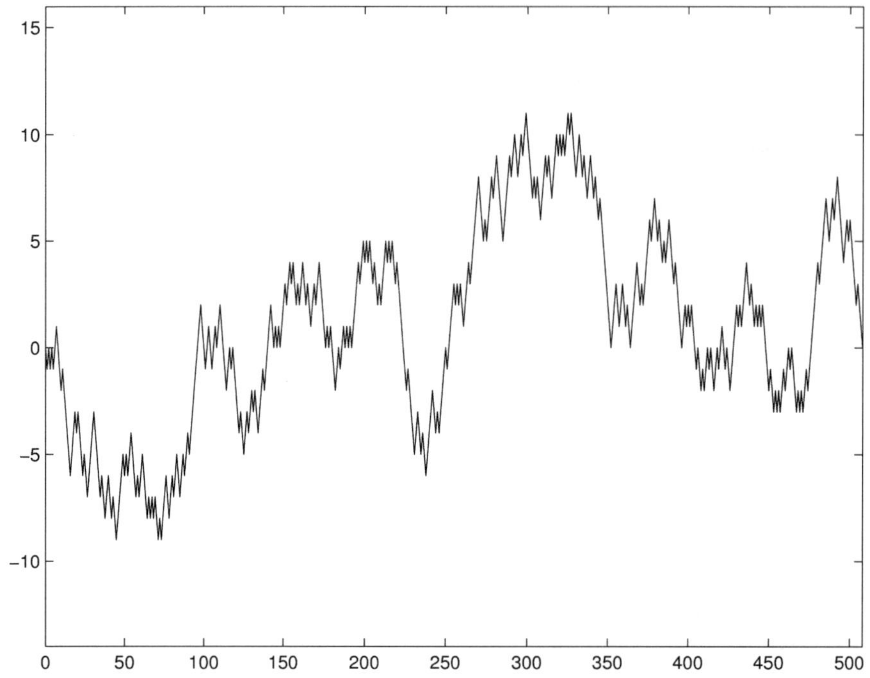

FIGURE 13. TM sequence with insertion, deletion, and substitution probabilities $p_i = p_d = 0.01$, $p_s = 0.05$, respectively.

$$d_{1,l}^{(1)} = s_{0,2l+1} - s_{0,2l},$$
$$s_{1,l} = s_{0,2l} + \lfloor d_{1,l}^{(1)}/2 \rfloor,$$
$$d_{1,l} = d_{1,l}^{(1)} + \lfloor \alpha_{-1}(s_{1,l-2} - s_{1,l-1}) + \alpha_0(s_{1,l-1} - s_{1,l}) + \alpha_1(s_{1,l} - s_{1,l+1}) - \beta_1 \, d_{1,l+1}^{(1)} \rfloor.$$

Unfortunately, extensive tests did not produce a collection of real-valued weighting factors $\alpha_1, \alpha_0, \alpha_1$, and β capable of achieving good compression results for the HUMHBB sequence. It remains a challenging open problem to develop a wavelet transform that performs well on the HUMHBB sequence.

There exist many other methods that can be used for handling long-range correlations in DNA sequences. One is based on the idea that long range correlations can be observed through interleaving. Here, a sequence is broken into subsequences that are written row-wise, and read column-wise. The column-wise readout is encoded by a runlength scheme. For illustration, we tested a part of the HUMGHCSA sequence (a non-coding region of the human growth hormone gene on chromosome 17):

AAAGAGAGAAAGAAAGAAAGAAAGAAAGAAAGAAAGAGAG
AGAGAGAGAGAGAGAGAGAGAGAAAGAAAGAAAGAAAGAA
AGAAAGAAAGAAAGAAAGAAAGAAAGAAAGAAAGAAAGAA
GGGAAAGAAAGAAAGGA.

Reading this sequence into a matrix with four columns row-wise, and reading it out column-wise produces the sequence

$$\mathbf{A}^{29}\mathbf{G}\mathbf{A}^{4}\mathbf{G}\mathbf{A}^{7}\mathbf{G}^{24}\mathbf{A}^{32}\mathbf{G}^{15}\mathbf{A}^{19},$$

where $\mathbf{N}^m$ denotes a string of m consecutive symbols **N**. Similar examples can be found in other sequences, including a subsequence of the PF sequence of length 1141. In this case, seven columns produce the optimal run-length distributions of the readout.

Many DNA sequences seem to obey generation rules of L-systems. For example, starting with the initial string **A** and using the rewriting rules $\mathbf{G} \to \mathbf{AG}$ and $\mathbf{A} \to \mathbf{GAA}$ five times, one obtains the sequence

GAAAGAGGAAGAAAGGAAGAAAGGAAGAAGAAAGAGGAAG
AAGAAAGGAAAGAGGAAGAAAGGAAGAAGAAAGAGGAAGA
AAGGAAGAAAGGAAGAAGAAAGGAAAGAGGAAGAAAGGAA
GAAGAAAGAGGAAGAAAGGAAGAA.

This sequence has small edit distance (< 23) from a subsequence of the HUMHBB region, and can be compressed by specifying the attributed of the L-system and the "edited innovation".

The techniques described above represent only a limited sampling of methods that are potentially useful for DNA compression. More details about ongoing work in this are can be found in [**2, 3, 70**].

5. The Information Content of a Shape

As described in the previous section, the problem of determining the information content of DNA sequences remains a challenge. Even less is known about the mechanism of information storage in molecular shapes. Entropy, as a measure of uncertainty and information, is a property of the probability distribution governing the formation of shapes, and not of the shapes themselves. As a consequence, it is important to develop good probability distribution models for molecular structures encountered in cells. In our analysis, we focus on the most simple form of shapes – two-dimensional RNA folds.

WC bonding of bases on the same RNA molecule leads to folding of the strand in two or three dimensions. Formations obtained in this way are referred to as the *secondary* and *tertiary* structures of the RNA sequence, respectively. An example of a secondary structure is shown in Figure 5.

The fold in Figure 5 contains several distinct structural elements, known as *stems*, *dangling ends*, and *loops*. A stem is a collection of paired bases that resembles a ladder. A dangling end is a sequence of unpaired bases that appears at a terminal of the fold. A loop is a collection of unpaired bases, and loops can be classified as *hairpins*, *interior loops*, *bulges*, and *branching loops*. Hairpin loops are loops that consist of one sequence of consecutive unpaired bases, enclosed by one stem. Interior loops are loops enclosed by two stems, while a bulge is a sequence of consecutive, unpaired bases, that protrudes from one side of the fold only. Similarly, branching loops are loops encircled by multiple stems.

The first mathematical model for a secondary structure was proposed in [**79**], using the simple notion of the adjacency matrix of a graph.

DEFINITION 5.1. [**79**] A secondary structure of size n is a graph on a set of n labeled vertices, for which the adjacency matrix $\mathcal{A}$, with entries $a_{i,j} \in \{0,1\}$, $i,j = 1,\ldots,n$, has the following three properties:

- $a_{i,i+1} = 1$, $1 \le i \le n-1$;
- For a given i, $1 \le i \le n$, there exists at most one index j such that $j \notin \{i-1, i+1\}$ and $a_{i,j} = 1$;
- $a_{i,j} = a_{k,l} = 1$ with $i < k < j$ implies that $i \le l \le j$;

The first property reflects the fact that bases in the strands are ordered, and that each base has at most two neighbors on the sugar-phosphate backbone. The second property enforces the constraint that no base can form more than one set of hydrogen bonds. Finally, the third constraint ensures that the folded structure lies in two-dimensions. Base pairings violating the third constraint often lead to the formation of *pseudo-knots*, one of the basic components of tertiary structures. Pseudo-knots will not be discussed in this section.

From the perspective of introducing the notion of the entropy of folds, the model described above has two drawbacks: first, it is too broad to capture intricate properties of RNA folds that arise due to bio-chemical constraints imposed on the backbone of the molecules. As an illustration, from the 17 secondary structures of length $n = 6$, accounted for by the model in [**79**], only one fold is stable at a temperature of 37 °C [**76**]. This is due to the fact that the model 5.1 does not take into account that loops have destabilizing effects on folds, and that this effect has to be compensated for by the presence of sufficiently long stems.

A second drawback of the model is that it does not provide a natural setup for defining a random process responsible for generating folds defined through adjacency matrices.

One can overcome both of these problems in terms of describing folds by constrained *context-free* and stochastic context-free grammars. Stochastic context-free grammars were first used for the purpose of secondary structure prediction in [**33**], and for constrained RNA fold enumeration in [**42**].

DEFINITION 5.2. A grammar is a four-tuple $\mathcal{G} = (V, R, P, \epsilon)$, where V and R are two disjoint alphabets, called the *non-terminal* and the *terminal* alphabet, respectively. The symbol ϵ represents a special element known as the *axiom*, which serves as a terminal symbol. The set P is a collection of *production rules*, which are pairs of the form (Σ, Θ), with $\Sigma \in V$ and $\Theta \in (V \cup R)^*$, where A^* denotes the free monoid over the alphabet A[9]. Production rules are usually denoted by $\Sigma \to \Theta$.

A *regular grammar* is a grammar with production rules of the form:

$$N \to \epsilon; \quad N \to T; \quad N \to T \cdot N; \tag{6}$$

Note that in regular grammars, a non-terminal symbol N appearing on the right hand side of a production rule must necessarily be to the right of a terminal symbol T. A *context-free grammar* is a grammar in which each production rule is allowed to include non-terminal symbols both at the left and right hand side of terminal symbols, i.e.

$$N \to \epsilon; \quad N \to Z_1 \cdot Z_2 \ldots \cdot Z_n; \tag{7}$$

[9]The free monoid over A is the set of all finite sequences of zero or more elements from A.

Here, the symbols $Z_i, i = 1, \ldots, n$, represent either terminal or non-terminal symbols, while n is an arbitrary integer.

DEFINITION 5.3. The language $\mathcal{L}$ of a grammar is the set of words over the alphabet A, $|A| = w$, that can be obtained from an arbitrary sequence of production rules. The generating function of the language $\mathcal{L}$, $G_{\mathcal{L}}(x_1, \ldots, x_w)$, is defined as

$$G_{\mathcal{L}}(x_1, \ldots, x_w) = \sum_{i_1, \ldots, i_w \geq 0} \ell_{i_1, \ldots, i_w} \, x_1^{i_1} \ldots x_w^{i_w}, \tag{8}$$

where $\ell_{i_1, \ldots, i_w}$ denotes the number of words in the language $\mathcal{L}$ that consist of i_1 symbols r_1, i_2 symbols r_2, etc., and i_w symbols r_w, $r_i \in A$, $i = 1, \ldots, w$. For $x_1 = x_2 = \ldots = x_w = x$, $G_{\mathcal{L}}(x)$ reduces to the generating function for the words in the language, counted according to their lengths.

In order to develop grammars describing secondary structures, these structures have first to be converted into one-dimensional strings. This can be accomplished by fixing a *reading direction* for the bases in the fold, say from the $3'$ to the $5'$ terminals of the strand, as shown in Figure 5. Then, the step $(1, 1)$ is assigned to the first base encountered in a pairing, when the sequence is traversed in the predefined reading direction. Similarly, the step $(1, -1)$ is assigned to the second base in a pairing. The step $(1, 0)$ is reserved for unpaired bases. Sequences obtained in this manner have special properties, and are known as *Motzkin* paths (words).

DEFINITION 5.4. A lattice path of length n is a sequence of points $P_1, P_2, \ldots, P_n$, with $n \geq 1$, such that each point P_i belongs to the planar integer lattice $\mathcal{Z} \times \mathcal{Z}$ and consecutive points P_i and P_{i+1} are connected by a line segment. A *Motzkin path* is a lattice path in the planar integer lattice, with steps $\Lambda = (1, 1)$, $\Gamma = (1, -1)$, and $\Delta = (1, 0)$, which never passes below the x-axis.

To see that the read-out of a secondary structure represents a Motzkin path, it suffices to observe that in any prefix of the sequence, one has to encounter more first than second bases, or the same number of first and second bases in a pairing. An example of a Motzkin path corresponding to an RNA fold is shown in Figure 5.

Motzkin paths have a simple description via context-free grammars, with terminal symbols $\{\lambda, \gamma, \delta\}$ (representing the steps Λ, Γ, and Δ, respectively), and production rules

$$M \to \epsilon; \quad M \to \lambda \cdot M \cdot \gamma \cdot M; \quad M \to \delta \cdot M;, \tag{9}$$

where M is a non-terminal symbol representing Motzkin paths.

Another set of production rules was used for RNA secondary structure prediction in [**33**], of the form:

$$\begin{aligned} &S \to L \cdot S; \; S \to L; \\ &F \to d \cdot F \cdot d; \; F \to L \cdot S; \\ &L \to d \cdot F \cdot d; \; L \to s; \, . \end{aligned} \tag{10}$$

Here, F, L, and S are non-terminal symbols, while s and d denote terminal symbols. The terminal s denotes an unpaired symbol, while d corresponds to a paired symbol. The non-terminal symbol S initiates stems, F produces loops, while L is used to specify if a position within the loop corresponds to an unpaired base or the initiation site of a new stem.

To determine the information content of a two-dimensional RNA fold, one can proceed in two ways. In the first case, one can assume that all shapes are equally likely, and that the entropy of the shape distribution equals $\log_2 N(n)$, where $N(n)$ is the number of different DNA shapes of length n. In the second case, one can assign probabilities to the production rules, and instead work with the *derivational entropy* [**16**]. In what follows, we briefly discuss both of these approaches.

Enumeration of RNA shapes can be performed based on the production rules only. The idea behind the approach is to determine the generating function of a context-free language by using a technique known as the *Delest-Schützenberger-Viennot (DSV)* method [**14, 17, 60**]. Through the DSV technique, a production rule is converted into an equation involving generating functions for the words of the language. The way in which this is achieved is purely automatic, and best described in terms of an example.

Consider the following production rules of a context-free language:

$$V_1 \to \epsilon; \quad V_1 \to x \cdot y \cdot V_2 \cdot x; \quad V_2 \to V_1 \cdot x \cdot x; \tag{11}$$

where V_1 and V_2 are non-terminals, while x and y are terminal symbols.

The DSV method applied to the production rules (11) can be summarized as follows.

STEP 1: Add all terms with the same non-terminal symbol on the left hand side of the production rules:

$$V_1 \to \epsilon + x \cdot y \cdot V_2 \cdot x; \qquad V_2 \to V_1 \cdot x \cdot x;$$

STEP 2: Convert all non-commutative variables, corresponding to both terminal and non-terminal symbols, into commutative variables:

$$V_1 \to \epsilon + x^2\, y\, V_2, \qquad V_2 \to x^2\, V_1;$$

STEP 3: Replace all commutative terminal variables with one variable, t, and replace all non-terminal variables with generating functions of the objects they refer to. Convert ϵ to 1 and the production rules into equations:

$$V_1(t) = 1 + t^2\, t\, V_2(t) = 1 + t^3\, V_2(t), \qquad V_2(t) = t^2\, V_1(t).$$

The specialization of terminal variables to t is performed in order to produce generating functions that enumerate sequences according to their length. For other types of generating functions, one can choose a different specialization.

STEP 4: Find the generating functions of non-terminal variables by solving the system of equations obtained in STEP 3:

$$V_1(t) = \frac{1}{1-t^5}, \qquad V_2(t) = \frac{t^2}{1-t^5}.$$

Applying the DSV approach to the production rules in (9) and (10) produces the following generating functions, respectively:

$$M \to \epsilon + \lambda \cdot M \cdot \gamma \cdot M + \delta \cdot M \;\Rightarrow M(t) = 1 + t^2\, M^2(t) + tM(t)$$
$$\Rightarrow M(t) = \frac{1 - t - \sqrt{1-2t-3t^2}}{2t^2}.$$

and

$$t^2\, S^2(t) - (t^3 - t^2 - t + 1)S(t) + t - t^3 = 0,$$
$$L(t) = \frac{S(t)}{1+S(t)}, \qquad F(t) = \frac{S^2(t)}{(1-t^2)(1+S(t))}. \tag{12}$$

DEFINITION 5.5. A generating function $T(t)$ is said to be algebraic if there exist polynomials $p_i(t)$, $i = 0, \ldots, l$, such that $\sum_{i=0}^{l} p_i(t)\, T^i(t) = 0$. The *order* of an algebraic function is the largest index i for which $p_i(t) \neq 0$.

It can be shown that the generating function of a context-free grammar is algebraic. For a special class of algebraic generating functions, one can determine the asymptotic growth rate of the number of sequences in the language in terms of the following two results.

THEOREM 5.6. *(Exponential Growth Formula) If $f(z)$ is analytic at zero and ρ is the modulus of a singularity nearest to the origin, in the sense that*

$$\rho := \sup\{r \geq 0 \mid f(z) \text{ is analytic in } |z| < r\},$$

then the coefficient $f_n = [z^n]f(z)$ satisfies

$$f_n \sim (1/\rho)^n, \tag{13}$$

where $A(n) \sim B(n)$ stands for $\lim_{n\to\infty}(A(n)/B(n)) = 1$.

For algebraic generating functions $G(t)$ of order two, an asymptotic estimate of its coefficient can also be found by first computing the discriminant $D(t)$ of the defining quadratic equation $a(t)G(t)^2 + b(t)G(t) + c(t)$, $D(t) = b(t)^2 - 4a(t)c(t)$, and then determining the smallest positive real root of the discriminant, R. Then, $[t^n]G(t) = O(R^{-n})$.

For Motzkin paths, $R = 1/3$, and the number of Motzkin paths of length n, $\mathcal{M}_n$, satisfies $\mathcal{M}_n = O(3^n)$. The exact asymptotic formula for Motzkin numbers was derived in [**7**], showing that

$$\mathcal{M}_n \sim \sqrt{3}\,3^{n+1}\,\frac{1 + 1/(16n)}{(2n+3)\sqrt{(n+2)\pi}}$$

As a consequence, the entropy of RNA folds of length n with a uniform distribution equals $H(\mathcal{M}(n)) \sim n \log 3$.

For the grammar in (10), the discriminant of the generating function $S(t)$ equals

$$t^6 + 2t^5 - t^4 - t^2 - 2t + 1,$$

and the value of its smallest positive real-values root is 0.4142. The asymptotic growth rate of the coefficients of $S(t)$ is 2.41^n.

The shapes enumerated by Motzkin paths fail to capture some intrinsic biological constraints imposed on RNA folds. Each loop is required to have length at least three, due to the *no sharp turn* constraint imposed on the backbone of RNA strands. In addition, one has to guarantee that each loop is stabilized by a sufficiently long stem.

Loops and stems in secondary structures can be identified with sub-paths in Motzkin paths. It is in this context that one can introduce the *stem-loop* constraint that allows to more accurately describe secondary structures of RNA folds.

DEFINITION 5.7. Let $\Lambda, \Upsilon, \Delta$ denote the $(1,1)$, $(1,-1)$, and $(1,0)$ steps in a Motzkin lattice path. A *maximal trapezoid* of height m and width s in a Motzkin path is a sequence of steps of the form $\Lambda^m\, \Delta^s\, \Upsilon^m$, not immediately preceded and followed by the symbols Λ and Υ, respectively.

Hairpins (consisting of a hairpin stem and hairpin loop) correspond to maximal trapezoids. The length of the hairpin stem equals the height of the pyramid, while the length of the hairpin loop equals the width of the trapezoid.

DEFINITION 5.8. An RNA sequence is said to obey a *stem-loop constraint*, if its corresponding Motzkin path has the following property. The height l_λ and width l_δ of each maximal trapezoid satisfy $\alpha \leq l_\delta \leq \beta\, l_\lambda$, for some absolute constant $\alpha > 2$ and some non-negative β that is allowed to depend on l_λ.

As an example, consider a stem-loop constraint with the following parameters. The parameter α is fixed to $\alpha = 3$, and for $3 \leq l_\lambda \leq k$, $\beta = 1$, while for $l_\lambda > k$, $\beta = k/l_\lambda$. In order to enumerate Motzkin paths obeying this stem-loop constraint, one needs to distinguish between several different subclasses of Motzkin lattice paths:

- M - the set of Motzkin paths;
- M^+ - the set of non-empty Motzkin paths.
- N - the set of non-empty non-trapezoids;
- $T_{(k)}$ - the set of non-empty maximal trapezoids of height h in $[3, k]$, and width w in $[3, h]$.
- $T^{(k)}$ - the set of non-empty maximal trapezoids of height $h > k$, and width w in the range $[3, k]$.

Motzkin paths obeying the given stem-loop constraint can be generated from the production rules described below:

$$M \to M^+ + \epsilon;$$

$$M^+ \to y \cdot M;$$

$$N \to z \cdot N \cdot \overline{z} \cdot M + T^{(k)} \cdot M^+ + T_{(k)} \cdot M^+;$$

$$T_{(k)} \to z^3 \cdot y^3 \cdot \overline{z}^3 + z^4 \cdot y^3 \cdot \overline{z}^4 + z^4 \cdot y^4 \overline{z}^4 + \dots$$
$$+ z^k \cdot y^3 \cdot \overline{z}^k + \dots + z^k \cdot y^k \cdot \overline{z}^k;$$

$$T^{(k)} \to z^{k+1} \cdot y^3 \cdot \overline{z}^{k+1} + \dots + \to z^{k+1} \cdot y^k \cdot \overline{z}^{k+1} + z \cdot T^{(k)} \cdot \overline{z};$$

These rules are to be interpreted as follows: a Motzkin path is either empty or non-empty. A non-empty Motzkin path can be obtained by inserting the symbol y in front of any other Motzkin path. A non-trapezoid can be obtained by "lifting" a non-trapezoid in terms of left and right augmentation by z and $\overline{z}$, and then appending to it an arbitrary Motzkin word. One can also form a non-trapezoid by appending to a trapezoid a non-empty Motzkin path. Finally, each trapezoid can only take a form which is not forbidden by the underlying stem-loop constraint, captured by the last two production rules. The derivations of the two-variate generating function of the described Motzkin paths can be found in [**42**].

A more accurate method for estimating the entropy of RNA folds consists in using *stochastic context-free grammars* (SCFG). A SCFG is a pair $(\mathcal{G}, P)$, where $\mathcal{G}$ is a grammar, and P is a probability function that maps each production rule into the interval $[0, 1]$. In a SCFG, it is assumed that if $p_{S\to\alpha}$ denotes a rule with the non-terminal symbol S on the left hand side, then $\sum_\alpha p_{S\to\alpha} = 1$.

DEFINITION 5.9. [**16**] Let T be the *parsing tree* of a sentence, i.e. a tree that describes the syntactic structure of a word generated by the production rules of a grammar. The probability p_T of a parsing tree T is the product of the probabilities of all production rules in the tree, counted with their multiplicities. The *derivational entropy* of the SCFG is defined as

$$H_d = -\sum_T p_T \log p_T.$$

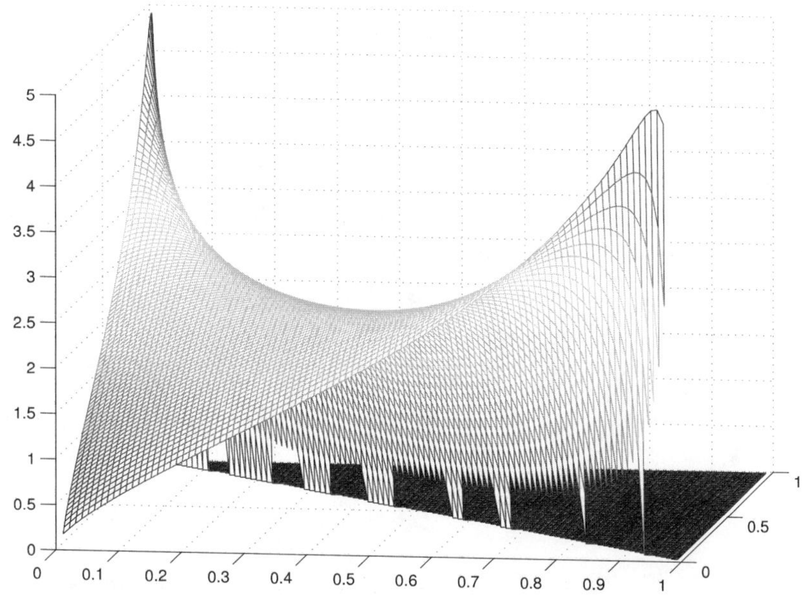

FIGURE 14. Derivational entropy of the Motzkin language.

The derivational entropy of Motzkin paths is hard to compute in the form stated in the definition above. Nevertheless, is is easy to compute a special relaxation of this notion of entropy. Assume that the production rules in (9) have probabilities $(1-p-q), p$ and q, respectively, with $0 \leq p, q \leq 1$. Since the first production rule in the Motzkin grammar corresponds to the termination rule, the probability $1-p-q$ captures the length of typical RNA folds. Similarly, the probabilities of the second and third rule are a measure of the likelihood of encountering paired and unpaired bases, respectively. For simplicity, we consider a model which assigns to each parsing tree a probability $(1-p-q)\binom{i}{l} p^l q^{i-l}$, where $i \geq 0$ denotes the number of joint occurrences of the second and third rule in 9, while $0 \leq l \leq i$ denotes the number of occurrences of the second rule [10]. In this case,

$$H_d^\star(\mathcal{M}) = -\sum_{i\geq 0}\sum_{0\leq l\leq i}(1-p-q)\binom{i}{l} p^l\, q^{i-l}\log\left((1-p-q)\binom{i}{l} p^l\, q^{i-l}\right).$$

After some straightforward algebraic manipulation, it follows that

$$H_d^\star(\mathcal{M}) = -\log(1-p-q) - \frac{(p+q)\log(p+q)}{1-p-q} + (1-p-q)\sum_{i\geq 0}(p+q)^i\, H_B^{(i)}\left(\frac{p}{p+q}, \frac{q}{p+q}\right),$$

[10]Observe that this model does not take into account that the parsing probability of an expression involving i terms depends on the particular ordering of the production rules applied. Furthermore, in a general model, the number of uses of the production rule $M \to \epsilon$ must equal $l+1$, since the second production rule introduces two non-terminal symbols.

where $H_B^{(i)}(a, 1-a)$ denotes the Shannon entropy of the binomial distribution with support size i and probability parameter a. There is no convenient closed-form expression for this entropy, although it is straightforward to show that

$$H_B^{(i)}\left(\frac{p}{p+q}, \frac{q}{p+q}\right) = \frac{1}{2}\log\left(2\,\pi\, e\,\frac{p\,q}{p+q}\right) + O\left(\frac{1}{i}\right). \tag{14}$$

The numerical values of the derivational entropy are plotted in Figure 14.

A similar analysis for the production rules in (10) is significantly more complicated. Based on a large number of training RNA folds, the probabilities of the production rules are known to equal [**33**]

$$\begin{aligned} &S \to_{0.869} L \cdot S,\ S \to_{0.131} L,\\ &F \to_{0.788} d \cdot F \cdot d,\ F \to_{0.212} L \cdot S,\\ &L \to_{0.895} d \cdot F \cdot d,\ L \to_{0.105} s. \end{aligned} \tag{15}$$

The main challenge in computing the derivational entropy of the SCFG in the above formula lies in compactly describing all parsing trees for production rules that involve more than one non-terminal symbol. This problem will be addressed elsewhere.

6. The Information Content of a Network

RNA and protein folds assume specific shapes in order to increase their stability, perform a given function, or interact with other molecules, thereby conveying important biological information. At any given time, there exist many different protein structures in one given cell, all of which interact according to a prescribed set of rules. As a consequence, the most important information processing in a cell occurs at the level of molecular interactions - or more specifically, at the level of protein-protein and regulatory network interactions.

The first network model of interaction between genes, and their underlying proteins was described in [**62, 63**], and is known as the NK model. The NK model is centered around a random, discrete-time, directed, dynamical *Boolean network*.

DEFINITION 6.1. A Boolean function $\mathcal{F}_B^K$ of K variables is a mapping with domain $\{0,1\}^K$ and range $\{0,1\}$. Similarly, a S-function $\mathcal{F}_S^K$ of K variables is a mapping with domain $\{0,1,...,S-1\}^K$ and range $\{0,1,...,S-1\}$. All operations in the Boolean domain are performed modulo two.

DEFINITION 6.2. Let $G = (V, E)$ be a directed graph with a set of vertices V and a set of edges E. Let the cardinality of the vertex set be N and let the in-degree of a vertex $v \in V$ be $\deg_v$. A Boolean network is the graph G, along with a set of Boolean functions $\mathcal{F}_{B,v}^{\deg_v}$ assigned to the vertices in V. The initial state of the Boolean network $\mathcal{S}_0$ is an assignment of binary values to the vertex set V, i.e. $V \to \{0,1\}^N$. The state of the Boolean network at time T, $\mathcal{S}_T$, is an assignment of binary values to the vertices in V obtained by applying the Boolean functions $\mathcal{F}_{B,v}^{\deg_v}$ to the values of the vertices at time $T-1$. A similar setup holds for S networks, by replacing the binary values and functions by values from the alphabet $\{0,1,...,S-1\}$ and S-functions, respectively.

In the NK model it is assumed that the N vertices in a Boolean or S network represent genes, and that the direction of an edge determines which gene influences the other. Furthermore, it is assumed that the incoming degree of each vertex in the graph is K.

If for each vertex $v \in V$ the corresponding Boolean function is chosen randomly, the model is known as a random NK model. In such Boolean networks, the state value "1" corresponds to a gene that is transcribed (i.e. that is active), while the value "0" corresponds to an inactive gene. The Boolean function itself determines when a gene will be active, based on the activity states of co-dependent genes. By starting from one initial state of gene activity, and by iteratively evaluating all Boolean functions assigned to the vertices, one obtains a time-varying set of activity values. These patterns describe when and how genes are activated or deactivated.

As an illustrative example, we refer to the mechanism of transcription regulation. As already pointed out, a promoter region of a gene is a set of bases to which transcription factors must bind in order to initiate transcription. On the other hand, there exist enzymes which bind to the promoter region so as to prevent the RNA-based transcription process from taking place. If such an enzyme, which is a protein, is generated by transcription of a gene indexed by the vertex v, and it deactivates the gene indexed by the vertex w, then the Boolean model has to take into account that $S_v = 1$ at time T enforces $S_w = 0$ at time $T + 1$. Clearly, transcription levels (also known as expression levels) are not binary valued, since a gene my be transcribed very often or very rarely in a given time period. This is why the S model is frequently used instead of the Boolean network model. Nevertheless, we focus our attention on the latter class of models. A set of time-dependent expression level patterns for four genes involved in regulating the process of cell replication is shown in Figure 15. Here, the threshold is used to distinguish between active and inactive genes.

An important observation is that the scope of gene interaction is limited: the activity of a gene depends only on the activity of a *small subset* of "control" and "co-expressed" genes.

The NK model can be analyzed with tools from non-linear dynamics and classical probability theory, including random walks and Brownian bridges techniques [**35**]. This analysis produced some interesting insight into various phenomena such as cell differentiation and evolutionary changes of the fitness of biosystems.

For example, it is well known that different cell types have exactly the same set of genes, which leads to the following question: how is it possible for cells to appear in forms as diverse as skin cells, blood cells, or nerve cells?

An answer to this question can be provided by the NK model. A Boolean network with parameters N and K has a finite number of 2^N possible state sequences, so that after a certain number of iterations the initial sequence transforms itself into a stable sequence that does not change any further (a *point attractor*), or starts transforming itself periodically through a small set of sequences (a *periodic attractor*). Networks with small values of the parameter K are known to closely approximate the high degree of dynamical order that exists in living organisms. In such a scenario, most genes settle into "frozen states", while others repeat short periodic activities. In the language of chaos theory, a sequence of genes is trapped "at the edge of chaos" [**22**], [**29**], and such type of order is omnipresent in nature [**66**]. In biological systems, and for each cell structure, different genes are switched

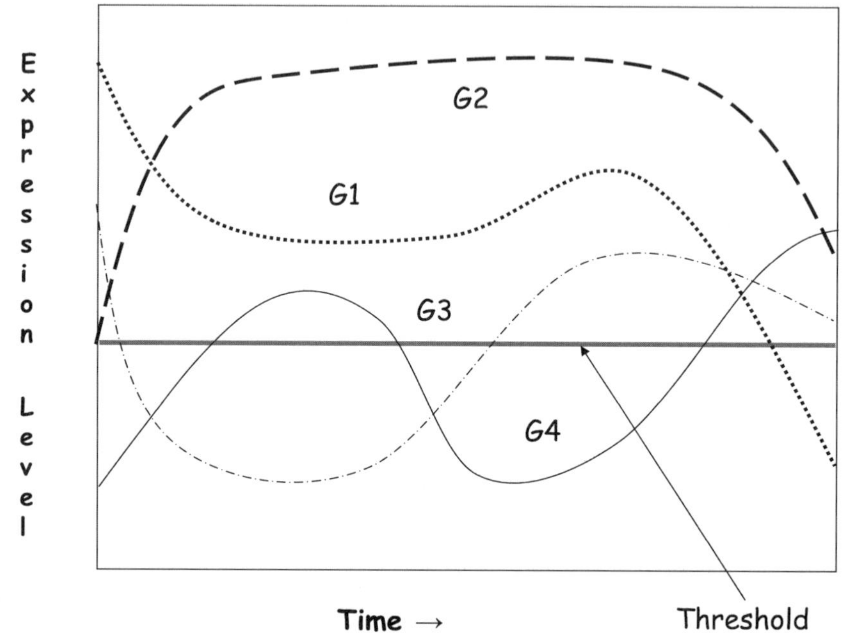

FIGURE 15. Expression levels, measured in terms of rate of transcription, for four genes.

on or off in a timely manner, forming one of the possible stable attractor configurations. For an estimated number of 25000 genes in the human genome, there are about 244 different attractors and roughly 260 different cell types.

Although Boolean network models represent coarse simplifications of genetic networks, it is straightforward to extend the underlying concepts to non-binary systems, corresponding to quantized gene expressions [**30, 63**]. Both binary and non-binary Boolean networks are closely related to well-studied objects in information and coding theory known as factor graphs and cellular automata[11]. Gene expression regulation can be seen as a form of message (information) passing through the gene regulatory (GR) Boolean network, and the network topology and Boolean function represent important biological information.

6.1. Information Passing in GR Networks. The techniques used for analyzing GR networks and related Boolean networks are largely taken from the theory of *discrete dynamical systems* [**61**]. Very often, the term dynamical system is reserved for entities governed by differential equations, but we use it to describe the most general class of systems with time-varying characteristics.

In the context of GR networks, the set V can be used to represent genes or other functional DNA subregions. The Boolean functions describe the activity state of a gene G, based on the activities of the genes for which a directed edge towards G exists. One such graph with $N = 3$ and $K = 2$ is shown in Figure 16

[11]Compared to cellular automata, Boolean networks exhibit more degrees of uncertainty. For example, cellular automata usually have deterministic topology (defined in terms of Von Neumann, Moore neighborhoods), and/or unique updating rules.

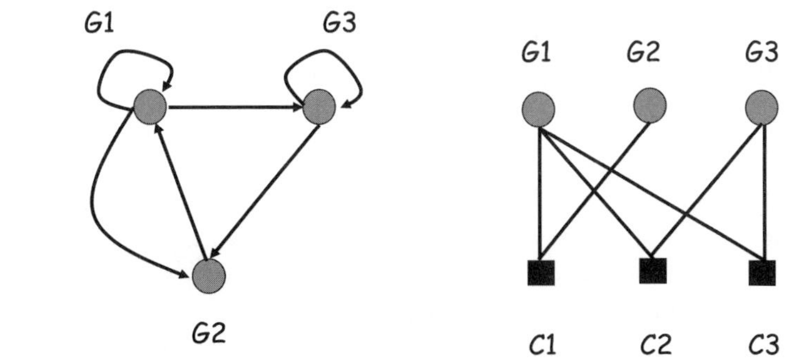

FIGURE 16. A gene interaction network and its control graph.

a). A Boolean network can also be defined in terms of state transition tables, describing the dynamics of the system. The state transition table for the network in Figure 16a), for one possible choice of Boolean functions, is shown below.

$$\mathcal{F}^2_{B,G_1} = \overline{G_1}\, G_2;$$
$$\mathcal{F}^2_{B,G_2} = G_1\, G_3;$$
$$\mathcal{F}^2_{B,G_3} = \overline{G_1}\;\overline{G_3} + G_1\, G_3 + \overline{G_1}\, G_3;$$

T	**T+1**
$G_1\, G_2\, G_3$	$G_1\, G_2\, G_3$
0 0 0	0 0 1
0 0 1	0 0 1
0 1 0	1 0 1
0 1 1	1 0 1
1 0 0	0 0 0
1 0 1	0 1 1
1 1 0	0 0 0
1 1 1	0 1 1

The eight states of the network can be separated into two sets of states. State 1 0 0 leads to the state 0 0 1 via the state 0 0 0. Once this state is reached, the network remains in it during all future time instances. As a consequence, this network state is a point attractor. The states 1 0 1 and 0 1 1 in the above example represent a periodic attractor. All other states belong to the *basin of attraction* of one of these two attractors, i.e. they transform themselves after a certain number of steps into one of the two attractors.

In a GR network, each attractor corresponds to one function performed by the cell. Similarly to the problem of estimating the information content of a shape, one can pose the problem of estimating the information content of a Boolean network. The most straightforward way to accomplish this task is as follows.

DEFINITION 6.3. Assume that all attractor states in a Boolean network are equally likely, and that their number equals A. Then the entropy of the Boolean network is defined as $\log A$. Similarly, if according to some probabilistic distribution on the initial state of the networks one can assign probabilities p_i to the attractors $\mathcal{A} = \{a_j\}_{i=1}^{A}$, then the Shannon entropy of the network is defined as $-\sum_{i=1}^{A} p_i \log p_i$.

EXAMPLE 6.4. There exist two attractors in the network of example (16). One is the point attractor 0 0 0, and the other is the periodic attractor of the states 0 1 1 and 1 1 1. According to the definition above, the entropy of the Boolean network equals log 2 = 1 bit. On the other hand, one can also assume that the initial state S of the Boolean network equals 0 0 0, or 1 1 0, or 1 1 1, with probability 1/3. Then the point attractor has probability 2/3, since both states 0 0 0 and 1 1 0 are in its basin of attraction. Similarly, the probability of the periodic attractor equals 1/3. As a consequence, the entropy of the Boolean network is $H(1/3)$, where H denotes Shannon's binary entropy.

The number of attractors of a random Boolean network with N vertices can be shown to be of the order of $\sqrt{N}$ [**29, 30, 31**]. Consequently, the entropy of the network equals $(1/2)\log N$.

In our subsequent analysis, we focus on describing efficient methods for finding the number of attractors of a Boolean network. These methods have their origin in dynamical systems theory [**67**], statistical physics [**51**], and iterative coding theory [**20**]. We note that the problem of characterizing attractors in a network is, in general, a very challenging task.

One can describe the genetic interaction graph in terms of a bipartite graph with the same cardinality of left and right vertices. In such a graph, the nodes on the left hand side represent genes, while nodes on the right hand side represent *controls* for the gene. The genes connected to control node C_i are those that exhibit an influence on the operation of gene G_i. The *control* bipartite graph of Figure 16 a) is shown in Figure 16 b). The incoming degrees of control nodes may differ, and henceforth it will be assumed that C_i has degree d_i. In this case, $K = \sum d_i/N$ denotes the average number of inputs of a GRN Boolean function.

DEFINITION 6.5. A canalizing Boolean function is a binary function in which a single input, in one of its states 0 or 1, determines the output of the function, irrespective of the value of the other inputs. A Boolean function is biased if the fraction p of ones that it generates exceeds 1/2. The function is unbiased if $p = 1/2$.

Several properties of GR networks can be seen to influence its number of attractors and operational characteristics:

- The number and probabilities of the initial state of the graph;
- The average connectivity of the graph, K; and
- The Boolean functions canalizing properties and their bias p.

The influence of each of these parameters on the properties of the networks is described in more detail in [**6**]. In general, the larger the average connectivity, and, the larger the bias, the larger the number of attractors of the network. The bias determines the *critical connectivity* of the graph, which represents the value of K for which a phase transition occurs in the number of attractors of a random network.

For the purpose of analyzing Boolean networks, specialized discrete dynamical systems methods were developed in [**4, 8**]. The most important such results pertain to the possible structures of network attractors, and are briefly described below.

Boolean Derivatives and Jacobians: For a Boolean function, $\mathcal{F}_B^k$, of k binary variables $x_1, x_2, ..., x_k$, the derivative with respect to x_i is defined as

(16)
$$\mathcal{F}_B^{k,(i)} = \frac{\partial \mathcal{F}_B^k}{\partial x_i} = \mathcal{F}_B^k(x_1, ..., x_{i-1}, 0, x_{i+1}, ..., x_k) + \mathcal{F}_B^k(x_1, ..., x_{i-1}, 1, x_{i+1}, ..., x_k).$$

For a given set of not necessarily distinct Boolean functions $\mathcal{F}_{j,B}^{k_j}, j = 1, ..., N$, assigned to the control nodes of the bipartite regulatory graph, the Boolean Jacobian $\mathbf{J}$ is a $N \times N$ matrix for which the entry indexed by (i,j) equals $\mathcal{F}_{i,B}^{k_i,(j)}, i = 1, ..., N$. The Boolean Jacobian is a time-evolving zero-one matrix with entries depending on the current state of the network. For Jacobian matrices one can develop an analogue of the Perron-Frobenius and mean-field theory from statistical mechanics [**51**].

The Perron-Frobenius theory specifies when a point in the state space is an attractor of all points at Hamming distance one from it. The necessary and sufficient conditions for this claim to hold true are that J has at most one "1" in each column; and, that there exists an integer $0 < m \leq N$ such that $J^m = \mathbf{0}$, where $\mathbf{0}$ denotes the all-zero matrix.

If an attractor of a network is known, its basin of attraction can be determined by adding random perturbations to it. If the perturbation vanishes in the limit as time goes to infinity, then the perturbed vector lies in the basin of attraction of the attractor. A formal description of this approach is described below.

DEFINITION 6.6. Let $X(T)$ be the state of a Boolean network at time T. A perturbed state vector $Y(T)$ of $X(T)$ at time T is any vector at non-zero Hamming distance from $X(T)$. The perturbation is defined as the modulo-two sum of $X(T)$ and $Y(T)$.

DEFINITION 6.7. The iterative Jacobian product $IJ(T)$ is a matrix defined as

$$IJ(T) = J(O) \otimes J(1) \otimes \ldots \otimes J(T),$$

where it is assumed that the network state is updated at the discrete time intervals kT, $k = 1, 3, \ldots$.

The iterative Jacobian captures the dynamics of the transformation of a perturbed state $Y(T)$ back to $X(T)$, or its transformation into another attractor. Sparse Jacobian matrices at different time intervals lead, under certain conditions, to an all-zero iterative Jacobian matrix. In this case, the initial perturbation vanishes, and the perturbed state belongs to the basin of attraction of state $X(T)$.

The rate with which the transformation of a perturbed state occurs is measured by the *Lyapunov exponent* of the Boolean network. This exponent is also a measure of the degree of instability of an attractor, and the Boolean network as a whole.

DEFINITION 6.8. The maximal Lyapunov exponent of a Jacobian is defined as:

$$\ell(T) = \frac{1}{t} \sum_{T \leq t} \log \eta(T), \tag{17}$$

where $\eta(T) = |IJ(T+1)|/(IJ(T)|$, and $|M|$ is used to denote the matrix norm of a $N \times N$ matrix M, $|M| = 1/N^2 \sum_{i,j} M_{i,j}$.

Different vertices (genes) in a Boolean network exhibit different influence on the speed of transition from perturbed states to stable attractors. The notion of *influence* can be formally defined as follows.

DEFINITION 6.9. The influence of variable x_i on Boolean function $f(x_1, \ldots, x_n)$ is the expectation of the partial derivative of f with respect to the joint distribution of its variables, i.e.,

$$I_i(f) = E\left[\frac{\partial f(x_1,\ldots,x_n)}{\partial x_i}\right] = P\{\frac{\partial f(x_1,\ldots,x_n)}{\partial x_i} = 1\}.$$

If the values of vertices with large influence are changed, the attractor is very likely to transform into a point in the state space that belongs to the basin of attraction of another attractor. This leads to a simple method for probing the state space for possible attractors.

The behavior of Boolean networks, regarding phase transitions and limiting properties can also be analyzed by using classical results from statistical mechanics. As an example, the *mean-field theory* allows one to replace Jacobian matrices at any given time by randomly chosen matrices with the same number of non-zero entries. This study is beyond the scope of this exposition, but the interested reader is referred to [**51**] for more details regarding the theory of mean-fields.

We conclude this exposition by describing a method for analyzing attractors in Boolean networks in terms of *factor graphs.*

6.2. Factor Graphs as Boolean Networks. As described above, there exist well developed mathematical methods for analyzing random Boolean networks and GR networks. Nevertheless, many of these techniques are very hard to apply to Boolean network models corresponding to measured GR network data. This is due to the fact that GR networks exhibit correlation patterns in their corresponding Boolean functions that *cannot* be considered random-like. Furthermore, the graph of GRNs is also non-random in nature, due to many biological constraints, one of which imposes some proximity constraints on interacting genes.

This suggests considering an alternative approach to dynamical network analysis. This alternative is based on the idea that codes on graphs, along with a given decoding algorithm, represent instances of Boolean or S-networks. Hence, analytic techniques from coding theory, such as Density Evolution (DE) or Extrinsic Information Chart (EXIT Chart) analysis [**53, 54**] can be used to provide more insight into the operation of both random and non-random GR networks. A detailed description of these techniques can be found in [**45**].

To highlight the connection between Boolean networks and factor graphs, let us first define the class of low-density parity-check (LDPC) codes. LDPC codes are bipartite graphs with n left hand side nodes and $n-k$ right hand side nodes, where $k \leq n$, and with a number of edges significantly smaller than $k(n-k)$. An LDPC code is said to be *regular* if all vertices on the left hand side have the same degree, and a similar property holds true for nodes on the right hand side. LDPC codes are special instances of the more general class of *factor graphs* [**53, 54**]. Factor graphs are systems used for describing local co-dependencies between random variables.

Let $\mathcal{L}$ be a regular LDPC code, and let d_v and d_c denote the degrees of the variable and check nodes of the bipartite code graph, respectively. For demonstrative purpose, a very simple example of a regular $(d_v = 2, d_c = 2)$ graph with four nodes both on the left hand and right hand side is shown in Figure 17 a). Such a graph clearly does not represent a practically useful LDPC code, but the examples to follow can be generalized for any type of regular or irregular, structured or random-like LDPC code with positive rate k/n.

For simplicity, assume that an LDPC code is used in conjunction with Gallager's Decoding Algorithm A [**20**]. In the *classical version* of the A algorithm, parity check

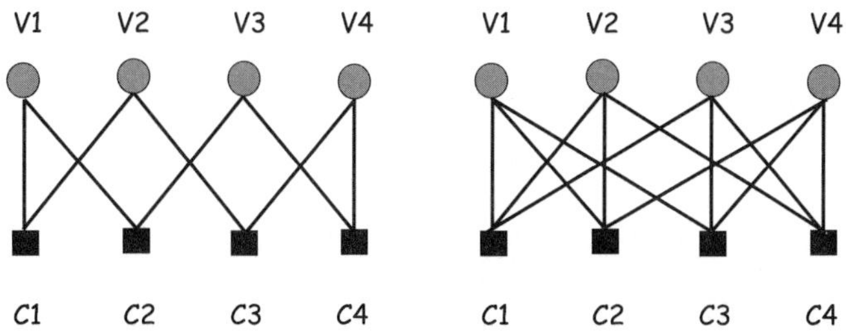

FIGURE 17. An LDPC code graph its control node representation.

nodes send a message to a variable node indicating the modulo-two sum of other neighboring variable nodes. The variable nodes send their received value unless the incoming messages are unanimous, in which case the unique value suggested by the incoming messages is sent. In the *flip version* of the algorithm, the variables flip their values when the incoming messages are unanimous in their decision (which differs from the current value of the variable).

From the exposition above, it is apparent that the LDPC decoding operations can be described by Boolean functions at the control nodes of the equivalent control graph. Observe that in such a setting, the control node C_i for variable G_i has as its input all variable nodes at distance exactly two from node G_i. Additionally, the control graph is symmetric in the sense that if variable i influences variable j, then variable j influences variable i as well. The LDPC code graph shown in Figure 17 a) can be transformed into a control bipartite graph, as shown in Figure 17 b).

THEOREM 6.10. *If the LDPC graph of a code is regular and if it contains no cycles of length four, then all Boolean control functions for both versions of Gallager's decoding algorithm A are identical, unbiased and non-canalizing. The generic Boolean function has the form:*

(18)

$$G_i^v\Big(\sum_{l_1 \in \mathcal{N}(G_i)} G_{l_1} + \sum_{l_1 \neq l_2 \in \mathcal{N}(G_i)} G_{l_1} G_{l_2} + \ldots + \sum_{l_1 \neq l_2 \neq \ldots \neq l_{d_c-1} \in \mathcal{N}(G_i)} G_{l_1} G_{l_2} \ldots G l_{d_c-1} \Big) + \prod_j \left(\sum_{l \in \, \phi_j(G_i)/G_i} G_l \right),$$

where $\mathcal{N}(G_i)$ denotes the two-neighborhood of the variable G_i (i.e. all variable nodes at distance two from G_i in the code graph, excluding G_i), $\phi_j(G_i)$ denotes the indices of the variables G_l involved in the j-th check equation of G_i; furthermore, $G_i^v = G_i(0)$ is the channel output for the classical version of the A algorithm, while $G_i^v = G_i$ holds for the flip version of the algorithm. If, on the other hand, the LDPC code is irregular and/or has cycles of length four, then the Boolean functions have different, but non-biased, forms.

For the LDPC code shown in Figure 17, the Boolean function for the variable G_1 are of the form:

$$\mathcal{F}_B^2 = \begin{cases} G_1G_2 + G_1G_3 + G_2G_3, & \text{(flip)} \\ G_1(0)\, G_2 + G_1(0)\, G_3 + G_2G_3, & \text{(classical)} \end{cases} \tag{19}$$

The corresponding Jacobian matrix for the flip version of the A algorithm is

$$J = \begin{pmatrix} G_2+G_3 & G_1+G_3 & G_1+G_2 & 0 \\ G_2+G_4 & G_1+G_4 & 0 & G_1+G_2 \\ G_3+G_4 & 0 & G_1+G_4 & G_1+G_3 \\ 0 & G_3+G_4 & G_2+G_4 & G_2+G_3 \end{pmatrix}$$

Based on the Jacobian matrix J one can determine the attractors of the network, their basins of attraction, the attractors periods etc, as described in the previous section.

The results described in this section imply that Boolean networks and LDPC codes are closely related entities. In this setting, gene regulation can be seen as one form of message (information) passing on a genetic graph. There exist many methods for analyzing the attractor landscape of LDPC codes[12] and the phase transitions of iterative message passing decoders. All of these schemes can be adapted for Boolean networks, and a sampling of ideas regarding this problem can be found in the more recent work [**45**].

7. Conclusion

We described the physical mechanisms of genetic data storage, and provided three new measure of the information content of a genetic data. We also described how ideas from information and coding theory can be used for the purpose of data compression, secondary RNA structure enumeration, and analysis of Boolean networks.

Acknowledgment: The author is grateful to her students, Stefan Laendner, Shashi Chilappagari, James Hartley, and Lloyd Rochester for generating some of the examples presented in the manuscript. The author also gratefully acknowledges several discussions with Dr. Bane Vasic.

References

[1] G. Abramson, H. Cerdeira, and C. Bruschi, "Fractal properties of DNA walks," *BioSystems*, vol. 49, no. 1, pp. 63–70, 1999.

[2] D. Adjeroh and F. Nan, "On compressibility of protein sequences," *Proceedings of the Data Compression Conference (DCC)*, pp. 422–434, 2006.

[3] D. Adjeroh, Y. Zhang, A. Mukherjee, and M. Powell, "DNA sequence compression using the Burrows-Wheeler transform," *Proceedings of the IEE Computer Society Bioinformatics Conference*, p. 303, 2002.

[4] T. Akutsu, S. Miyano, and S. Kuhara, "Algorithms for inferring qualitative models of biological networks," *Pacic Symposium on Biocomputing*, vol. 5, pp. 290–301, 2000.

[5] R. Astudillo, "On a class of Thue-Morse type sequences," *Journal of Integer Sequences*, vol. 6, pp. 1-11, 2003.

[6] F. Bagnoli, R. Rechtman, and S. Ruffo, "Damage spreading and Lyapunov exponents in cellular automata," *Physics Letters A*, vol. 172, no. 34, pp. 34-38, 1992.

[7] E. Barcucci, "From Motzkin to Catalan permutations," *Discr. Math.*, vol. 217, pp. 33–49, 2000.

[8] U. Bastola and G. Parisi, "Closing probabilities in the Kauffman model: An annealed computation," *Physica A*, vol. 98, pp. 1–25, 1996.

[9] R. Bundschuh and T. Hwa, "Statistical mechanics of secondary structures formed by random RNA sequences," *Physical Review Letter E*, vol. 65, (031903), 2002.

---

[12]Attractors in LDPC codes correspond to codewords and trapping sets [**53**]. Trapping sets can be identified by the *impulse method* and other related techniques [**54**].

[10] A. R. Calderbank, I. Daubechies, W. Sweldens, and B.-L. Yeo, "Wavelet transforms that map integers to integers," *J. Appl. Comput. Harmonic Anal.*, vol. 5, no. 3, pp. 332-369, 1997.

[11] T. Chen, H. He, and G. Church, "Modeling gene expression with differential equations," *Pacific Symp. Biocomp.*, vol. 99, no. 4, pp. 29–40, 1999.

[12] X. Chen, S. Kwong, and M. Li, "A compression algorithm for DNA sequences and its applications in genome comparison," *Genome Informatics*, vol. 10, pp. 51–61, 1999.

[13] N. Cherniavsky and R. Ladner, "Grammar-based compression of DNA sequences,", UW CSE Technical Report 2007-05-02.

[14] N. Chomsky, *Syntactic structures*, The Hague, Mouton, 1965.

[15] A. Condon, B. Davy, and F. Tarrant, "Classifying RNA pseudoknotted structures," *Theoretical Comp. Science*, vol. 320, pp. 35-50, 2004.

[16] A. Corazza and G. Satta, "Cross-entropy and estimation of probabilistic context-free grammars," *Proceedings of the Human Language Technology Conference of the North American Chapter of the ACL*, pp. 335–342, New York, 2006.

[17] M. Delest, "Algebraic languages: a bridge between combinatorics and computer science," *DIMACS Series in Discrete Mathematics and Theoretical Computer Science*, vol. 24, pp. 71–88, 1996.

[18] M. Duc, C. Trevor, I. Dix, L. Allison, and C. Mears, "A simple statistical algorithm for biological sequence compression," *Proceedings of the Data Compression Conference (DCC)*, pp. 43–52, 2007.

[19] M. Eisen, P. Spellman, P. Brown, D. Botstein, "Cluster analysis and display of genome-wide expression patterns," *Proc. Natl. Acad. Sci. USA* 95, pp. 14863–14868, 1998.

[20] R. Gallager, *Low-density parity-check codes*, MIT Press, Cambridge MA, 1963.

[21] W. Gibbs, "The unseen genome: gems among the junk," *Scientific American*, vol. 289, no. 5, pp. 46–53, 2003.

[22] Y. Gao and J. Culberson, "An analysis of phase transition in NK landscapes," *Journal of Artificial Intelligence Research*, vol. 17, pp. 309–332, 2002.

[23] L. Gransson and T. Koski, "Using a dynamic Bayesian network to learn genetic interactions," *Technical report*, Graduate School of Biomedical Research and Department of Mathemathics, Linkping University, 2001.

[24] S. Grumbach and F. Tahi, "A new challenge for compression algorithms: genetic sequences," *Information Processing and Management*, vol. 30, pp. 875–886, 1994.

[25] E. Hartuv, A. Schmitt, J. Lange, S. Meier-Ewert, H. Lehrach, and R. Shamir, "An algorithm for clustering cDNAs for gene expression analysis," *Proceedings of the International Conference on Research in Computational Molecular Biology (RECOMB) 99*, pp. 188–197, 1999.

[26] A. Hategan and I. Tabus, "Protein is compressible," *Proceedings of the 6th Nordic Signal Processing Symposium (NORSIG) 2004*, Espoo, Finland, pp. 192–195, 2004.

[27] J. Hopfield, "Kinetic proofreading: A new mechanism for reducing errors in biosynthetic processes requiring high specifity," *Proceedings of the National Academy of Science*, vol. 71, no. 10, pp. 4135–4139, 1974.

[28] J. Hopfield, "The energy relay: a proofreading scheme based on dynamic cooperativity and lacking all characteristics of kinetic proofreading in DNA replication and protein synthesis," in *Proceedings of the National Academy of Science*, vol. 77. no. 9, pp. 5248–5252, 1980.

[29] S. Kauffman, "Adaptation on rugged fitness landscapes," in *Lectures in the Science of Complexity, SFI Studies in the Science of Complexity*, Lecture Volume I, ed. D. Stein, Addison-Wesley, Redwood City, pp. 527–618, 1989.

[30] S. Kaufman, *The origins of order: Self-organization and selection in evolution*, Oxford University Press, Oxford 1993.

[31] S. Kauffman and S. Levin, "Towards a general theory of adaptive walks on rugged landscapes," *Journal of Theoretical Biology*, vol. 128, pp. 11–45, 1987.

[32] L. E. Kay, *Who wrote the book of life?: Information and the transformation of molecular biology*, Science in Context 8, vol. 4, pp. 601–634, 1998.

[33] B. Knudsen and J. J. Hein, "Using stochastic context-free grammars and molecular evolution to predict RNA secondary structure," *Bioinformatics*, vol. 15, no. 5, pp. 446–454, 1999.

[34] Y. Kobayashi and N. Saiyo, "Secondary structure prediction based on statistical mechanics," *Genome Informatics*, vol. 9, pp. 344–346, 1998.
[35] V. Limic, and R. Pemantle, "More rigorous results on the Kauffman-Levin model of evolution," *Annals of Probability*, vol. 32, no. 3, pp. 2149–2178, 2004.
[36] A. Lindenmayer, "Mathematical models for cellular interaction in development: Filaments with one-sided inputs," *Journal of Theoretical Biology*, vol. 18, pp. 280–289, 1968.
[37] S. Linn, R. Stephen-Lloyd, R. Roberts, *Nucleases*, Cold Spring Harbor Laboratory Press, 1993.
[38] D. MacKay, *Information Theory, inference and learning algorithms*, Cambridge University Press, 2003.
[39] F. MacWilliams and N. Sloane, *The theory of error-correcting codes*, North-Holland Publishing Company, Amsterdam, 1977.
[40] G. Maroni, "Molecular and genetic analysis of human traits," *Blackwell Science*, 2001.
[41] H. McAdams and A. Arkin, "Stochastic mechanisms in gene expression," *Proc. Natl. Acad. Sci. USA* 94, pp. 814–819, 1997.
[42] O. Milenkovic, "Constrained coding via context-free grammars with applications to RNA sequence analysis," *Proceedings of the International Symposium on Information Theory (ISIT) 2007*, Nice, France, pp. 1686–1691, 2007.
[43] O. Milenkovic, *The three faces of DNA/RNA sequence hybridization*, *Bioinformatics: An Engineering Case-Based Approach*, Artech House, pp. 285–313, 2007.
[44] O. Milenkovic and B. Vasic, "On the information processing mechanism of DNA and efficient DNA storage," *DIMACS Workgroup on Theoretical Advances in Information Recording*, New Brunswick, NJ, Mar. 2004.
[45] O. Milenkovic and B. Vasic, "Information theoretic problems in genetics," in *Proceedings of the Information Theory Workshop (ITW) 2004*, San Antonio, TX, pp. 60–65, Sept. 2004.
[46] R. Mukhopadhyay, E. Emberly, C. Tang, and N. Wingreen, "Statistical mechanics of RNA folding," *Physical Review E*, vol. 68, (041904), 2003.
[47] C. Nevill-Manning and I. Witten, "Protein is incompressible," *Proceedings of the Data Compression Conference (DCC) 1999*, Los Alamitos, CA, pp. 257–266, 1999.
[48] G. Ochoa, "On genetic algorithms and Lindenmayer systems," *Lecture Notes in Computer Science*, vol. 1498, *Proceedings of the 5th International Conference on Parallel Problem Solving from Nature*, pp. 335–344, 1998.
[49] C. Oosawa and M. Savageau, "Statistical properties of randomly constructed Boolean networks that resemble the transcription factor network of Escherichia Coli", *Genome Informatics*, vol. 13, pp. 375–376, 2002.
[50] H. Orland, "DNA, RNA, and protein folding," *AAPPS Bulletin*, vol. 13, no. 2, pp. 19–21, Apr. 2003.
[51] G. Parisi, *Statistical field theory*, Addison-Wesley, Reading, MA, 1988.
[52] C. Peng, S. Buldyrev, A. Goldberg, S. Havlin, F. Sciortino, M. Simons, and H. Stanley, "Long-range correlations in nucleotide sequences," *Nature*, vol. 356, p. 168, 1992.
[53] T. Richardson, A. Shokrollahi, and R. Urbanke, "Design of capacity-approaching irregular low-density parity-check codes," *IEEE Trans. Inform. Theory*, vol. 47, no. 2, pp. 619–638, Feb. 2001.
[54] T. Richardson and R. Urbanke, "The capacity of low-density parity-check codes under message-passing decoding," *IEEE Trans. on Inform. Theory*, vol. 47, no. 2, pp. 599–618, Feb. 2001.
[55] R. Rigatti, J-H. Jia, N. J. Samani, and I. C. Eperon, "Exon repetition: a major pathway for processing mRNA of some genes is allele-specific," *Nucleic Acids Res.*, vol. 32, no. 2, pp. 441–446, Jan. 2004.
[56] J. Robinson, P. J. Robinson, A. Gupta, A. J. Bleasby, B. A. Whitton, and A. P. Morby, "Singular over-representation of an octameric palindrome, HIP1, in DNA from many cyanobacteria," *Nucleic Acid Research*, vol. 23, no. 5, pp. 729–735, 1995.
[57] S. Sarkar, *Biological information: A skeptical look at some central dogmas of molecular biology*, in *The Philosophy and History of Molecular Biology: New Perspectives*, edited by S. Sarkar, Dordrecht, The Netherlands, *Boston Studies in the Philosophy of Science*, pp. 199–202, 1996.

[58] M. Savageau, "Rules for the evolution of gene circuitry," *Pacific Symp. Biocomp.* vol. 98, no. 3, pp. 55–65, 1998.

[59] K. Sayood, *Introduction to data compression*, Morgan Kaufmann, 2000.

[60] M. P. Schützenberger, "Context-free language and pushdown automata," *Information and Control*, vol. 6, pp. 246–264, 1963.

[61] M. Schroeder, *Fractals, chaos, power Laws,* W.H. Freeman and Company, New York 1997.

[62] I. Shmulevich, E. Dougherty, and W. Zhang, "From Boolean to probabilistic Boolean networks as models of genetic regulatory networks," *Proceedings of the IEEE*, vol. 90, no. 11, pp. 1778–1792, 2002.

[63] I. Shmulevich, E. Dougherty, S. Kim, and W. Zhang, "Probabilistic Boolean networks: a rule-based uncertainty model for gene regulatory networks," *Bioinformatics*, vol. 18, pp. 261–274, 2002.

[64] S. Sivashankari and P. Shanmughavel, "Comparative genomics - a perspective," *Bioinformation*, vol. 1, no. 9, pp. 376–378, 2007.

[65] R. Sokal and C. Michener, "A statistical method for evaluating systematic relationships," *Univ. Kansas Sci. Bull.*, vol. 38, pp. 1409–1438, 1958.

[66] R. Sole and B. Goodwin, *Signs of life, or how complexity prevails biology*, Basic Books, 2000.

[67] S. Strogatz *Nonlinear dyanmics and chaos, with applications to physics, biology and engineering*, Westview, 2000.

[68] N. Sourlas, "Spin-glass models as error-correcting codes," *Nature*, vol. 339, p. 693, 1989.

[69] T. Strachan and A. Read, *Human molecular genetics 2*, Garland Science, 2006.

[70] I. Tabus, G. Korodi, and J. Rissanen, "DNA sequence compression using the normalized maximum likelihood model for discrete regression," *Proceedings of Data Compression Conference (DCC) 2003*, pp. 253–262, 2003.

[71] P. Tamayo, D. Slonim, J. Mesirov, Q. Zhu, S. Kitareewan, E. Dmitrovsky, E. Lander, and T. Golub, "Interpreting patterns of gene expression with self-organizing maps: methods and application to hematopoietic differentiation," *Proc. Natl. Acad. Sci. USA*, vol. 96, pp. 2907–2912, 1999.

[72] H. Tanaka, D. Bergstrom, M-C. Yao, S. Tapscott, "DNA palindromes as a common form of structural chromosome aberrations in human cancers," *23rd Annual Meeting of the Japan Human Cell Society*, Tsukuba, Japan, Aug. 2005.

[73] D. Thieffry and R. Thomas, "Qualitative analysis of gene networks," *Pacific Symp. Biocomp.* 98, 3, pp. 77–88, 1998.

[74] P. Toronen, M. Kolehmainen, G. Wong, and E. Castren, "Analysis of gene expression data using self-organizing maps," FEBS L. 451, pp. 142–146, 1999.

[75] J. Tsang, "Gene expression, DNA arrays, and genetic networks," *unpublished manuscript*, 1999, available at http://monod.uwaterloo.ca/papers.

[76] M. Zuker, "The use of dynamic programming algorithms in RNA secondary structure prediction," *Mathematical Methods for DNA Sequences*, Edited by M. S. Waterman, CRC Press, Inc., pp. 159–184, 1989.

[77] A. Wagner, "Evolution of gene networks by gene duplications: a mathematical model and its implications on genome organization," *Proc. Natl. Acad. Sci. USA* 91, pp. 4387–4391, 1994.

[78] L. Wessels, E. van Someren, and M. Reinders, "A comparison of genetic network models," *Pac. Symp. on Biocomputing*, vol. 6, pp. 508–519, 2001.

[79] M. S. Waterman, "Combinatorics of RNA hairpins and cloverleaves," *Studies in Applied Mathematics*, vol. 1, pp. 91–96, 1978.

[80] L. Z. Yu, C. Birky, and R. Adam, "The two nuclei of giardia each have complete copies of the genome and are partitioned equationally at cytokinesis," *Eukaryotic Cell*, vol. 1, no. 2, pp. 191–199, 2002.

[81] L. Zhang, D. Yuan, S. Yu, Z. Li, Y. Cao, Z. Miao, H. Qian, and K. Tang, "Preference of simple sequence repeats in coding and non-coding regions of Arabidopsis thaliana," *Bioinformatics*, vol. 20, no. 7, pp. 1081–1086, 2004.

[82] J. Ziv and A. Lempel, "A universal algorithm for data compression," *IEEE Trans. on Inform. Theory*, vol. 23, no. 3, pp. 337-343, 1977.

[83] X. Zhou, X. Wang, E. R. Dougherty, "Construction of genomic networks using mutual-information clustering and reversible-jump MCMC predictor design," *Signal Processing*, vol. 83, no. 4, pp. 745–761, 2003.

DEPARTMENT OF ELECTRICAL AND COMPUTER ENGINEERING, UNIVERSITY OF COLORADO, BOULDER, COLORADO 92103

Current address: Center for Information Theory and Applications, University of California, San Diego, California, La Jolla 92103

E-mail address: milenkov@colorado.edu

DIMACS Series in Discrete Mathematics
and Theoretical Computer Science
Volume **73**, 2008

Ghostbusting: Coding for Optical Communications

Navin Kashyap and Paul H. Siegel

ABSTRACT. This paper is meant to be an introduction to the problem of combating the effect of spurious "ghost" pulses that arise due to a nonlinear phenomenon known as intrachannel four-wave mixing in the context of high bit-rate, long-haul optical communications. We share our understanding of this highly complex phenomenon, and survey some of the existing techniques in the literature that are designed to tackle this problem. We build a framework for a systematic approach to designing coding and phase modulation schemes for ghost pulse suppression, and show how techniques from the theory of constrained coding can be applied to design and analyze codes developed within this framework.

1. Introduction

What, you may well ask, is an article on coding techniques for optical communications doing in a volume focusing on the theoretical advances in information recording? The response we offer is that the optical fiber channel and the information recording channel share certain problems which require the use of common tools for solution. In this article, we explore the applicability of constrained coding techniques, which are commonly used in the magnetic and optical recording channels, to solve inter-symbol interference (ISI) problems arising in the very high bit-rate, long-haul optical fiber channel.

High bit-rate ($\geq$ 40 Gbps) optical communication presents several interesting challenges to a communications theorist, because the diverse set of impairments peculiar to the optical channel require the development of new techniques capable of combating the effects of these impairments. The main challenge posed by the high bit-rate optical channel is that it is inherently and strongly nonlinear. As a result, traditional digital communications and coding techniques, which typically assume a linear channel model, become less effective in the scenario of high bit-rate optical communication.

One of the nonlinearities encountered in the optical fiber channel is an effect known as intrachannel four-wave mixing (FWM) [**19**],[**6**],[**16**]. The FWM effect

2000 *Mathematics Subject Classification.* 37B10, 68P30, 94A40, 94B12.

Key words and phrases. Optical communications, coding, ghost pulses, ghostbusting.

This work was supported by the UC Discovery Grant program and Applied Micro Circuits Corporation, San Diego, and was carried out while the first author was at the University of California-San Diego.

©2008 American Mathematical Society

results in strong ISI between the symbols in a bitstream being transmitted across the optical fiber. It is widely accepted that at bit rates of 40 Gbps and beyond, FWM plays a major role in limiting the information-carrying capacity and the propagation distance of a dispersion-managed optical transmission system [**16**],[**15**],[**22**].

The ISI caused by FWM is a highly nonlinear phenomenon, as we describe in more detail in Section 2. Therefore, it is not clear that it can be realistically approximated by a conventional finite-state ISI channel model. As a result, equalization and coding techniques developed in the communications literature for the finite-state ISI channel are not immediately applicable to the optical scenario.

The optics literature has seen the emergence of some simple modulation schemes aimed at reducing the impact of FWM in an optical communication system. These schemes are based on the fact that FWM is a phase-sensitive effect, and therefore, can be controlled by modulating the phase of the pulses being transmitted. We describe some of these phase modulation schemes in Section 3.1.

Coding, *i.e.*, the introduction of redundancy in the transmitted bits, as a means of controlling errors has only very recently been considered as an approach to mitigate the FWM effect. To the best of our knowledge, the only work in this area, aside from our own, is that reported in [**20**], which we briefly describe in Section 3.2.

In Section 4, we describe the application of techniques from constrained coding in designing and analyzing some schemes we propose to combat FWM. Our approach tries to be as general as possible by combining coding and phase modulation, and lays a foundation for a systematic treatment of the subject.

We conclude the paper with Section 5, which contains a summary and suggestions for further research directions in this area.

At this point, the astute reader may have noted that there has been no explanation given yet for the use of the term "ghostbusting" in the title. While the reason for the use of this term will be abundantly clear from context in the next section, we nevertheless provide a note of explanation here. The primary effect of FWM on a train of light pulses being transmitted across an optical fiber is the creation of spurious "ghost" pulses where there should be none. Much of this article discusses techniques to suppress the formation of ghost pulses. Hence, ghostbusting.

2. Intrachannel Four-Wave Mixing

Transmission of return-to-zero (RZ) pulses in optical fibers with strong dispersion management is a key component of high bit-rate ($\geq$ 40 Gbps) optical communication systems. Strong dispersion management has been found to control certain fiber nonlinearities such as self-phase modulation and interchannel crosstalk in wavelength-division-multiplexed systems. However, a residual nonlinearity in such systems was reported in a series of papers [**19**],[**6**],[**16**], which was found to cause amplitude fluctuations of pulses in '1' slots and spurious "ghost" pulse generation in '0' slots. This nonlinearity, dubbed intrachannel four-wave mixing, was quickly realized to be the limiting penalty in long-haul, high bit-rate optical transmission [**15**],[**22**], and effective suppression of the effects of FWM is the subject of active research.

Consider a train of light pulses corresponding to a sequence of bits that is sent across the fiber optic medium that constitutes the optical channel (see Figure 1). Each bit in the sequence is allocated a time slot of duration T, and a 1 or 0 is marked by the presence or absence of a pulse in that time slot. The effect of

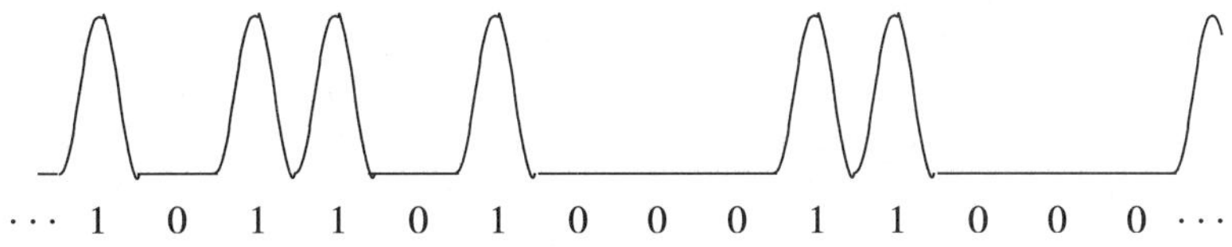

FIGURE 1. Train of pulses in optical transmission.

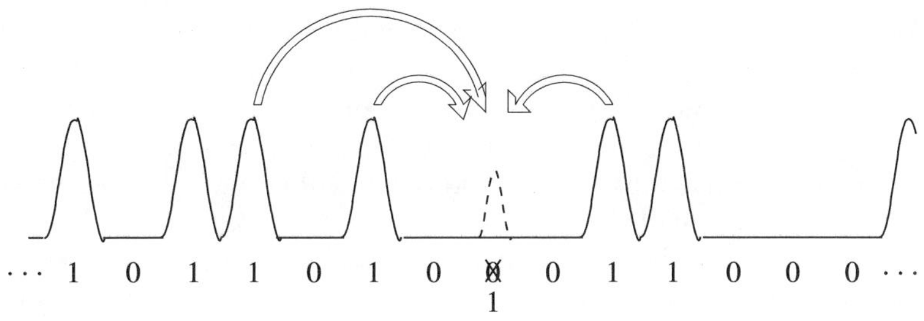

FIGURE 2. Ghost pulse formation due to the interaction of three pulses.

intrachannel FWM is to transfer energy from triples of pulses in '1' slots into a fourth time slot. It has been observed that the interaction of pulses in the kth, lth and mth time slots (k, l, m need not all be distinct) in the pulse train pumps energy into the $(k + l - m)$th time slot. If this slot originally did not contain a pulse, *i.e.*, if the $(k + l - m)$th bit was a 0 in the original sequence of bits, then the transfer of energy creates a spurious *ghost pulse* in the slot, which could cause the original 0 to be read as a 1 (see Figure 2). Since energy must be conserved, some of the pulses in the kth, lth and mth time slots lose energy, resulting in a lowering of their amplitude (intensity). On the other hand, if the $(k+l-m)$th slot already contained a pulse, then there is an exchange of energy between the pulses in the kth, lth, mth and $(k + l - m)$th slots, resulting in amplitude fluctuations in the pulses. An analytic explanation of this phenomenon can be derived via the nonlinear Schrödinger equation that describes pulse propagation in optical fibers [**1**],[**2**],[**22**].

While ghost pulses clearly lead to $0 \to 1$ errors, pulse amplitude fluctuations caused by FWM may cause $1 \to 0$ errors. For instance, a "true" pulse may be involved in the formation of several ghost pulses, and the cumulative energy leakage from all its interactions may cause it to weaken to an extent that it is not detected at the receiving end. However, it seems that this is a much rarer event, and therefore much less a cause for concern, than ghost pulse formation.

There are, in general, multiple (k, l, m) triples giving rise to the same integer $k + l - m$. So, it is possible to have several pulse triples generating a ghost pulse at the same '0' slot. Of course, in reality, the number of pulse triples involved in ghost pulse formation at a certain '0' slot is quite small. This is because, as one would expect from physical considerations, the interaction between pulses that are sufficiently far apart in the transmitted pulse train is weak. Indeed, for typical optical transmission parameters, pulses that are more than 8 to 10 time slots apart do not contribute significantly to the formation of ghost pulses [**15**]. In any case, when multiple pulse triples generate a ghost pulse at the same '0' slot, the resulting ghost pulse at that slot is the superposition of the ghost pulses formed by each of the pulse triples. The superposition of multiple ghost pulses may result in a stronger ghost pulse, or sometimes, due to destructive interference, a weaker ghost pulse, as will be clear from the following discussion on the role of phase in FWM.

The phases of the original pulses play a vital (and, as yet, little understood) role in determining which pulses lose energy and which gain energy in the course of the energy transfer induced by FWM. Furthermore, the phase of a ghost pulse created by a pulse triple depends on the phases of the pulses in the triple. Thus, in the case of a superposition of multiple ghost pulses, the relationship of the phase of the resultant ghost pulse to that of all the pulses involved in its creation can be quite complex. Indeed, even the amplitude of a ghost pulse depends on the phases of the pulse triples involved in its creation, since the superposition of ghost pulses with opposing phases at the same location will actually suppress ghost pulse formation at that location [**15**].

Physically, a ghost pulse is just another pulse of light. So, it is possible that ghost pulse formation may propagate, in the sense that the interaction of a ghost pulse with actual pulses or other ghost pulses may lead to the creation of even more ghost pulses.

It should be noted that FWM is primarily a problem with long-haul (several tens of kilometers) optical communications. This is because the amplitude of ghost pulses grows linearly with propagation distance, and for typical optical transmission parameters, ghost pulse amplitude only reaches significant proportions over tens of kilometers. The simulations reported in the literature were typically carried out over fibers of lengths 50–100 km [**19**],[**22**],[**15**].

3. Ghostbusting Schemes in the Literature

In this section, we survey some of the phase modulation schemes for the purpose of ghost pulse suppression developed in the optics literature, and also discuss the coding scheme proposed by Vasic *et al* [**20**] as an alternative to phase modulation.

3.1. Phase Modulation Schemes. As described in the last section, ghost pulse formation is a phase-sensitive effect, *i.e.*, the phase of a ghost pulse depends on the phases of the pulses involved in its creation. So, one method of suppressing ghost pulse formation would be to modulate the phases of the transmitted pulses in such a way as to cause destructive interference between ghost pulses formed at the same location.

The phase modulation schemes in the optics literature primarily consist of applying a phase shift of π to some of the pulses in the transmitted pulse train. We can effectively think of such a phase modulation scheme as a means of converting a binary sequence $b_0 b_1 \ldots b_{M-1}$ into a ternary sequence $c_0 c_1 \ldots c_{M-1}$, with $c_i \in \{-1, 0, 1\}$, such that $b_i = |c_i|$ for all i.

One popular modulation format is the duobinary format, which is based on the following method of converting a binary sequence $(b_i)_{i \in \mathbb{Z}} \in \{0,1\}^{\mathbb{Z}}$ into a ternary sequence $(c_i)_{i \in \mathbb{Z}} \in \{-1,0,1\}^{\mathbb{Z}}$: $c_i = b_i + b_{i-1} - 1$ for all $i \in \mathbb{Z}$. Of course, in general, this does not ensure that $b_i = |c_i|$, so some "pre-coding" is required to ensure that this holds. The duobinary format works as follows: given a binary sequence $b_0 b_1 \ldots b_{M-1}$, $b_i \in \{0,1\}$, first pre-code it into the binary sequence $a_0 a_1 \ldots a_{M-1}$ defined via $a_i = \sum_{j=0}^{i} \overline{b_i} \mod 2$, where $\overline{b_i}$ denotes the complement of b_i; then, let $c_i = a_i + a_{i-1} - 1$, $i = 0, 1, \ldots, M-1$, arbitrarily defining $a_{-1} = 0$. It is easily verified that we now have $|c_i| = b_i$ for all i. (A closely related modulation technique, also known as duobinary encoding or Class-1 partial-response signaling, has been used as a discrete-time model for the low-pass characteristics of optical recording channels [**8**].)

The duobinary format had previously been used successfully to reduce the effect of chromatic dispersion in an optical transmission system [**21**]. Cheng and Conradi [**4**] used simulations to demonstrate that this format is also useful in suppressing some of the stronger ghost pulses. They also considered a modified duobinary format which was comparable to the duobinary format in terms of ghost pulse suppression.

Liu *et al* [**15**] proposed a scheme expressly designed to suppress the intensity of the worst ghost pulses by selectively inverting the phases of certain runs of ones. As is to be expected based on our earlier description of ghost pulse formation, some of the worst ghost pulses are formed at isolated '0' slots that are surrounded by long runs of ones on either side. For example, consider the sequence of bits $b_{-3}b_{-2}b_{-1}b_0b_1b_2b_3 = 1110111$. A ghost pulse is formed at the central zero due to the superposition of the ghost pulses created at the position $k + l - m = 0$ for the following values of (k, l, m): $(-1, -2, -3)$, $(1, 2, 3)$, $(-1, -1, -2)$, $(1, 1, 2)$, $(1, -2, -1)$, $(-1, 2, 1)$, $(1, -3, -2)$, $(-1, 3, 2)$, $(-2, 3, 1)$ and $(2, -3, -1)$. Liu *et al* show that the ghost pulse energy in 1110111 grows more than 10 times faster than that in the 1110000 pattern. To counter such strong ghost pulses, they propose a phase inversion scheme where ones equidistant from a central zero are given opposite phases. For example, 1110111 may be converted to $\bar{1}\bar{1}\bar{1}0111$ or $\bar{1}1\bar{1}01\bar{1}1$, where $\bar{1}$ is a compact notation for -1, denoting a pulse whose phase differs from a '1' pulse by π. The logic here is that if pulse triples at positions (k, l, m) and $(-k, -l, -m)$ both generate ghost pulses at position 0, then the resultant ghost pulses have the same energy, but due to the phase inversion scheme, they have opposite phases. So, their superposition results in ghost pulse suppression due to destructive interference. This analysis is supported by simulation results as well, which show that with the proposed phase inversion scheme, the ghost pulse is fully suppressed in the 1110111 bit sequence, but it remains the same in the 1110000 sequence.

As an aside, the simulation results of Liu *et al* also show that longer runs of ones may not necessarily introduce a stronger ghost pulse. For example, the ghost pulse in the 1110111 bit pattern turns out to be stronger than that in the 1111011111 pattern. This is believed to happen for two reasons: (a) ones separated by roughly 8 or more bits do not contribute significantly to the FWM process, and (b) ghost pulses formed by different triples have different phases and they tend to interfere when too many ones are involved.

Alic and Fainman [**3**] added to the work of Liu *et al* by providing more phase modulation rules for ghost pulse suppression. For a number of commonly occurring bit patterns, they list the phase modulation patterns that are optimal in terms of ghost pulse suppression, based on simulation results. For example, they suggest that the bit pattern 11001 be converted to $1100\bar{1}$ or $1\bar{1}001$, and 110001 be converted to $1\bar{1}0001$, and so on, for maximal ghost pulse suppression. While their list of bit patterns is far from being exhaustive, they provide some rules of thumb for generating a good phase modulation format for an arbitrary bit pattern.

For the sake of completeness, we mention that phase modulation schemes are not the only ghostbusting schemes proposed in the optics literature. Kumar [**13**] proposed a method for suppressing intrachannel FWM by using unequally spaced pulses with a resulting sacrifice in spectral efficiency.

3.2. A Constrained Coding Scheme. We saw earlier how the appearance of certain bit patterns, *e.g.* 1110111, in the transmitted bit stream results in the formation of strong ghost pulses. Indeed, if a zero in the transmitted bit stream is preceded or followed by a long run of ones, then there is a superposition of multiple ghost pulses at that zero, creating a strong ghost pulse there. Instead of playing with phase modulation formats to control such ghost pulses, one can root out the problem at the source simply by not transmitting bit streams containing long runs of ones. With this in mind, Vasic *et al* [**20**] proposed a ghostbusting scheme in which an arbitrary (binary) data sequence is converted to a binary sequence satisfying a certain *maximum transition run (MTR) constraint*[1] before transmission.

In the language of constrained coding (*cf.* [**7**],[**17**]), a binary sequence, $\mathbf{x}$, is said to satisfy an MTR(j) constraint, j being a non-negative integer, if every run of ones in $\mathbf{x}$ is of length at most j [**18**],[**9**],[**5**]. In the scheme proposed by Vasic *et al*, a *constrained code* consisting of sequences satisfying the MTR(2) constraint is used for transmission. If an arbitrary, finite-length binary data sequence $b_0 b_1 \ldots b_{M-1}$ is to be sent across an optical fiber, then it is first encoded into a codeword $c_0 c_1 \ldots c_{N-1}$ that satisfies the MTR(2) constraint, which is then transmitted as a train of optical pulses. Thus, the sequence that is actually transmitted does not contain three ones in a row, which should result in the elimination of strong ghost pulses. The codeword $c_0 c_1 \ldots c_{N-1}$ can be decoded at the receiver end to recover the data sequence $b_0 b_1 \ldots b_{M-1}$.

Since the imposition of the MTR constraint implies that not all binary sequences can be used as codewords, there is a rate penalty incurred in using such a constrained code. This is in contrast to the phase modulation schemes surveyed earlier, which are all essentially codes of rate 1. Rate here is used to denote the number of data bits transmitted per coded symbol.

Vasic *et al* used an MTR(2) constrained code of rate 0.8 for simulation purposes[2]. To be precise, a block code consisting of $2^8 = 256$ codewords of length 10 was used, with encoding and decoding performed via a lookup table. (Although a simple MTR(2) block code with 16 codewords of length 5 also exists [**18**],[**9**], the use of longer codewords allows for the avoidance or elimination of certain binary strings detrimental to system performance.) Their simulation results show significant ghost pulse reduction with the use of their coding scheme. They conclude that "it is possible to successfully tackle the detrimental effects of FWM in 40 Gbps systems using simple [constrained] coding schemes."

4. A Systematic Approach to Ghostbusting

Note that all the phase modulation and coding schemes discussed in Section 3 involve uniquely mapping a binary data sequence $b_0 b_1 \ldots b_{M-1}$ to a sequence $c_0 c_1 \ldots c_{N-1}$ that is less susceptible to degradation due to ghost pulse formation.

[1]MTR constraints were originally introduced to improve the performance of magnetic recording channels characterized by certain higher-order partial-response models [**18**].

[2]The *capacity* of the MTR(2) constraint, which defines the maximum rate possible for a code using sequences satisfying the constraint, is known to be 0.8791.

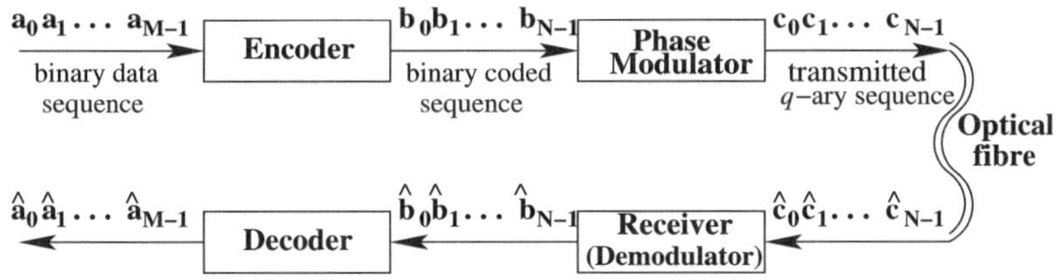

FIGURE 3. Schematic of an optical coding scheme.

In the case of the phase modulation schemes, $c_0c_1 \ldots c_{N-1}$ is a ternary sequence with $N = M$ and $|c_i| = b_i$ for all i, constructed in such a way that ghost pulse formation can be kept under control. In the case of the coding scheme of Section 3.2, $c_0c_1 \ldots c_{N-1}$ is a binary sequence satisfying the MTR(2) constraint. Thus, in all cases, $c_0c_1 \ldots c_{N-1}$ is a q-ary sequence (q being 2 or 3) with certain properties conducive to ghost pulse suppression. This naturally leads us to consider a generalized model for ghostbusting schemes, which combines phase modulation and coding, as outlined below.

We shall use the term "optical coding scheme" to denote a scheme for communicating across the optical fiber channel that combines coding and phase modulation. In other words, an optical coding scheme is a method of mapping an arbitrary sequence of data bits onto a train of light pulses that is possibly phase-modulated, so that if the pulse train passes through an optical fiber channel without being corrupted, then the original data sequence can be correctly retrieved by an optical receiver at the channel output. We have deliberately left the outcome undefined in the scenario when the pulse train is actually corrupted by the channel. In a good optical coding scheme, the receiver should be able to retrieve the original data sequence even when the optical signal undergoes some degradation in the channel.

There is an essential difference between an optical coding scheme and a traditional coded modulation scheme. In an optical coding scheme, phase modulation can be used to combat channel impairments while the pulse train is in transit along the fiber, but it cannot be used at the channel input to encode information or at the channel output to correct errors. This is due to the fact that an optical receiver can only detect the amplitude of the optical signal at the channel output, not its phase. So, two distinct sequences of light pulses that differ only in phase cannot be used to encode two distinct binary data sequences.

Thus, an optical coding scheme must have separate coding and phase modulation components (see Figure 3). In such a scheme, at the transmitter end, a binary data sequence, $a_0a_1 \ldots a_{M-1}$, would first be mapped to a binary coded sequence, $b_0b_1 \ldots b_{N-1}$, which determines the positions of the pulses in the transmitted pulse train. The phase modulation component would then convert the coded binary sequence to a sequence $c_0c_1 \ldots c_{N-1}$ over the q-ary alphabet $\mathcal{A}_q = \{0, 1, 2 \ldots, q-1\}$, for some integer $q \geq 2$, such that $c_i = 0$ if and only if $b_i = 0$. We shall think of the integers $1, 2, \ldots, q-1$ as a set of $q-1$ phases, with each '1' in $b_0b_1 \ldots b_{N-1}$ being assigned one of these phases. For example, the phase modulation schemes of Section 3.1 use the ternary alphabet $\mathcal{A}_3 = \{0, 1, 2\}$, with the integers 1 and 2 representing the phases 0 and π, respectively.

The sequence $c_0c_1 \ldots c_{N-1}$ is transmitted as a pulse train across the optical fiber channel, a pulse being in the jth time slot iff $c_j \neq 0$. The phase of a pulse in the jth time slot is determined by the actual value of c_j. The pulse train may get corrupted by the channel, so that at the channel output, the receiver detects a binary sequence $\hat{b}_0\hat{b}_1 \dots \hat{b}_{N-1}$, which it then decodes (if possible) to obtain a reconstruction, $\hat{a}_0\hat{a}_1 \dots \hat{a}_{M-1}$, of the original data sequence. Naturally, the coding scheme should be designed so that the number of errors in the reconstruction is minimized.

The approach we take to ensure that errors are minimized is to design the encoder and phase modulator in such a way that the sequences $c_0c_1 \dots c_{N-1}$ that are actually transmitted have some 'nice' structure that allows them to pass through the channel virtually uncorrupted by ghost pulses. In particular, we consider optical coding schemes in which the sequences used for transmission satisfy a certain class of "ghost pulse constraints," which we shall define next.

4.1. The q-ary Ghost Pulse Constraint. It was made clear in Section 2 that the process that results in the creation of ghost pulses is quite complex in nature. In order to establish reasonable criteria for the design of optical coding schemes within the framework outlined above, we make a simplifying assumption on the FWM process. We shall assume that the strongest ghost pulses are created due to the interaction between pulses of the same phase. To be precise, we shall assume that the transmitted q-ary sequence $c_0c_1 \dots c_{N-1}$ is most severely corrupted by ghost pulses when there are indices k, l, m such that c_k, c_l and c_m are nonzero and equal, and $c_{k+l-m} = 0$. Equivalently, the most serious problems are created by situations where there are pulses in the kth, lth and mth time slots, all having the same phase, and the $(k+l-m)$th slot is empty. Recall that the interaction of pulses in the kth, lth and mth slots results in an energy transfer to the $(k+l-m)$th slot, causing a ghost pulse to be formed there. To counteract the formation of these strong ghost pulses, the coding schemes we consider only transmit sequences which are constrained in such a way that the situation described above does not occur. The all-ones sequence, the all-zeros sequence, and the sequences of alternating zeros and ones are all examples of such constrained sequences.

To describe the constraints we impose on transmitted sequences (which are always finite in length), it is most convenient to first define the constraints on *bi-infinite* sequences, *i.e.*, sequences indexed by the set of integers, $\mathbb{Z}$. For $\mathbf{x} = (x_k)_{k\in\mathbb{Z}} \in \mathcal{A}_q^{\mathbb{Z}}$, we define the *support* of $\mathbf{x}$ to be $\text{supp}(\mathbf{x}) = \{k \in \mathbb{Z} : x_k \neq 0\}$.

DEFINITION 4.1 (The q-ary Ghost Pulse (qGP) constraint). A sequence $\mathbf{x} \in \mathcal{A}_q^{\mathbb{Z}}$ satisfies the qGP constraint if for all $k, l, m \in \text{supp}(\mathbf{x})$ (k, l, m not necessarily distinct) such that $x_k = x_l = x_m$, we also have $k + l - m \in \text{supp}(\mathbf{x})$.

We shall denote by $\mathcal{T}_q$ the set of all $\mathbf{x} \in \mathcal{A}_q^{\mathbb{Z}}$ that satisfy the qGP constraint. A *finite-length* q-ary sequence $c_0c_1 \dots c_{N-1}$ is said to satisfy the qGP constraint if it is a subblock of some sequence in $\mathcal{T}_q$, *i.e.*, if $c_0c_1 \dots c_{N-1} = x_ix_{i+1} \dots x_{i+N-1}$ for some $i \in \mathbb{Z}$ and $\mathbf{x} = (x_k)_{k\in\mathbb{Z}} \in \mathcal{T}_q$. We shall denote by $T_q(n)$, $n \in \mathbb{Z}^+$, the set of all q-ary sequences of length n that satisfy the qGP constraint. Note that under the simplifying assumption made above, the structure of the sequences in $T_q(n)$ allows them to pass through an optical fiber channel without being significantly corrupted by ghost pulses.

Now, let $\mathcal{S}_q$ denote the set of all *binary* sequences $\mathbf{y} \in \{0,1\}^{\mathbb{Z}}$ such that there exists an $\mathbf{x} \in \mathcal{T}_q$ with $\text{supp}(\mathbf{x}) = \text{supp}(\mathbf{y})$. Also, let $S_q(n)$, $n \in \mathbb{Z}^+$, denote the set of length-n subblocks of sequences in $\mathcal{S}_q$. The sequences in $\mathcal{S}_q$ and $S_q(n)$ are just the "phaseless" versions of the sequences in $\mathcal{T}_q$ and $T_q(n)$. Thus, if $T_q^* = \bigcup_{n\geq 1} T_q(n)$ constitutes the set of sequences that can be transmitted across an optical fiber channel, then $S_q^* = \bigcup_{n\geq 1} S_q(n)$ is the set of codewords that can be used to encode information, since these are the sequences that are actually seen by an optical receiver at the channel output.

The coding rate of any optical coding scheme that uses qGP-constrained sequences for transmission is limited by the *capacity*, $h(\mathcal{S}_q)$, of the set $\mathcal{S}_q$, which is defined as

$$h(\mathcal{S}_q) = \lim_{n\to\infty} \frac{\log_2 |S_q(n)|}{n} \tag{1}$$

The closer $h(\mathcal{S}_q)$ is to 1, the more efficiently such coding schemes can in principle transmit information per code symbol.

While it can easily be shown that $h(\mathcal{S}_q)$ is a non-decreasing function of q, we will primarily be interested in the cases when $q = 2$ and $q = 3$. These are the cases of practical interest because phase modulation schemes involving anything more than simple phase inversion are not easy to implement in practice. When $q = 2$, we shall refer to the qGP constraint as the *binary ghost pulse (BGP)* constraint, and when $q = 3$, the corresponding constraint will be called the *ternary ghost pulse (TGP)* constraint.

The BGP constraint is straightforward to analyze. Indeed, it can be shown [**10, 11**] that the sequences that satisfy the BGP constraint are exactly those whose support set forms an arithmetic progression. The following theorem makes this statement precise.

THEOREM 4.2. *A bi-infinite binary sequence* $\mathbf{x}$ *is in* $\mathcal{S}_2$ *if and only if* $\text{supp}(\mathbf{x}) = \emptyset$ *or* $\text{supp}(\mathbf{x}) = a + k\mathbb{Z}$ *for some* $a, k \in \mathbb{Z}$.

It easily follows from the above theorem that $|S_2(n)| = O(n^2)$, and hence, (1) implies that $h(\mathcal{S}_2) = 0$. Thus, any coding scheme based on BGP-constrained sequences is bound to be inefficient in terms of rate.

It turns out that the TGP constraint is much harder to analyze than its binary counterpart. Ideally, we would like to be able to find a simple characterization of the sequences in $\mathcal{S}_3$, along the lines of that given in Theorem 4.2 for sequences in $\mathcal{S}_2$. This would then enable us to determine the capacity $h(\mathcal{S}_3)$. Unfortunately, we only have a partial characterization of the sequences in $\mathcal{S}_3$, which we state in Theorems 4.3 and 4.4 below. The proof of these theorems can be found in [**11**]. Recall that $\mathbf{y} = (y_m)_{m\in\mathbb{Z}} \subset \{0,1\}^{\mathbb{Z}}$ is *periodic* if there exists a $k \in \mathbb{Z}^+$ such that $y_m = y_{m+k}$ for all $m \in \mathbb{Z}$. The integer k is referred to as a *period* of $\mathbf{y}$. The *fundamental period* of a periodic sequence, $\mathbf{y}$, is the smallest $k \in \mathbb{Z}^+$ that is a period of $\mathbf{y}$. An *aperiodic* sequence is a sequence that is not periodic.

THEOREM 4.3. *Let* $\mathbf{y} \in \{0,1\}^{\mathbb{Z}}$ *be aperiodic. Then,* $\mathbf{y} \in \mathcal{S}_3$ *iff* $\text{supp}(\mathbf{y})$ *is one of the following:*

(i) *a set with either 1 or 2 elements;*
(ii) $(k\mathbb{Z} + i) \cup \{j\}$ *for some* $k \in \mathbb{Z}^+$, $i \in [0, k-1]$, *and* $j \in \mathbb{Z}$, $j \not\equiv i \pmod{k}$;
(iii) $(3t\mathbb{Z} + i) \cup V$ *for some* $t \in \mathbb{Z}^+$, $i \in [0, 3t-1]$, *and* $V \subset \mathbb{Z}$, $|V| = 2$, $V \equiv \{t+i, 2t+i\} \pmod{3t}$.

The above theorem shows that any binary sequence $\mathbf{y} \in \mathcal{S}_3$ can be made periodic by changing at most *two* ones to zeros.

THEOREM 4.4. *Let* $\mathbf{y} \in \{0,1\}^{\mathbb{Z}}$ *be periodic with fundamental period* p *prime. Then,* $\mathbf{y} \in \mathcal{S}_3$ *iff one of the following two conditions holds:*

(i) $\mathrm{supp}(\mathbf{y}) = \bigcup_{i\in I}(p\mathbb{Z}+i)$, *with* $|I| \leq 2$;

(ii) $p = 5$ *and* $\mathbf{y}$ *is* $(01111)^{\mathbb{Z}}$ *or one of its shifts.*

The classification of periodic sequences in $\mathcal{S}_3$ with non-prime period remains an open problem. Now, recall our definition of $S_3(n)$ as the set of all length-n subblocks of $\mathcal{S}_3$. It can be inferred from Theorem 4.3 that aperiodic sequences in $\mathcal{S}_3$ contribute $O(n^4)$ blocks to $S_3(n)$. Numerical evidence presented in [**11**],[**12**] seems to suggest that the number of blocks contributed to $S_3(n)$ by periodic sequences in $\mathcal{S}_3$ is also polynomial in n. Consequently, we conjecture that $h(\mathcal{S}_3) = 0$, just as in the BGP case.

The conclusion to be drawn from this is that the qGP constraint is too severe a constraint to impose on sequences, as it results in highly inefficient coding schemes. Therefore, we need to considers means of weakening the constraint, and we discuss one way of doing this next.

4.2. The qGP(t) Constraint. As mentioned in Section 2, pulses that are more than 8 to 10 time slots apart in the pulse train do not contribute significantly to the formation of ghost pulses. So, if we weaken the qGP constraint by disregarding the interactions between nonzero symbols that are separated by more than some fixed distance, then the sequences satisfying the weakened constraint can still be transmitted across an optical fiber without significant degradation due to ghost pulse formation. This brings us to our definition of the qGP(t) constraint.

DEFINITION 4.5 (The qGP(t) constraint). Let t be a positive integer. A sequence $\mathbf{x} \in \mathcal{A}_q^{\mathbb{Z}}$ satisfies the qGP(t) constraint if for all $k, l, m \in \mathrm{supp}(\mathbf{x})$ (k, l, m not necessarily distinct) such that $x_k = x_l = x_m$ and $\max\{|k-l|, |l-m|, |k-m|\} \leq t$, we have $k + l - m \in \mathrm{supp}(\mathbf{x})$.

Thus, in the qGP(t) constraints, only indices that are within a distance of t from each other are allowed to be a part of the constraint. The quantity t is referred to as the *memory* of the constraint. As usual, BGP(t) and TGP(t) will be used to denote the qGP(t) constraints with $q = 2$ and $q = 3$, respectively.

Analogous to our previous definitions, we shall let $\mathcal{T}_{q,t}$ denote the set of all $\mathbf{x} \in \mathcal{A}_q^{\mathbb{Z}}$ that satisfy the qGP(t) constraint. A finite-length q-ary sequence is said to satisfy the qGP(t) constraint if it is a subblock of some sequence in $\mathcal{T}_{q,t}$. For $n \in \mathbb{Z}^+$, the set of all q-ary sequences of length n that satisfy the qGP(t) constraint will be denoted by $T_{q,t}(n)$. We let $\mathcal{S}_{q,t}$ be the set of all binary sequences $\mathbf{y} \in \{0,1\}^{\mathbb{Z}}$ such that there exists an $\mathbf{x} \in \mathcal{T}_{q,t}$ with $\mathrm{supp}(\mathbf{x}) = \mathrm{supp}(\mathbf{y})$. Finally, $S_{q,t}(n)$, $n \in \mathbb{Z}^+$, denotes the set of length-n subblocks of sequences in $\mathcal{S}_{q,t}$.

As in the qGP case, $T^*_{q,t} = \bigcup_{n\geq 1} T_{q,t}(n)$ constitutes the set of sequences that can be transmitted across an optical fiber, and $S^*_{q,t} = \bigcup_{n\geq 1} S_{q,t}(n)$ is the set of codewords that can be used to encode information. Thus, the rate of any coding scheme using qGP(t)-constrained sequences for transmission is limited by the capacity of $\mathcal{S}_{q,t}$, which is defined as

$$h(\mathcal{S}_{q,t}) = \lim_{n\to\infty} \frac{\log_2 |S_{q,t}(n)|}{n} \tag{2}$$

For fixed q, the sequence, $h(\mathcal{S}_{q,t})$, $t = 1, 2 \ldots$, is a non-increasing sequence, since $\mathcal{S}_{q,t} \supset \mathcal{S}_{q,t+1}$, and so, $\lim_{t\to\infty} h(\mathcal{S}_{q,t})$ exists. In fact, since $\mathcal{S}_q = \bigcap_{t=1}^{\infty} \mathcal{S}_{q,t}$,

TABLE 1. $h(\mathcal{S}_{2,t})$ for $1 \le t \le 20$.

t	$h(\mathcal{S}_{2,t})$	t	$h(\mathcal{S}_{2,t})$
1	0.6942	11	0.2301
2	0.5515	12	0.2180
3	0.4650	13	0.2073
4	0.4057	14	0.1977
5	0.3620	15	0.1891
6	0.3282	16	0.1813
7	0.3011	17	0.1742
8	0.2788	18	0.1678
9	0.2600	19	0.1618
10	0.2440	20	0.1564

it follows [**14**, Proposition 4.4.6] that $\lim_{t\to\infty} h(\mathcal{S}_{q,t}) = h(\mathcal{S}_q)$. This gives us an alternative way of computing, or at least approximating, $h(\mathcal{S}_3)$, which is difficult to compute directly, as we noted earlier. We will later discuss an algorithm that is implementable in principle, to determine $h(\mathcal{S}_{q,t})$ for any given q and t. Unfortunately, the algorithm is computationally too intensive to be useful in practice.

The BGP(t) constraint is closely related to the (t,∞) *runlength-limited (RLL) constraint*, which is well-studied in the constrained coding literature (see *eg.*, [**7**]). A bi-infinite binary sequence is said to be (t,∞)*-RLL constrained* if any two successive ones in the sequence are separated by at least t zeros. Let $\mathcal{X}_{t,\infty}$ denote the set of all (t,∞)-RLL constrained binary sequences. The following theorem, proved in [**12**], establishes the relationship between $\mathcal{S}_{2,t}$ and $\mathcal{X}_{t,\infty}$.

THEOREM 4.6. *For any $t \in \mathbb{Z}^+$, $\mathcal{S}_{2,t} = \mathcal{X}_{t,\infty} \cup \mathcal{Y}_t$, where $\mathcal{Y}_t$ is the set of all sequences $\mathbf{x} \in \{0,1\}^{\mathbb{Z}}$ such that* $\mathrm{supp}(\mathbf{x}) = a + d\mathbb{Z}$ *for some integers $a, d \in [0,t]$.*

Now, the sequences in $\mathcal{Y}_t$ contribute at most $(t+1)^2$ blocks to $S_{2,t}(n)$. Hence, it follows from (2) that $h(\mathcal{S}_{2,t}) = h(\mathcal{X}_{t,\infty})$, where $h(\mathcal{X}_{t,\infty})$ is the capacity of the (t,∞)-RLL constraint, which is defined analogously to (2). It is well known [**7**, p. 89] that $h(\mathcal{X}_{t,\infty}) = \log_2 \rho_t$, where ρ_t is the largest-magnitude root of the polynomial $z^{t+1} - z^t - 1$. This root is always real and lies in the open interval $(1,2)$, so that $0 < h(\mathcal{X}_{t,\infty}) < 1$. We thus have the following corollary to Theorem 4.6.

COROLLARY 4.7. For any $t \in \mathbb{Z}^+$,

$$h(\mathcal{S}_{2,t}) = \log_2 \rho_t,$$

where ρ_t is the largest-magnitude root of the polynomial $z^{t+1} - z^t - 1$.

For the sake of reference, we list the values of $h(\mathcal{S}_{2,t})$, rounded to four decimal places, for $1 \le t \le 20$, in Table 1. As can be seen from the table, for $t \ge 8$, $h(\mathcal{S}_{2,t})$ is less than 0.28, which implies that codes consisting of sequences satisfying the BGP(t) constraint are also inefficient in terms of rate.

Shifting our focus on to the TGP(t) constraint, we remark at the outset that this too is a difficult constraint to analyze completely. We have a clear understanding of the constraint in the cases when t is 1 or 2, but this does not extend to higher values of t. We will suggest a systematic approach to tackle the general case, which can in principle be programmed into a computer.

A detailed analysis of the cases $t = 1$ and $t = 2$ allows us to prove the following result, which is the TGP(t)-analogue of Theorem 4.6 for these values of t.

THEOREM 4.8. (a) $\mathcal{S}_{3,1} = \{0,1\}^{\mathbb{Z}}$.
(b) $\mathcal{S}_{3,2}$ *is the set of all sequences* $\mathbf{y} \in \{0,1\}^{\mathbb{Z}}$ *such that* $\mathbf{y}$ *contains none of the strings* 011100, 001110 *and* 001111100 *as a subblock.*

We sketch a proof for part (a) of the theorem, referring the reader to [**12**] for a complete proof of the theorem. For ease of notation, we shall take the ternary alphabet to be $\{-1,0,1\}$. Given a ternary sequence $\mathbf{x} = (x_i)_{i\in\mathbb{Z}}$, we shall denote by $|\mathbf{x}|$ the binary sequence $(|x_i|)_{i\in\mathbb{Z}}$. Part (a) is proved by constructing a "phase modulation" mapping, Φ, that takes an arbitrary $\mathbf{y} \in \{0,1\}^{\mathbb{Z}}$ to a sequence $\Phi(\mathbf{y}) \in \mathcal{T}_{3,1}$ such that $|\Phi(\mathbf{y})| = \mathbf{y}$. It then follows from the definitions that $\mathcal{S}_{3,1} = \{0,1\}^{\mathbb{Z}}$.

Let $\phi : \{0,1\}^4 \to \{-1,0,1\}$ be the function defined by the following rule:

$$\phi(y_{-2}y_{-1}y_0y_1) \quad = \quad \begin{cases} 0 & \text{if } y_0 = 0, \\ -1 & \text{if } \; y_{-2}y_{-1}y_0 = 011 \\ & \text{or } \; y_{-2}y_{-1}y_0y_1 = 1111, \\ 1 & \text{otherwise} \end{cases}$$

We extend ϕ to a *sliding-block map*, $\Phi : \{0,1\}^{\mathbb{Z}} \to \{-1,0,1\}^{\mathbb{Z}}$, as follows: For $\mathbf{y} = (y_i)_{i\in\mathbb{Z}}$, $\Phi(\mathbf{y}) = \mathbf{x} = (x_i)_{i\in\mathbb{Z}}$ with $x_i = \phi(y_{i-2}y_{i-1}y_iy_{i+1})$ for all $i \in \mathbb{Z}$. It follows from the definitions that for any $\mathbf{y} \in \{0,1\}^{\mathbb{Z}}$, $\Phi(\mathbf{y})$ is a ternary sequence such that $|\Phi(\mathbf{y})| = \mathbf{y}$. Furthermore, it may be verified that $\Phi(\mathbf{y})$ does not contain any of the strings 011, 110, $0\bar{1}\bar{1}$ and $\bar{1}\bar{1}0$ as a subblock (as before $\bar{1}$ denotes the symbol -1), which is enough to guarantee that $\Phi(\mathbf{y}) \in \mathcal{T}_{3,1}$. This proves part (a) of the theorem.

The mapping Φ constructed above explicitly shows how the phase of an arbitrary binary sequence can be modulated to yield a sequence satisfying the TGP(1) constraint. A corresponding construction for a phase modulation function that maps an arbitrary binary sequence in $\mathcal{S}_{3,2}$, as characterized by Theorem 4.8(b), to a sequence in $\mathcal{T}_{3,2}$ is given in [**12**].

It is worth pointing out that the MTR(2) constraint used for ghost pulse reduction by Vasic *et al* [**20**] is contained in the set $\mathcal{S}_{3,2}$. This is clear from Theorem 4.8(b), since a binary sequence satisfies the MTR(2) constraint if and only if it does not contain 111 as a subblock, and so any MTR(2) constrained sequence then cannot contain 011100, 001110 or 001111100 as a subblock.

The result of Theorem 4.8 allows us to determine the exact values of $h(\mathcal{S}_{3,1})$ and $h(\mathcal{S}_{3,2})$, as stated in the following corollary to the theorem.

COROLLARY 4.9. (a) $h(\mathcal{S}_{3,1}) = 1$.
(b) $h(\mathcal{S}_{3,2}) = \log_2 \rho$, where ρ is the largest-magnitude root of the polynomial $z^{10} - 2z^9 + z^5 - z^4 + 2z^3 - z^2 - 2z + 1$. Numerically, $h(\mathcal{S}_{3,2}) \approx 0.96048$.

Part (a) of the above result is clear from Theorem 4.8(a). Part (b) follows from the fact that $z^{10} - 2z^9 + z^5 - z^4 + 2z^3 - z^2 - 2z + 1$ is the characteristic polynomial of the adjacency matrix of the graph in Figure 4, which gives a *minimal deterministic presentation* of $\mathcal{S}_{3,2}$. Recall that a *finite, labeled, directed graph* $\mathcal{G}$ consists of a finite set of vertices V, a finite set of directed edges $E \subset V \times V$, and an edge labeling $L : E \to \mathcal{A}$, where $\mathcal{A}$ is some finite alphabet. We say that such a graph $\mathcal{G}$ is a *presentation* of $\mathcal{S}$, if $\mathcal{S}$ is the set of sequences obtained from reading the labels of paths in $\mathcal{G}$. A presentation, $\mathcal{G}$, of $\mathcal{S}$ is said to be *deterministic* if at each

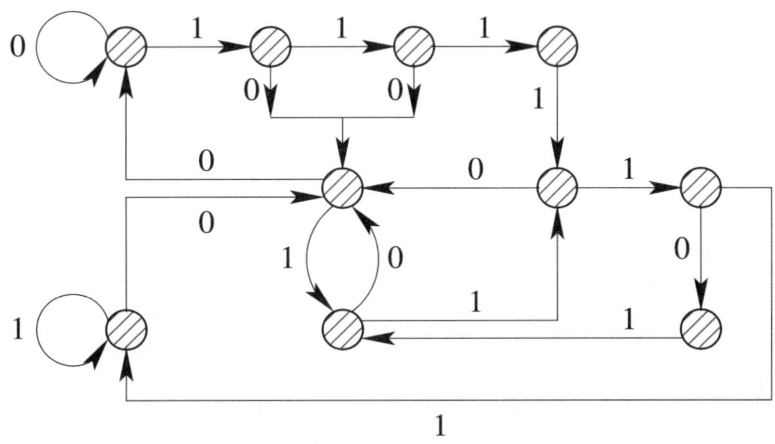

FIGURE 4. A minimal deterministic presentation of $S_{3,2}$.

vertex of $\mathcal{G}$, the outgoing edges are labeled distinctly. A deterministic presentation of $\mathcal{S}$ is *minimal* if it has the smallest number of vertices among all deterministic presentations of $\mathcal{S}$. It is well known [**14**, Theorem 4.4.4] that if $\mathcal{G}$ is a deterministic presentation of a constrained system, $\mathcal{S}$, of bi-infinite sequences, then the capacity of $\mathcal{S}$ is equal to $\log_2 \lambda(A_{\mathcal{G}})$, where $\lambda(A_{\mathcal{G}})$ is the largest eigenvalue of the adjacency matrix, $A_{\mathcal{G}}$, of $\mathcal{G}$.

It is interesting to note that for $t = 1, 2$, $h(\mathcal{S}_{3,t})$ is much greater than $h(\mathcal{S}_{2,t})$, as can be seen by comparing Corollary 4.9 with Table 1, and also that the drop from $h(\mathcal{S}_{3,1})$ to $h(\mathcal{S}_{3,2})$ is much smaller than that from $h(\mathcal{S}_{2,1})$ to $h(\mathcal{S}_{2,2})$. If this trend continues for larger values of t as well, say at least until t's of around 8 to 10, we can have reasonably efficient codes that effectively mitigate the formation of ghost pulses in a typical optical communication scenario.

Unfortunately, the techniques used to prove Theorem 4.8 cannot be easily generalized to arbitrary values of t, and so the problem of precisely analyzing the TGP(t) constraint for $t > 2$ remains largely open. We can provide an algorithmic procedure [**12**] to construct a deterministic presentation for $\mathcal{S}_{3,t}$, or indeed, $\mathcal{S}_{q,t}$, for any t. Given such a presentation for $\mathcal{S}_{q,t}$, there are well-established techniques (see *e.g.*, [**14**],[**17**]) to compute the capacity $h(\mathcal{S}_{q,t})$, and to construct efficient encoders that convert an arbitrary binary sequence to a sequence in $\mathcal{S}_{q,t}$.

Given $q, t \in \mathbb{Z}^+$, we define a finite, labeled, directed graph, $\hat{\Gamma}_{q,t}$, as follows. The set of vertices, $V_{3,t}$, of $\hat{\Gamma}_{3,t}$ is the set of all sequences $\mathbf{x} = (x_{-t}x_{-t+1} \dots x_0 \dots x_{2t}) \in \mathcal{A}_q^{3t+1}$ that satisfy the following condition: for all $k, l, m \in \text{supp}(\mathbf{x}) \cap [0, t]$ such that $x_k = x_l = x_m$, $x_{k+l-m} \in \text{supp}(\mathbf{x})$. For each pair of vertices $\mathbf{x} = (x_{-t}x_{-t+1} \dots x_{2t})$ and $\hat{\mathbf{x}} = (\hat{x}_{-t}\hat{x}_{-t+1} \dots \hat{x}_{2t})$ ($\mathbf{x}, \hat{\mathbf{x}}$ need not be distinct), we draw a single directed edge from $\mathbf{x}$ to $\hat{\mathbf{x}}$ if and only if the last $3t$ symbols of $\mathbf{x}$ are the same as the first $3t$ symbols of $\hat{\mathbf{x}}$, *i.e.*, $(x_{-t+1}x_{-t+2} \dots x_{2t}) = (\hat{x}_{-t}\hat{x}_{-t+1} \dots \hat{x}_{2t-1})$. Moreover, this directed edge is labeled with the symbol $\hat{x}_{2t}$. It can be shown [**12**] that $\hat{\Gamma}_{q,t}$ is a deterministic presentation of $\mathcal{T}_{q,t}$.

Now, let $\Gamma_{q,t}$ be the labeled directed graph obtained from $\hat{\Gamma}_{q,t}$ by simply replacing each nonzero edge label in $\hat{\Gamma}_{q,t}$ by the label '1'. More precisely, $\Gamma_{q,t}$ is the graph which has the same sets of vertices and edges as $\hat{\Gamma}_{q,t}$, but whose edges are labeled such that if $x \in \mathcal{A}_q$ is the label of an edge in $\hat{\Gamma}_{q,t}$, then the label of the corresponding edge in $\Gamma_{q,t}$ is 0 if $x = 0$, and 1 if $x \neq 0$. It should be clear that $\Gamma_{q,t}$ is a presentation of $\mathcal{S}_{q,t}$. However, this presentation is, in general, not deterministic. Fortunately, there is a well-defined procedure that, given an arbitrary presentation of a constrained system, finds a deterministic presentation for it. This method is called the *subset construction* method, and is described in [**17**, Section 2.2.1, p. 1649] and [**14**, Theorem 3.3.2]. Applying this method to $\Gamma_{q,t}$, we obtain a deterministic presentation, $\mathcal{G}_{q,t}$, for $\mathcal{S}_{q,t}$. We can then use the Moore algorithm [**17**, Section 2.6.2] to reduce $\mathcal{G}_{q,t}$ to a minimal deterministic presentation, $\mathcal{H}_{q,t}$, of $\mathcal{S}_{q,t}$.

The drawback to the above procedure is that it is computationally very intensive, and most of its complexity is due to the subset construction technique. The subset construction technique, when applied to a graph with r vertices, yields a graph with $2^r - 1$ vertices. Now, in general, the graph $\Gamma_{q,t}$ has substantially more than q^t vertices, since it always contains as vertices the q^{2t} q-ary sequences of the form $(x_{-t}x_{-t+1} \ldots x_{-1}\, 00 \ldots 0\, x_{t+1} \ldots x_{t+2} \ldots x_{2t})$. As a result, the graph $\mathcal{G}_{q,t}$ obtained above has at least (and this is a vast underestimate) $2^{q^{2t}}$ vertices. Thus, when $q \geq 3$, this procedure for constructing a deterministic presentation fails to be useful even for $t = 2$.

In theory, $\mathcal{H}_{q,t}$ can be used to compute $h(\mathcal{S}_{q,t})$ by determining the largest eigenvalue of the adjacency matrix of $\mathcal{H}_{q,t}$, and to construct finite-state encoders for converting unconstrained binary sequences to sequences in $\mathcal{S}_{q,t}$. But it is clear that, in general, this is practically unviable due to the sheer immensity of the graphs involved.

For the sake of completeness, we would like to mention that the graphs $\hat{\Gamma}_{q,t}$ and $\Gamma_{q,t}$ constructed above also give us a method for modulating the phase of an arbitrary sequence, $\mathbf{y}$, in $\mathcal{S}_{q,t}$ to yield a sequence, $\mathbf{x}$, satisfying the qGP(t) constraint. Given a $\mathbf{y} \in \mathcal{S}_{q,t}$, there is a path in $\Gamma_{q,t}$ whose sequence of labels is $\mathbf{y}$. We may then take $\mathbf{x}$ to be the sequence of labels of the corresponding path in $\hat{\Gamma}_{q,t}$. The practicality of this method depends on the existence of a systematic procedure for finding a path in $\Gamma_{q,t}$ that generates $\mathbf{y}$.

5. Summary and Future Research Directions

This paper is meant to introduce the communications and coding communities to the problem of ghostbusting, *i.e.*, combating the effect of ghost pulses that arise due to a nonlinear phenomenon known as intrachannel four-wave mixing (FWM) in the context of high bit-rate, long-haul optical communications. We have shared our own understanding of the problem, tried to illustrate its complex nature, and surveyed some of the existing techniques in the literature that are designed to tackle this problem.

We also lay the foundation for a systematic approach to designing coding and phase modulation schemes for ghostbusting. We demonstrate how techniques from the theory of constrained coding, whose development was motivated to a large extent by problems in information storage technology, can be applied to design and analyze codes for ghostbusting. Our analysis shows that it is possible to design efficient coding schemes using sequences that satisfy a certain constraint we refer to as the TGP(t) constraint.

Intrachannel FWM remains the major bottleneck in communication over a high bit-rate, long-haul optical transmission system. The lack of a reasonably simple, yet realistic, model for this effect has meant that there only exist *ad hoc* criteria for designing ghostbusting schemes. As a result, the performance of the ghostbusting schemes found in the literature tends to be variable at best. Thus, the problem that needs to be primarily resolved is that of finding a good model for FWM that, for example, takes into account the role played by optical phase in the formation of ghost pulses. Given such a model, it should be possible to use the wide range of techniques available in communications and coding theory to design efficient and reliable coding schemes for ghostbusting.

It would be useful to explore the usefulness of error-correcting codes in dealing with signal degradation caused by ghost pulses. The most obvious approach here would be to view ghost pulse formation as a noise source, and determine via simulations the resultant bit error rate or signal-to-noise ratio at the channel output. Powerful error-correcting codes could then be used to clean up the channel to an acceptable level.

There are several open problems left to be solved in the constrained coding approach we have taken in this paper. There are the theoretical questions of capacities of the qGP and qGP(t) constraints for $q > 2$ and arbitrary t, and the practical questions of designing efficient encoders and decoders for these constrained systems. Finally, it remains to actually test these codes in typical operating environments to evaluate their performance in terms of ghost pulse suppression.

References

[1] M.J. Ablowitz and T. Hirooka, "Intrachannel pulse interactions in dispersion-managed transmission systems: energy transfer," *Opt. Lett.*, vol. 27, no. 3, pp. 203–205, Feb. 2002.

[2] M.J. Ablowitz and T. Hirooka, "Resonant intrachannel pulse interactions in dispersion-managed transmission systems," *IEEE J. Sel. Topics Quant. Electron.*, vol. 8, no. 3, pp. 603–615, May/June 2002.

[3] N. Alic and Y. Fainman, "Data-dependent phase coding for suppression of ghost pulses in optical fibers," *IEEE Photon. Technol. Lett.*, vol. 16, no. 4, pp. 1212–1214, Apr. 2004.

[4] K.S. Cheng and J. Conradi, "Reduction of pulse-to-pulse interaction using alternative RZ formats in 40-GB/s systems," *IEEE Photon. Technol. Lett.*, vol. 14, no. 1, pp. 98–100, Jan. 2002.

[5] R.D. Cideciyan, E. Eleftheriou, B.H. Marcus and D.S. Modha, "Maximum transition run codes for generalized partial response channels," *IEEE J. Select. Areas Commun.*, vol. 19, no. 4, pp. 619–634, Apr. 2001.

[6] R.-J. Essiambre, B. Mikkelsen and G. Raybon, "Intra channel cross-phase modulation and four-wave mixing in high-speed TDM systems," *Electron. Lett.*, vol. 35, no. 18, pp. 1576–1578, Sept. 1999.

[7] K.A.S. Immink, *Coding Techniques for Digital Recorders*, Prentice Hall, New York, 1991.

[8] K.A.S. Immink, P.H. Siegel and J.K. Wolf, "Codes for digital recorders," *IEEE Trans. Inform. Theory*, vol. 44, no. 6, pp. 2260–2299, Oct. 1998.

[9] R. Karabed, P.H. Siegel and E. Soljanin, "Constrained coding for binary channels with high intersymbol interference," *IEEE Trans. Inform. Theory*, vol. 45, no. 6, pp. 1777–1797, Sept. 1999.

[10] N. Kashyap, P.H. Siegel and A. Vardy, "A Ramsey theory approach to ghostbusting," *Proc. IEEE Symp. Inform. Theory (ISIT)*, Chicago, USA, p. 190, 2004.

[11] N. Kashyap, P.H. Siegel and A. Vardy, "An application of Ramsey theory to coding for the optical channel," submitted to *SIAM J. Discrete Math*, 2004. Preprint available on request.

[12] N. Kashyap, P.H. Siegel and A. Vardy, "Coding for the optical channel — the ghost pulse constraint," submitted to *IEEE Trans. Inform. Theory*, 2004. Preprint available on request.

[13] S. Kumar, "Intrachannel four-wave mixing in dispersion managed RZ systems," *IEEE Photon. Technol. Lett.*, vol. 13, no. 8, pp. 800–802, Aug. 2001.

[14] D. Lind and B. Marcus, *An Introduction to Symbolic Dynamics and Coding*, Cambridge Univ. Press, Cambridge, UK, 1995.

[15] X. Liu, X. Wei, A.H. Gnauck, C. Xu, and L.K. Wickham, "Suppression of intrachannel four-wave-mixing induced ghost pulses in high-speed transmissions by phase inversion between adjacent marker blocks," *Opt. Lett.*, vol. 27, no. 13, pp. 1177–1179, July 2002.

[16] P. V. Mamyshev and N. A. Mamysheva, "Pulse-overlapped dispersion-managed data transmission and intrachannel four-wave mixing," *Opt. Lett.*, vol. 24, no. 21, pp. 1454–1456, Nov. 1999.

[17] B.H. Marcus, R.M. Roth and P.H. Siegel, "Constrained Systems and Coding for Recording Channels," in *Handbook of Coding Theory*, R. Brualdi, C. Huffman and V. Pless, Eds., Elsevier, Amsterdam, The Netherlands, 1998.

[18] J. Moon and B. Brickner, "Maximum transition run codes for data storage systems," *IEEE Trans. Magn.*, vol. 32, no. 5, pp. 3992–3994, Sept. 1996.

[19] I. Shake, H. Takara, K. Mori, S. Kawanishi and Y. Yamabayashi, "Influence of inter-bit four-wave mixing in optical TDM transmission," *Electron. Lett.*, vol. 34, no. 16, pp. 1600–1601, Aug. 1998.

[20] B. Vasic, V.S. Rao, I.B. Djordjevic, I. Gabitov and R.K. Kostuk, "Ghost pulse reduction in 40 Gb/s systems using line coding," preprint, 2004.

[21] K. Yonenaga and S. Kuwano, "Dispersion-tolerant optical transmission system using duobinary transmitter and binary receiver," *J. Lightwave Technol.*, vol. 15, no. 8, pp. 1530–1537, Aug. 1997.

[22] J. Zweck and C.R. Menyuk, "Analysis of four-wave mixing between pulses in high-data-rate quasi-linear subchannel-multiplexed systems," *Opt. Lett.*, vol. 27, no. 14, pp. 1235–1237, July 2002.

Department of Mathematics and Statistics, Queen's University, Kingston, Ontario K7L 3N6, Canada
E-mail address: nkashyap@mast.queensu.ca

Department of Electrical & Computer Engineering, University of California San Diego, La Jolla, California 92093-0407, USA
E-mail address: psiegel@ucsd.edu

List of Working Group Presentations

Macro-Molecular Data Storage with Petabyte/cm^3 Density, Highly Parallel Read/Write Operations, and Genuine 3D Storage Capability
M. Mansuripur, University of Arizona, Tucson, AZ

How Random is the Human Genome?
P. Winkler, Bell Laboratories, Murray Hill, NJ, and Institute for Advanced Study, Princeton, NJ

Can We Explain the Faithful Communication of Genetic Information?
G. Battail, École Nationale Supérieure des Télécommunications, Paris, France

The Information Processing Mechanism of DNA and Efficient DNA Storage
O. Milenkovic, University of Colorado, Boulder, CO

Optimal Block-Decodable Encoders for Constrained Systems
B. H. Marcus, University of British Columbia, Vancouver, Canada

Iterative Timing Recovery
A. Kavčić, Harvard University, Cambridge, MA

Information Rates for Two-Dimensional ISI Channels
P. H. Siegel, University of California, San Diego, La Jolla, CA

Coding and Signal Processing for Two-Dimensional Optical Storage
W. M. J. Coene, Philips Research Laboratories, Philips, Eindhoven, The Netherlands

Capacity and Beyond
E. Kurtas, Seagate Research, Pittsburgh, PA

Millipede: A Nanotechnology-Based Approach for Highly-Parallel, Ultra-Dense Data Storage
G. Cherubini, IBM Research, Zürich, Switzerland

ET Might Write not Radiate
C. Rose, Rutgers University, Piscataway, NJ

List of Workshop Presentations

Towards the Optimal Bit Aspect Ratio in Magnetic Recording
W. RYAN, UNIVERSITY OF ARIZONA, TUCSON, AZ

Iterative Timing Recovery
J. R. BARRY, GEORGIA INSTITUTE OF TECHNOLOGY, ATLANTA, GA

Soft Decision Decoding of RS Codes Using Adaptive Parity Check Matrices
K. NARAYANAN, TEXAS A&M UNIVERSITY, COLLEGE STATION, TX

Constrained Systems with Unconstrained Positions: Graph Constructions and Trade-off Functions (part I)
P. CHAICHANAVONG, UNIVERSITY OF CALIFORNIA, SAN DIEGO, LA JOLLA, CA

Constrained Systems with Unconstrained Positions: Graph Constructions and Trade-off Functions (part II)
L. POO, STANFORD UNIVERSITY, STANFORD, CA

Modulation Codes for the Deep Space Optical Channel
B. E. MOISION, JET PROPULSION LABORATORY, PASADENA, CA

Timing Recovery at Low SNR
A. NAYAK, GEORGIA INSTITUTE OF TECHNOLOGY, ATLANTA, GA

Asymptotic Capacity Bounds for Magnetic Recording
R. VENKATARAMANI, SEAGATE RESEARCH, PITTSBURGH, PA

Ghostbusting – Constrained Coding for Optical Communication
N. KASHYAP, QUEEN'S UNIVERSITY, KINGSTON, ON, CANADA

Belief-Propagation with Information Correction: Near Maximum-Likelihood Decoding of Low-Density Parity-Check Codes
N. VARNICA, HARVARD UNIVERSITY, CAMBRIDGE, MA

Titles in This Series

73 **Paul H. Siegel, Emina Soljanin, Adriaan J. van Wijngaarden, and Bane Vasić, Editors,** Advances in Information Recording

72 **Regina Y. Liu, Robert Serfling, and Diane Souvaine, Editors,** Data Depth: Robust Multivariate Analysis, Computational Geometry and Applications

71 **Zhilan Feng, Ulf Dieckmann, and Simon Levin, Editors,** Disease Evolution: Models, Concepts, and Data Analyses

70 **James Abello and Graham Cormode, Editors,** Discrete Methods in Epidemiology

69 **Siemion Fajtlowicz, Patrick W. Fowler, Pierre Hansen, Melvin F. Janowitz, and Fred S. Roberts, Editors,** Graphs and Discovery

68 **A. Ashikhmin and A. Barg, Editors,** Algebraic Coding Theory and Information Theory

67 **Ravi Janardan, Michiel Smid, and Debasish Dutta, Editors,** Geometric and Algorithmic Aspects of Computer-Aided Design and Manufacturing

66 **Piyush Gupta, Gerhard Kramer, and Adriaan J. van Wijngaarden, Editors,** Advances in Network Information Theory

65 **Santosh S. Vempala,** The Random Projection Method

64 **Melvyn B. Nathanson, Editor,** Unusual Applications of Number Theory

63 **J. Nešetřil and P. Winkler, Editors,** Graphs, Morphisms and Statistical Physics

62 **Gerard J. Foschini and Sergio Verdú, Editors,** Multiantenna Channels: Capacity, Coding and Signal Processing

61 **M. F. Janowitz, F.-J. Lapointe, F. R. McMorris, B. Mirkin, and F. S. Roberts, Editors,** Bioconsensus

60 **Saugata Basu and Laureano Gonzalez-Vega, Editors,** Algorithmic and Quantitative Real Algebraic Geometry

59 **Michael H. Goldwasser, David S. Johnson, and Catherine C. McGeoch, Editors,** Data Structures, Near Neighbor Searches, and Methodology: Fifth and Sixth DIMACS Implementation Challenges

58 **Simon Thomas, Editor,** Set Theory: The Hajnal Conference

57 **Eugene C. Freuder and Richard J. Wallace, Editors,** Constraint Programming and Large Scale Discrete Optimization

56 **Alexander Barg and Simon Litsyn, Editors,** Codes and Association Schemes

55 **Ding-Zhu Du, Panos M. Pardalos, and Jie Wang, Editors,** Discrete Mathematical Problems with Medical Applications

54 **Erik Winfree and David K. Gifford, Editors,** DNA Based Computers V

53 **Nathaniel Dean, D. Frank Hsu, and R. Ravi, Editors,** Robust Communication Networks: Interconnection and Survivability

52 **Sanguthevar Rajasekaran, Panos Pardalos, and D. Frank Hsu, Editors,** Mobile Networks and Computing

51 **Pierre Hansen, Patrick Fowler, and Maolin Zheng, Editors,** Discrete Mathematical Chemistry

50 **James M. Abello and Jeffrey Scott Vitter, Editors,** External Memory Algorithms

49 **Ronald L. Graham, Jan Kratochvíl, Jaroslav Nešetřil, and Fred S. Roberts, Editors,** Contemporary Trends in Discrete Mathematics

48 **Harvey Rubin and David Harlan Wood, Editors,** DNA Based Computers III

47 **Martin Farach-Colton, Fred S. Roberts, Martin Vingron, and Michael Waterman, Editors,** Mathematical Support for Molecular Biology

46 **Peng-Jun Wan, Ding-Zhu Du, and Panos M. Pardalos, Editors,** Multichannel Optical Networks: Theory and Practice

45 **Marios Mavronicolas, Michael Merritt, and Nir Shavit, Editors,** Networks in Distributed Computing

For a complete list of titles in this series, visit the
AMS Bookstore at **www.ams.org/bookstore/**.